D1714388

# A Black Congressman in the Age of Jim Crow

*New Perspectives on the History of the South*

UNIVERSITY PRESS OF FLORIDA

Florida A&M University, Tallahassee
Florida Atlantic University, Boca Raton
Florida Gulf Coast University, Ft. Myers
Florida International University, Miami
Florida State University, Tallahassee
University of Central Florida, Orlando
University of Florida, Gainesville
University of North Florida, Jacksonville
University of South Florida, Tampa
University of West Florida, Pensacola

New Perspectives on the History of the South
Edited by John David Smith

*"In the Country of the Enemy": The Civil War Reports of a Massachusetts Corporal*, edited by William C. Harris (1999)

*The Wild East: A Biography of the Great Smoky Mountains*, by Margaret L. Brown (2000; first paperback edition, 2001)

*Crime, Sexual Violence, and Clemency: Florida's Pardon Board and Penal System in the Progressive Era*, by Vivien M. L. Miller (2000)

*The New South's New Frontier: A Social History of Economic Development in Southwestern North Carolina*, by Stephen Wallace Taylor (2001)

*Redefining the Color Line: Black Activism in Little Rock, Arkansas, 1940-1970*, by John A. Kirk (2002)

*The Southern Dream of a Caribbean Empire, 1854-1861*, by Robert E. May (2002)

*Forging a Common Bond: Labor and Environmental Activism during the BASF Lockout*, by Timothy J. Minchin (2003)

*Dixie's Daughters: The United Daughters of the Confederacy and the Preservation of Confederate Culture*, by Karen L. Cox (2003)

*The Other War of 1812: The Patriot War and the American Invasion of Spanish East Florida*, by James G. Cusick (2003)

*"Lives Full of Struggle and Triumph": Southern Women, Their Institutions and Their Communities*, edited by Bruce L. Clayton and John A. Salmond (2003)

*German-Speaking Officers in the United States Colored Troops, 1863-1867*, by Martin W. Öfele (2004)

*Southern Struggles: The Southern Labor Movement and the Civil Rights Struggle*, by John A. Salmond (2004)

*Radio and the Struggle for Civil Rights in the South*, by Brian Ward (2004, first paperback edition, 2006)

*Luther P. Jackson and a Life for Civil Rights,* by Michael Dennis (2004)

*Southern Ladies, New Women: Race, Region, and Clubwomen in South Carolina, 1890-1930,* by Joan Marie Johnson (2004)

*Fighting Against the Odds: A Concise History of Southern Labor Since World War II*, by Timothy J. Minchin (2004, first paperback edition, 2006)

*"Don't Sleep With Stevens!": The J. P. Stevens Campaign and the Struggle to Organize the South, 1963-80*, by Timothy J. Minchin (2005)

*"The Ticket to Freedom:" The NAACP and the Struggle for Black Political Integration*, by Manfred Berg (2005)

*"War Governor of the South": North Carolina's Zeb Vance in the Confederacy*, by Joe A. Mobley (2005)

*Planters' Progress: Modernizing Confederate Georgia*, by Chad Morgan (2005)

*The Officers of the CSS* Shenandoah, by Angus Curry (2006)

*The Rosenwald Schools of the American South*, by Mary S. Hoffschwelle (2006)

*Honor in Command: The Civil War Memoir of Lt. Freeman Sparks Bowley, 30th United States Colored Infantry*, edited by Keith P. Wilson (2006)

*A Black Congressman in the Age of Jim Crow: South Carolina's George Washington Murray*, by John F. Marszalek (2006)

# A Black Congressman
# in the Age of Jim Crow

South Carolina's George Washington Murray

JOHN F. MARSZALEK

Foreword by John David Smith

University Press of Florida
Gainesville/Tallahassee/Tampa/Boca Raton
Pensacola/Orlando/Miami/Jacksonville/Ft. Myers

Copyright 2006 by John F. Marszalek
Printed in the United States of America on acid-free paper

11 10 09 08 07 06   6 5 4 3 2 1

A record of cataloging-in-publication data is available from the
Library of Congress
ISBN 0-8130-3002-1

The University Press of Florida is the scholarly publishing agency
for the State University System of Florida, comprising Florida A&M
University, Florida Atlantic University, Florida Gulf Coast University,
Florida International University, Florida State University, University
of Central Florida, University of Florida, University of North Florida,
University of South Florida, and University of West Florida.

University Press of Florida
15 Northwest 15th Street
Gainesville, FL 32611-2079
http://www.upf.com

For John, Chris, and Jamie,
Shannon 1 and Shannon 2,
Will, Emily, and Col

# Contents

# Foreword

Historians and writers from Ulrich Bonnell Phillips, C. Vann Woodward, and Howard Zinn to Wilbur J. Cash, William Faulkner, and Lee Smith have underscored the South's distinctiveness. For many persons the South signifies more than a region. For them it represents an idea, an abstraction, even an ideology. For some the South has become an obsession. Since the colonial period, the South has been both connected to and distanced from the rest of North America. Its settlement pattern, its crops, and, most significantly, its commitment to racial slavery earmarked the Old South as different from the rest of the nation. As Woodward noted in 1960, the South has many "burdens." Its defeat in the Civil War and its experiences during and after Reconstruction left an indelible blot on the fabric of southern history. Yet in the twenty-first century, the South seems very much "American"—more like the rest of the country, not some mythic land apart.

Dating back to the 1880s, historians and critics have defined and redefined southern history in innumerable ways. The "Nationalist" historians, the "Dunning School," the "Agrarians," the "Revisionists," the "Postrevisionists," the Marxists, and, today, all manner of postmodernists have tried to squeeze some contemporary meaning from southern history. Historians and others regularly interpret the region's history and culture in such varied journals and magazines as the *Journal of Southern History*, *Southern Review*, *Southern Humanities Review*, *Southern Living*, *Southern Exposure*, and *Southern Cultures*. In 1979 the *Encyclopedia of Southern History* appeared, followed ten years later by the *Encyclopedia of Southern Culture*. Both within and beyond the region, there seems to be an insatiable appetite for information on the South and its people.

In fact, no region in America, including New England and the West, has received as much in-depth analysis and reflection as has the American South. Insiders (native southerners) and outsiders (non-southerners, including an unusually large number of northern and European specialists on the South) agree that the Southland has a particular Weltanschauung, one loaded with irony, pathos, paradox, and racial and class conflict. In some universities southern history long has reigned as a major research specialty. They confer doctorates in the field. Many academic publishers consider "southern studies" a strong part of their list. Books about the South sell on both sides of the Mason-Dixon line and overseas. Associations and institutions sponsor regular symposia and conferences regionally, nationally, and internationally on the South's past.

In the last century, when the South ranked as "the nation's economic problem No. 1," sociologists dissected the region's pathologies, especially its historic race problem and poverty. Today, social scientists and economists marvel at the "Sun Belt"—its thriving and alluring prosperity built atop longstanding anti-union sentiment, its daunting skyscrapers, its rapid transit systems, its social and racial progress. Atlanta, the region's bourgeois Mecca, has numerous lesser rivals throughout the former Confederacy—Dallas, New Orleans, Miami, Nashville, Charlotte, Raleigh, and Richmond. Cable television, chain restaurants, New York department stores, malls and their accompanying outlet shops—even the "national edition" of the New York *Times* (printed in several southern cities and delivered to the doorsteps of thousands of southerners)—dot the southern landscape like the proverbial cotton plants of old.

An appreciation of the South's distinctiveness and its diversity lies at the heart of the University Press of Florida's *New Perspectives on the History of the South* series. This broadly based series publishes the highest quality new scholarship on the history of the American South. The books cover all aspects and periods of the southern past, with special emphasis on the region's cultural, economic, intellectual, and social history.

John F. Marszalek's *A Black Congressman in the Age of Jim Crow: South Carolina's George Washington Murray*, the latest volume in the series, carefully unravels the role of race, class, and political factionalism in one state at the fin de siècle.

Marszalek employs biography as a means to explore the determined but ultimately unsuccessful efforts of George Washington Murray (1853–1926) and other black southerners to retain voting rights during the flurry of local disfranchisement legislation and practice that blanketed the South during the last decades of the nineteenth century. Murray, born a slave in Sumter County, South Carolina, was a self-made man. He succeeded as a teacher, farmer, inventor, and politician, serving two terms (1893–95, 1896–97) in Congress. Murray was one of the last two post–Civil War African Americans to serve in Congress before Jim Crow laws virtually disfranchised black southerners. Not until 1928 did another African American serve in the House of Representatives. It took the 1965 Voting Rights Act to widen the possible number of blacks in Congress.

Marszalek interprets Murray as a competent and conscientious politician who, when necessary, cooperated with Democrats but who consistently sought to improve the plight of blacks by favoring federal civil rights legislation. Murray urged blacks to participate in politics but, like Booker T. Washington, also endorsed industrial education for the children of the freed people. Murray opposed emigration, initially voted for the free and unlimited coinage of silver, and consistently encouraged blacks to acquire property and to combat white prejudice by patronizing black businesses.

In charting Murray's political rise and fall, Marszalek also dissects the internecine struggles that killed South Carolina's Republican party as it lost battle after battle against the Democrats' white supremacy campaigns. While Marszalek explains how skin color differentiation contributed to the factionalism that plagued the state's black leadership, he insists that the "color issue was not a major issue of Republican factional division and conflict." Rather the "crushing prejudice" of whites unleashed self-destructive tendencies among African American leaders. According to Marszalek, the factions "blamed each other for their own plight even though, in truth, the real blame lay with a prejudiced South Carolina white society."

Marszalek's meticulously researched biography of Murray emphasizes the seemingly unlimited power of white racism and the powerlessness of black Republicans during the rise of Jim Crow. The evolution from rigid segregation to desegregation and the triumph of biracial democracy in the last century comprise essential elements in the history of today's decidedly distinctive and diverse South.

*John David Smith*
*Series Editor*

# Preface

The last paragraph of a standard book on nineteenth-century black congress-men summarizes the traditional view of George W. Murray and the other black men who served in Congress. Writing in 1940, Samuel Denny Smith said: "They served to keep alive race friction, and they were used as a political football by white political groups of all persuasions." Though they "were rather well equipped by education, previous political experience, and wealth, and . . . most of them had considerable white blood in their veins and were frequently aided by white friends," they were still failures. "Their lack of ac-complishment," Smith concluded, "was an argument that the Negro would do well, for a time at least, to forego political ambition in this realm and to con-fine his efforts to other vocations where he had a better chance of success."[1]

A famous study of the post-Reconstruction Republican party in South Carolina takes a similar view. James Welch Patton wrote in 1949 that Pal-metto State Republicans were conspicuous only for their venality. Though admitting that white violence was partially to blame for Republican failure in those years, he said, "especial importance must be attached to the nature and composition of the party itself." South Carolina Republicans were "a political fiction," he insisted, "an aggregation of federal office holders and placemen, held together by a desire to catch such crumbs as might fall from the national Republican table when that party was in power." They opposed any reformers, Patton wrote, and they failed "to adopt a positive program based upon perti-nent local issues and in the interest of a more wholesome state government." Their conventions had a "racial texture" and "moral complexion" that were "mottled" and filled with "wild Gullah oratory," and their political activities in general were "a repetition of some of the more lurid phases of the Recon-struction era." Republican candidates, such as Murray whom Patton listed by name, "if not downright dishonest were certainly believed to be."[2]

Writing in 1992, Harris M. Bailey, Jr. expressed similar beliefs. "Leader-ship was the greatest failing of the state's Republican party. The leadership was unable to quash the flare-up of personal disputes in the party or control the growth of factionalism. If the leadership had adopted coalition strategies, fu-sion tickets with factional elements in the Democratic party might have made the party more competitive in statewide elections. . . . The black and white leadership *allowed* the Democrats to dictate the content of political debate in South Carolina. Substantial questions of policy and ideology were subjugated to questions of race and, to a subliminal degree, questions of caste."[3]

The standard historical view of Murray and the South Carolina Republican Party, therefore, was that both Murray and his party were venal failures. They were typical descendants of their Reconstruction predecessors, so hostilely characterized in traditional but now discredited Reconstruction historiography.

Most modern historical accounts of Republican Party and black life in the post-Reconstruction South have corrected many such erroneous views. George B. Tindall's and I. A. Newby's excellent books on South Carolina blacks during the late nineteenth century and the early twentieth are examples of this much needed revisionism. Why, then, is a new book on George W. Murray and South Carolina Republicans needed? Most books on black life in the South do not deal with the unique South Carolina situation in depth, while Newby and Tindall do not analyze Murray, the Republicans, or disfranchisement in any detail. Loren Schweninger's excellent study of southern black property holders does not mention Murray, despite the large tracts of land he owned. A book on Murray and South Carolina Republicans will fill a genuine need by providing information and insight not available elsewhere.

South Carolina is a state whose race relations were particularly contentious in the late nineteenth century and the early twentieth. It had the highest percentage of black citizens of any state in the Union, and the cries for white supremacy were consequently shriller there than anywhere else in the South. The legend of South Carolina Reconstruction and the "redemption" led by Wade Hampton created a historical mythology that gave black-white interaction a sharp edge. A dread of "black domination" existed that made white South Carolinians more virulently opposed to Republicans and black voters than were any other southern whites. Only in Mississippi, whose white population was second to South Carolina's did Republican disfranchisement come earlier. Similarly Florida blacks ceased being a factor in state politics by the middle of the 1880s. Other southern states, however, were less uncompromisingly anti-Republican: for example, the Republican Party in Louisiana and Tennessee was heavily white. Texas, Alabama, Virginia, and Arkansas had active fusion movements in the 1890s, while, in Georgia the possibility of fusion caused two Democratic factions to appeal openly for black votes. North Carolina experienced a successful fusion of black and white Republicans and Populists, which merger briefly took control of the state government. In Maryland, Republicans were such an integral part of the two-party system that what racial attacks there were were considered an assault not only against black voters but also against the two-party system.

South Carolina never experienced such flexibility. After its bloody "redemption" from Reconstruction, the Palmetto State passed an anti-black registration and voting law in 1882, and it used every other available legal and illegal method to frustrate black voters. The fear of benefiting blacks and Republicans, be they white or black, kept any crack in white political solidarity from spreading. There was severe Democratic factionalism in the 1890s, but no fusion with Republicans resulted. South Carolina's animosity toward black voters and Republicans was too intense to permit such manipulation. South Carolina did not even have a Populist movement similar to that in other southern states to act as a focus for fusion with Republicans. Ben Tillman and his farmer group took control of the Democratic Party so early and so completely that they had little interest in Populism. The defeated Conservative Democratic faction despised the victorious Tillmanites, but fear of black domination kept them from appealing forcefully to black voters and fusing with Republicans in opposition to the Tillmanites.

Such racism also kept several of the state's so-called Lily White Republican movements from gaining success. For a white to become a Republican in South Carolina was to invite disgrace; therefore, few men, whatever their disagreement with Democratic leaders or policy, dared leave the Democratic Party to join the state Republicans. Anyone who became a Republican was immediately accused of undermining white political control and thus was considered a traitor to his race.

This book attempts to describe the life of a black congressman and his reaction and that of his political party to this suffocating political climate. George W. Murray's political career did not demonstrate criminal incompetence; it demonstrated determined effort to overcome his state's racist discrimination. The story of the state Republican Party, of which Murray was such a key member, is the tale of an organization attempting to survive systematic local disfranchisement and the complementary national GOP unconcern. White South Carolina society would not allow Republicans within the state to participate meaningfully in South Carolina's political life, while national Republican party leaders saw Palmetto State Republicans as having no function other than delegate votes at national conventions. Consequently, South

Carolina Republicans had to try to survive in any way they could. They rallied black voters while trying to attract disaffected or nonaligned whites; other times they tried to fuse with one or another of the continually feuding Democratic factions. They also looked to the national government to dispense life-giving patronage. They were neither uniquely incompetent nor venal in their response to the uncompromisingly racist white society they faced.

# Acknowledgments

Throughout the long research leading to this book, a host of libraries, archives, academic and public institutions, and individuals provided aid that made this publication possible. Some of the people are now deceased and no longer able to see the fruits of their encouragement. Others are enjoying retirement, while still others remain very much involved in their careers. All of them played important roles in my efforts to explain George W. Murray and the South Carolina Republican Party. My few words here can not repay them for their encouragement and support.

George W. Murray's family was most kind in welcoming me into their Norfolk, Virginia homes and providing information on their forebear. Thelma L. Murray, the widow of Murray's son, and June Davis, her daughter, both remembered important data about Murray, which Dr. Edward, his son, had told them. Mrs. Murray had known her father-in-law in Chicago, and both women knew his first wife in South Carolina and his second wife in Chicago. Evelyn R. Cuthbert of Sumter, South Carolina and Dorothy Westbrooks of Chicago knew members of the Murray family in those two locations and provided insight on their lives. The attorney George D. Shore, Jr. of Sumter not only provided information and aid but was also the first person to suggest I write this book. I met him in 1971 during a research visit when I was working on the life story of another former Sumter resident, the nineteenth-century West Point cadet Johnson C. Whittaker. More recently, Sumter attorney John S. Hoar, himself a long-time student of Sumter, South Carolina history in general and George W. Murray in particular, encouraged me to complete the book.

The staffs of a number of libraries provided major aid in the early days of the research: Mitchell Memorial Library, Mississippi State University; Gannon University Library; South Caroliniana Library, University of South Carolina; Schomburg Center for Research in Black Culture, New York; the Manuscript Division of the Library of Congress; the National Archives and Records Administration, Washington, D.C., and the National Archives and Records Administration, South East Region (Atlanta, Ga.); Robert Muldrow Cooper Library, Clemson University; South Carolina Department of Archives and History, Columbia; Archives and Manuscripts, Yale University Library;

Chicago Historical Society; Vivian G. Harsh Collection on Afro-American History and Literature, George C. Hall Branch, Chicago Public Library; Indianapolis Public Library; Indiana Historical Society; Princeton [Indiana] Public Library; South Carolina Supreme Court; United States Court of Appeals for the Fourth Circuit; Columbia University Library; University of Chicago Library; Moorland-Spingarn Research Center, Howard University; South Carolina Historical Society, Charleston; Charleston Library Society; and Beaufort [S.C.] County Library.

Thanks are also due to the staffs of a variety of other institutions: Clerk's Office, Sumter County, Marion County, and Charleston County, all in South Carolina; Supreme Life Insurance Company of Chicago; Department of Vital Statistics, Recorder of Deeds and Probate Division of Chicago and Cook County, Illinois; Department of Health and Property Records Office, Norfolk, Virginia; the Chicago *Defender*; former Mississippi congressman David Bowen for expediting access into the Records of the U.S. House of Representatives; and the former commissioner of Customs Vernon D. Acree for permission to consult U.S. Customs records.

Numerous historians answered my queries for information and several read all or parts of earlier drafts of the manuscript: Lawrence O. Christenson, University of Missouri-Rolla; Maurine Christopher, New York; John Hope Franklin, Duke University; William Gaboury, Southern Oregon College; Louis R. Harlan, University of Maryland; Daniel W. Hollis, University of South Carolina; August Meier, Kent State University; I. A. Newby, University of Hawaii; William E. Parrish, Mississippi State University; John T. Schlebecker, Smithsonian Institution; James F. Sefcik, Louisiana State Museum; Allan H. Spear, University of Minnesota; George B. Tindall, University of North Carolina. John David Smith, University of North Carolina, Charlotte and the editor of the series in which this book appears, Bobby L. Lovett, Tennessee State University, and two anonymous University Press of Florida readers provided excellent critiques in the final stages of this manuscript's revision.

I owe special thanks to a generation of student-assistants at Gannon University and Mississippi State University: at the former, Patrick Casey and Larry Maxted; at the latter, Helen Thompson, Tommy Norris, Marva Long, Cathryn T. Goree, Doris Lowrey, Charles Morris, and Marilyn Pegues. They have all long since gone on to a variety of successful careers, but their help to me during their time at Gannon and MSU was instrumental in my research and writing. Peggy Y. Bonner, long-time MSU History Department secretary and friend, provided essential help with formatting my prose.

I received a grant-in-aide from the American Council of Learned Societies, a Gannon University Faculty Research Grant, and travel aid from the Institute for the Humanities of Mississippi State University. Without this financial support, I could not have done the travel necessary to complete the research.

Numerous friends provided hospitality during research trips. They include James X. Kroll, formerly of Michigan City, Indiana, now of Denver, Colorado and Dr. and Mrs. Ronald Sadlowski, formerly of Chicago and now of Tampa, Florida.

My greatest debt is to my wife, Jeanne Kozmer Marszalek, who not only watched and encouraged me but also helped with the research and read and criticized the entire manuscript. The fact that this book is completed is a tribute to her faith that it would be done.

Our three sons grew up watching me work on this book. No father could be prouder of them and all that they have achieved. The daughters-in-law and grandchildren they brought into our family have made the joys of parenthood even greater.

# From Slavery to Public Life

On September 22, 1853, a slave woman whose name has been lost to history gave birth to a male child on a plantation somewhere in Sumter County, South Carolina. As she looked at her newborn baby and named him George Washington Murray, this mother could never have envisioned that he would become a U.S. congressman and one of the most famous persons in his state. This was simply beyond a slave's imagination in the 1850s. Slaves could not hope for much—certainly not for leadership in the white man's world.

Sumter County, located in the middle of South Carolina, is about forty miles east of Columbia, the state capital. A sandy loam soil covers the rolling terrain here, and hot summers and mild winters create a favorable growing environment year-round. Cotton, followed by corn, was the major crop in the pre–Civil War years, and here black slavery existed from the earliest white settlement.

The influx of white population into South Carolina and the expansion in the number of acres under cultivation resulted in a constant increase in the number of slaves in the state. The result was the passage of legislation in 1820 prohibiting the entry of free blacks and disallowing the freeing of slaves except by the legislature. The panic over the Denmark Vesey slave conspiracy resulted in even further restrictive legislation. Outnumbered whites were determined to keep control over the increasing black population. Yet there remained free blacks in Sumter County, some of whom were even able to purchase land. In 1838, William Ellison, a ginwright, bought the Sumter County home of a South Carolina governor, and the family held it for three generations.[1]

This was not the usual lot for black people in South Carolina. Most were slaves, bound to the land of their masters. As was the case everywhere in the South, the treatment of slaves varied according to the attitude and behavior of the slave owner. The education of slaves was prohibited by state law in 1834, but it occurred often enough to cause a Sumter grand jury in 1829 to complain about the danger of it happening so often. Law records also indicate that from 1827 to 1854 there were thirteen prosecutions of white people for cruelty to slaves. The only recorded punishment, however, was a $1 fine. Eleven slave holders were also indicted for murder, but, once again, they escaped punishment.[2]

Whites in Sumter County, like all white Carolinians, were deeply afraid that their slaves would some day rise in revolt as they knew had happened in the Caribbean. Consequently, they shared the universal southern worry about the abolitionist movement, constantly reacting to rumors about abolitionists infiltrating the state. In 1857, for example, a suspicious white woman came to Sumter, and local whites discovered that she was doing research for a book along the lines of *Uncle Tom's Cabin*. The slaves, no doubt, were watched even more carefully to see if the alleged female abolitionist had planted any dangerous notions of freedom in their hearts before she left town.[3]

The enslaved blacks in Sumter, like others throughout the South, used a variety of means to demonstrate their resistance to the institution. They ran away, as far as they could go or just to the nearby woods; they physically fought their white masters; they even murdered some. Normally, however, they demonstrated their displeasure in a variety of safer ways, such as goldbricking, destruction of tools, feigning illnesses, and general passive noncooperation. They protested within the oppressive system to survive as best they could, but slavery simply did not go away no matter what they did.[4]

Reflecting its white citizens' concern about slavery and particularly about its future stability, South Carolina was the first state to secede from the Union in 1861. In Sumter County, whites invited the leading advocate of secession, the fire-eater Edmund Ruffin, to speak to a crowd gathered to elect delegates to the state's secession convention. A brass band played, cannon fired, and 150 "Minute Men" greeted Ruffin. Four delegates represented Sumter County, joining with other individuals from throughout the state to pass unanimously the ordinance of separation on December 20, 1860.[5] George W. Murray was then only seven years old, and just beginning to realize what his life and future portended. He had to wonder what the secession excitement was all about. He had to have heard that whites were ready to break up the nation in order to keep people like him enslaved.

When Civil War came in April 1861, at Fort Sumter in Charleston harbor, just one hundred miles from Sumter County, a Sumter company of soldiers was already in Virginia. The battle of Bull Run in July resulted in the death or injury of Sumter soldiers, and this phenomenon came as a shock. Secession was supposed to be bloodless. The war stayed distant from the area, however, but many white Sumter males joined the Confederate Army and served on other distant battlefields. Wounded men found their way to Sumter as did civilian refugees. It was not until April 1865 after Robert E. Lee had already surrendered, however, that Union troops under Brigadier General Edward E. Potter, conducting a raid through the state, reached the area and fought a skirmish with local whites. Brushing them aside, Potter's force entered the city and systematically destroyed everything of military value, such as railroads and supplies of all sorts. At his approach, slaves fell in behind, Potter estimating, at one time, that five thousand black people were following his column during his two week raid through Sumter County. The war had waited almost to the end to come to Sumter, but its arrival was traumatic to the region's whites and a breath of hope to the now free blacks.[6]

It was within this context of the 1850s and the Civil War that George Washington Murray lived the first years of his life. Except for his birth date, county of origin, and the fact that he lived the hard life of a slave in mid–South Carolina, little, unfortunately, is known about him.[7] His mother and his father, his exact birth place, and the details of the first twelve years of his life are all unknown. Apparently he had an older half-brother named Prince James and a younger brother named Frank, later a Sumter County farmer. Nothing else is known of them. His father and mother died sometime before the end of the Civil War. The coming of freedom during that conflict found him, as he later expressed it, "bereft of both parents thrown upon the rugged shores of early emancipation."[8]

The end of slavery was a troubled time for all South Carolina black people.[9] From 1865 to the early 1900s, the approximately 415,000 Palmetto State blacks had to make the difficult transition from slavery to freedom within a turbulent political context: first a confusing Reconstruction, then the 1877 return of the Conservatives led by Wade Hampton, and finally the late-century agrarian revolt led by Benjamin R. Tillman. Difficult as the times were, however, freedom and the hope of continuing progress buoyed the freed people. No matter how difficult life was, it was better than being shackled in slavery.

Since most South Carolina blacks, Murray among them, had been plantation slaves, agriculture (that is mostly the growing of cotton and rice) was the extent of their economic experience. After emancipation most freed people envisioned a continued farming life, but now as independent agrarians. The newly emancipated slaves' great hope was land, their own land. A few were successful; they became land owners. Most, however, never achieved their dream. As late as 1910, only 21 percent of South Carolina's black farmers tilled their own soil.

Yet blacks were determined to resist any system that smacked of slavery.

Conversely, white land owners were equally determined to control the labor on their land. The result was the establishment of the sharecropping system in which blacks farmed with a minimum of supervision, and whites protected their investments by receiving a share of the harvested crop. Unfortunately, the crop lien system quickly evolved. The sharecropper had to mortgage his uncertain harvest in order to obtain the necessary supplies at planting time, and he often fell into debt and became tied to the land. By the end of the nineteenth century, peonage was a major fact of black life.

Financial slavery was thus the common lot of most South Carolina blacks in the post–Civil War period, and their desperate existence was clearly evident in their housing accommodations. As in slavery, houses for black people were inadequate. Their cabins or shacks of one to three rooms normally had no window glass, and the chimney was made of crossed sticks and clay. Nearby there might be a primitive well and a garden patch containing a variety of vegetables. Perhaps there would also be a small orchard with a few fruit trees. The prosperous black farmer had a few chickens and pigs. A milk cow was a luxury.

The major institutions in the black community were a country store, sometimes run by the white landowner himself, a church, the center of religious and social life, and perhaps a local school. The store provided the black farmer with those necessities he could not produce himself, but since harvests did not routinely cover the cost of purchases, the black farmer found himself and his family in perpetual debt. The black church was, as it had been in slavery, the place where blacks could unwind after a hard week of dealing with white society. Almost every sizable community had such an institution, because the need for religious consolation and group expression drew blacks together and gave them something they could call their own. There was widespread white opposition to educating blacks, so they continued to attend inferior segregated schools throughout the late nineteenth century. Although white public schools received better support than did the schools for blacks, white society constantly grumbled about the expense involved in educating black people. The white aversion to black education evident during the days of slavery remained in emancipation.

The state expended only a bare minimum on black education. Black teachers received little training, buildings were inadequate, and books, supplies, and equipment even as basic as desks were rare. Institutions conducted by religious groups were generally superior to public institutions, but they too were inadequate. Despite such impediments, blacks reached for education with an enthusiasm that astounded observers. In fact, next to land ownership, poor blacks looked to education as the surest way to improve their lives. Unfortunately, both education and land ownership were illusive commodities in a state that had witnessed the end of slavery but was determined to keep blacks subordinate.

Politics was also in a state of flux. The end of the Civil War saw the coming of Reconstruction, the attempt to bring the nation back together and include the former slaves now free as members of the reconstructed nation. In South Carolina, as in other southern states, former Confederate leaders were elected to federal and state offices, and the new state legislatures passed what came to be called "Black Codes," laws designed to insure that the freed people would remain subordinate in the postwar world. Such actions doomed the so-called Presidential Reconstruction of Andrew Johnson and brought about the passage of the Reconstruction Act of 1867, which terminated southern state governments and established military rule until southerners accepted the Fourteenth Amendment, which granted blacks citizenship. White southerners, South Carolinians included, called this period Radical or Black Reconstruction.

With the U.S. Army in control in 1868, South Carolina held a constitutional convention, and, to the shock of the state's whites, the delegation consisted of forty-eight whites and seventy-six blacks. These men produced a document that even some opponents had to admit had merit in its attempt to democratize the state's voting and office holding. The first election based on this new constitution resulted in twenty-one whites and ten blacks in the state senate, and forty-six whites and seventy-eight blacks in the state house. Public education, long established in the North, was constitutionally established in South Carolina, and a Land Commission, begun in 1869, bought up land and then resold it at affordable terms to freed people. All this activity was shocking to the white people of the state.

According to long-held mythology, Reconstruction was a time of unmitigated brutality and corruption. Never before or since, the tale goes, was there corruption of such magnitude. In truth, South Carolina's whites refused to accept the idea of an equal black participation in politics and life, so they labeled everything the Reconstruction governments did as corrupt. They called any non-native politicians corrupt carpetbaggers, any native whites who cooperated with Reconstruction traitorous scalawags, and all black politicians ignorant, venal scavengers. The word "Republican" became anathema to white voters because this was the party of carpetbaggers, scalawags, and blacks, and

no self-respecting white would ever vote for such people. This attitude continued until after the civil rights revolution of the 1960s.

To say that Reconstruction was merely a matter of white versus black,
Republican versus Democrat, is to oversimplify the situation. The tripartite
makeup of the Republican Party meant that there were serious policy and
personality disagreements among the so-called carpetbaggers, scalawags, and
blacks. As the historian Thomas Holt has shown, there were even disagreements among blacks themselves, between the light-skinned individuals (the
browns) and the dark-skinned people (the blacks). Many browns came from
elite free black or higher slave status and thus had skills and finances that
former field hands, the blacks, did not have. Such differing backgrounds and
experiences meant that browns and blacks frequently disagreed on the direction of their party and their race. Their emphasis on land, education, and civil
rights differed, and thus they did not present a united front against the powerful white society opposing them.[10]

George W. Murray grew to manhood during the whirlwind of Reconstruction, and he reflected these political conflicts, and, even more, he reflected
the general black desire to gain an education and own property. Family recollections indicate that Murray's slave masters, noticing his attempts to learn
to read, had violated the law and helped him. If this was true, he made little
progress, having to teach himself the alphabet by questioning neighborhood
school children and then practicing on anyone who would listen. In 1868, the
year of the constitutional convention, when he was fifteen years old, he was so
impressed with a speech delivered by George S. Boutwell, a Republican senator from Maine, that he memorized the section calling for the destruction of
pro-slavery ideas. Arithmetic was his best subject, however, and he could add
and subtract in his mind before he learned to write.

Sometime during his teenage years, he took up farming in the Rafting
Creek area of Sumter County on a piece of property east of present day High-
way 261, some twenty miles northwest of the city of Sumter.[11] In 1871, at the
age of eighteen, he decided to further his formal education and applied at a
nearby school. He was appointed the teacher instead. Demonstrating the poor
quality of education for blacks, the self-taught Murray was considered capable
of teaching others despite his own lack of formal training. For the next several
years, during the three or so months that classes were held each year,[12] he tilled
his fields in the early morning, taught his classes during the day, then hurried
back to the plow in the evening, sometimes working far into the night by the
light of the moon.

He maintained this rigorous schedule until the fall of 1874 when he passed a competitive examination and entered the temporarily integrated University of South Carolina, the institution still reeling from the turmoil surrounding the 1873 admission of its first black students.[13] Shocked white professors and students had reacted to the integration of their university by refusing to teach blacks or attend classes with them. The student body became predominately black, and a new faculty, mainly northern Methodists, replaced the departing teachers. The lone nonwhite professor was Harvard's first black graduate, Richard T. Greener.

This new "radical" university inherited a familiar problem from the old "conservative" school—a scarcity of students. As a remedy, the state offered scholarships to poor black and white scholars. Many of the scholarship winners could not meet the university's academic requirements, so the school had to establish a "subfreshman" class. Such financial and academic inducements only helped a little; the university's total enrollment in the fall of 1874 reached only 148 students, including 65 in the preparatory school. Of this total, 55 received financial aid.[14]

Scholarship winner Murray and twenty-four other students were placed in the sub-freshman section on October 5, 1874. They received instruction in arithmetic, composition, grammar, geography, history, and Latin. According to a February 17, 1875 university report, Murray's grade average during his first semester was 78 percent, good enough to rank him eighth in a class that had shrunk to twenty-three students. During his June 1875 examinations, his average rose to 81 percent, but his class standing dropped to ninth out of twenty-nine. He used his scholarship money of twenty dollars per month to pay debts incurred with merchant creditors for school expenses.[15]

After a summer back on his Sumter County farm, Murray returned to school for the fall semester in October 1875. He was now a freshman, a member of the graduating class of 1879. His average quickly dipped to 75 percent in the more difficult classical curriculum. Fellow students included Johnson C. Whittaker, later a West Point cadet, Thomas E. Miller, Murray's future political opponent, and Whitefield McKinlay, later an ally of Booker T. Washington. Murray lived in Columbia, although a long distance from the campus, and a few times he was late to mandatory morning prayers. His only unusual activity that year was his participation with twenty-one other students in petitioning for the reinstatement of an expelled classmate.[16]

His academic progress remained poor, his lack of formal education taking its toll. It took him until February 24, 1877, a year and a half, to advance to the sophomore class, and then he did not pass the March examinations. This academic record soon became irrelevant, however. Murray and his fellow black students were not allowed to complete their educations.[17]

Murray's expulsion from the University of South Carolina was the result of the collapse of Reconstruction and the return of the White Conservatives under the former Confederate general Wade Hampton. When the Republican governor, Daniel H. Chamberlain, opposed the legislative appointment of two controversial Republicans to the bench, white Carolina joined him in the protest. In Sumter at the beginning of January 1876, whites called for a mass meeting, but two thousand blacks rallied in support of the two Republican judicial appointees. Republicans were obviously splitting, but they still had enough power left to call out such a large crowd, and, fortunately, violence was averted.[18]

On July 4, 1876, however, an anti-black riot took place in another South Carolina town, Hamburg. Rumor had it that a black militia company, celebrating the national holiday, had prevented a wagon driven by two white men from passing. Outraged, several hundred whites, led by the former Confederate general Matthew C. Butler, demanded the disarming of the militia. When the blacks refused, gunfire erupted. Before the extended violence was over, seven blacks lay dead.

This bloody event served as the catalyst for the white takeover of South Carolina's government. The Democrats, who, up to this point, had been uncertain as to what to do, now nominated Wade Hampton for governor and, despite the Hamburg Massacre, he promised fair treatment for the state's black people. Violence exploded throughout the state, nonetheless. So-called Red Shirts, who accompanied Hampton on his tour of the state, intimidated blacks. Meanwhile, a variety of white rifle clubs broke up Republican gatherings. Throughout South Carolina, in activity reminiscent of the earlier Ku Klux Klan, whites beat, whipped, and shot black people in a campaign of violence to ensure Hampton's victory. Even the deployment of federal troops throughout the state, including briefly in Sumter, could not stop the violence. On election day itself, Red Shirts menacingly marched down the middle of streets throughout the state, making sure blacks did not vote. Despite such intimidation, the Republican candidate, Daniel Chamberlain, received the most Republican votes in the state's history up to that time, 91,127. But, Hampton was elected anyway, receiving 92,261. Chamberlain protested and tried to set up a rival government, but when the newly elected Republican president Rutherford B. Hayes withdrew federal troops from the state capital as part of the plan to insure his own disputed election over Samuel Tilden, Reconstruction was over in South Carolina. Anti-black violence had ensured the return of the old white power structure. Unlike the situation in other southern states, the new leaders came out of the past; they were former Confederate generals who wanted a return to the antebellum days when people like them ran the state.[19]

Murray's expulsion from the state's university demonstrated that blacks like him had been put in their place through the return of this white leadership. Murray returned to northwest Sumter County, to his life of school teaching and farming. Although he demonstrated no political ambitions, he no doubt was concerned about his right to vote, so the political changes he was witnessing in his county and his state had to be disturbing. But he had more personal matters on his mind. A twenty-four-year-old man of dark skin, he married a light-skinned twelve-year-old named Ella Reynolds. This 1877 marriage of adult and child never seemed to create any controversy, and the union lasted into the twentieth century. A son was born in December 1879 (later to become a physician) and a daughter arrived in 1881 (later to marry a Baptist minister). Another child, a girl, died in infancy.[20]

Murray's hard work behind the plow began to pay off. In 1880 he owned forty-nine acres of tilled land and fifteen acres of woodlands and forests; the land and the farm buildings were valued at $1,500. The farm's yearly production in 1879 was valued at $650. There were five acres of corn and twenty-one acres of cotton, one milk cow, four pigs, one horse, one mule, one working ox, eight chickens, eight peach trees, and four apple trees. The woodlands yearly produced twenty-five cords of wood. The farm operations were remunerative enough for Murray to afford a hired hand. He was a successful farmer by either white or black South Carolina standards of that age.[21]

Buttressed with his farm success, Murray began a political career in April 1880 as a delegate from Sumter County to the state Republican Party convention. That June he came to understand the benefit of such politics when he gained a patronage job as an enumerator for the U.S. census. He was a Republican, as were most blacks during those years, but his party was a floundering one. The South Carolina Republican Party had never been unified even during Reconstruction, and it was now staggering from the 1876 trouncing it had received at the hands of Wade Hampton and the resurgent Conservative Democrats. Anti-Republican violence, intra-party bickering, some of which included intra-race conflicts dating from Reconstruction days, Conservative accusations of corruption, and the death or removal of many key leaders all hurt the party. Republicans had a weak organization and most of the state's white citizens despised them besides.[22]

Murray's attendance at his first state Republican convention brought him face to face with these weaknesses. That April 1880 meeting was convened to elect delegates to the 1880 national GOP gathering, but other issues were also debated. Were the delegates elected to the national conclave to be instructed on how to vote? How should a resolution supporting Johnson C. Whittaker, a former University of South Carolina black student, in his battle with the West Point judicial system be worded? Whittaker was found in early April in his West Point room, the victim of a nighttime attack by three masked men. Military authorities, however, insisted that he had slashed his own ears, tied himself up, and feigned unconsciousness, all to avoid an examination two months into the future.[23]

The big issue was whether or not to support U. S. Grant for a third presidential term. The debate droned on interminably until Murray, though a newcomer, protested. He told the convention delegates that he was tired of all the haggling and just wanted to go home. Others must have felt the same way because his motion passed.[24] Murray's political debut began with a successful display of impatient frustration at his political party's vacillation, a display of temper that in later years would become even more evident in his political personality.

This show of impudent independence may very well have been the reason for the disappearance of his name from the political rolls for the next several years. When state Republicans held a meeting in March 1882 to protest some hostile state electoral changes, Murray was not present. He was not even involved in a meeting called in his hometown to form a biracial political party.

The state legislature had recently changed the state election procedure to make it more difficult for blacks to register to vote. If an individual did not register to vote during a prescribed period, he was barred forever from the suffrage.[25] The legislature also passed the "eight-box" law, which required a separate ballot box for each of the offices being contested in an election, a procedure meant to frustrate poorly educated black voters, although it adversely affected poor whites too. Congressional district boundaries were also gerrymandered to insure white victories in six of the seven districts. The Seventh Congressional District (the so-called Black District) contained a high preponderance of blacks; the white power structure risked the election of one black congressman from that district to guarantee six white ones elsewhere. The White Conservatives, whom Wade Hampton said would be fair to black people, were obviously working to eliminate them from the political process.

Murray was a delegate to the September 1882 convention of the newly created seventh congressional district,[26] indicating that his political limbo was short lived. Once again, he spoke out as though he were a powerful politician, which he was not. He threatened to "turn the district to the Bourbons," the White Conservative leaders, if the convention did not give the congressional nomination to Sam Lee, the Sumter County party chairman and former Reconstruction Speaker of the House. The delegates ignored Murray. No one was able to gain a majority, not E.W.M. Mackey, a white Republican leader, nor two blacks, Sam Lee and Robert Smalls, a Civil War naval hero. Day after day, ballot after ballot, the vote remained deadlocked, reflecting the deep Republican divisions even in the one congressional district that Republicans had a chance to win. On the 247th and the 250th ballots, two of Smalls delegates supported Mackey. The Lee forces immediately and angrily pushed through a resolution requiring a candidate who won by bribery to forfeit the nomination, obviously accusing Smalls of malfeasance. On the 251st ballot, a week after the balloting had begun, three more delegates switched to Mackey, and he won the nomination.[27]

The Lee forces, Murray included, were outraged and immediately petitioned the Republican State Committee to repudiate Mackey's nomination on the grounds of fraud. Since Mackey chaired the state committee, the petition went nowhere. In protest, Lee ran an independent race, but Mackey beat him easily, 18,469 to 10,017. The black congressional district had elected a white Republican. On the state level, a Republican alliance with the Greenback Party helped elect fifteen blacks to the state legislature, but the Conservative Democrats held on to the governorship and won just about everything else. Murray had supported losers both on the local and on the state level. More ominously, the restrictive 1882 eight-box law stood unchallenged and was sure to marginalize black voters in the future.[28]

Just two years later, in the 1884 elections, Republicans saw the first effect of the law. Black representation in the state legislature dropped from fifteen to seven. Instead of fostering unity, however, this result only increased Republican infighting, and Murray was in the thick of it. During a raucous debate in Sumter among candidates for the 1884 seventh district Republican congressional nomination, Murray tried to join in, but the meeting's chairman, Sam Lee, ruled him out of order. Angrily Murray excoriated Lee, the man he had so strongly supported in 1882. Lee gaveled for order; Murray responded by marching up and down the aisle demanding to be heard, and the delegates became increasingly restive. A reporter, trying to hear what was going on, moved to the front. Lee noticed the newsman and warned the gathering that, this time, a press description of Republican turmoil would not be Democratic mis-representation; it would be the truth. The delegates grew silent, and Murray sat down.[29]

This incident, like the deadlocked 1882 convention, clearly indicated the lack of Republican unity. Surrounded as they were by an oppressing white pop-ulace, Republicans reacted by feuding among themselves, black against black, white against black. They were unable to strike back effectively or safely at those discriminating against them, so they turned their anger onto themselves. Republicans vented their frustration through intramural squabbling.

The Sumter County Republican meeting of 1884, called to elect delegates to the state convention, erupted into similar disagreement. Murray, who re-mained angry at Lee for the snub at the prior meeting, unsuccessfully opposed the Lee slate of candidates and sought to gain a state delegate's seat for him-self and his slate. He called Lee's supporters "low-down scoundrels" and Lee himself a dishonest boss who was willing to do anything to maintain political power. A stunned Lee replied in his own defense with one of the convention's longest speeches. Murray lost, Republicans were split, but once again the new Sumter black politician gained recognition for his boldness.[30]

Murray now allied himself even more closely to the anti-Lee Sumter Coun-ty faction led by T. B. Johnston, an Irish-born former Union Army officer, and it paid off for him. At the September 1884 district congressional convention, he was elected Sumter County congressional chairman, the coordinator of the seventh congressional district's Republican effort in his county. When the vote was taken to nominate a candidate for the state legislature, he received only 106 votes, the lowest of any candidate and minuscule compared to the victor's 1,816. In 1885, however, he was elected for the first of his three terms as Sumter County Republican chairman.[31] He had risen to leadership status.

Unfortunately, his office was an empty honor. The 1882 registration restric-tions and the eight-box law made it impossible for Republicans to win any state office. At the congressional level, the gerrymandering of districts gave Republicans a chance in only one of the state's seven districts. The national party's loss of the White House to Grover Cleveland, a Democrat, was further disheartening, so discouraging, in fact, that the state party never even held a state convention during the Cleveland presidency. The Republicans reaction to their disfranchisement predicament was to withdraw from the political scene. Murray's newly acquired leadership role meant little in the face of the White Conservatives' increasingly successful electoral disfranchisement.

Murray still had his land to farm, and he continued teaching. Between 1884 and 1889 when Grover Cleveland was president and Republicans were in political limbo in South Carolina, he taught at School District No. 8–Rafting Creek. He earned $150 in 1886, but this fell to $50 in 1888. His farm remained the major source of his income. He also made some money on the stump. Beginning in 1881, he inaugurated his public speaking career. Before the 185 black teachers in attendance at a "Normal Institute," he delivered a paper on school discipline.[32]

While he taught and farmed, politics did not remain far from Murray's mind. Republicans had high hopes of recapturing the White House for their party, and Murray, as Sumter County Republican chairman, had no problem being elected one of the five county delegates to the state convention. Because of his teaching activities, one newspaper said that he was "the most intellectual negro [sic] in the county." He said nothing at the April state convention, however, demonstrating that he was not yet a major Republican figure, despite his solid local base.[33]

That summer, a hard fought Republican national convention nominated Benjamin Harrison for president, and Murray used the hoopla surrounding this event to extend his political influence beyond his home county. He took part in a ratification meeting in Berkeley County just outside Charleston, speaking in support of Harrison and defending the Republican policy of high tariffs. He rhetorically asked the audience if they preferred to have a tariff hat for $1 and wages of 75 cents per day or a free-trade hat for 75 cents and wages of 40 cents per day. A woman in the audience responded that she wanted the 75 cents hat. Murray was temporarily jolted, but he ended his first major political speech "amid great cheering," State Republicans began to take notice.[34]

Murray's blossoming political status matched the optimistic Republican attitude. The Republican share of the presidential vote in South Carolina had sunk to another low (13,740 for Harrison compared to 65,825 for Grover Cleveland 65,825), but Palmetto State Republicans were optimistic because of Harrison's victory and the return of a national GOP administration to Washington. In Sumter County, two thousand blacks attended a public meeting, complete with a one-hour parade. An incredulous newsman, seeing this mass of humanity, wrote that the state Republican Party might be dead, but it was "a lively corpse" in Sumter County. Murray not only presided over this successful four-hour event, but he was also its first major speaker. He denied that the state Republican Party was dead; it had "only [been] snowed under by a pile of ballot-box frauds." Mocking the White Conservatives, he said that they "claimed to be our friends and proved it by a hundred years of slavery" and now by ballot-box cheating. A strong Republican organization was the only way to counteract such fraud, he roared. He warned the crowd that the American eagle would leave the South "where it was not healthy for it to live" and instead go to places like Oregon, Vermont, and Maine, solid Republican strongholds. This statement earned him a nickname he would carry throughout his political career: the "black bold eagle" of South Carolina.[35]

He quickly demonstrated continued boldness and his rising political stock. A few weeks after Benjamin Harrison's election, Murray sent the president-elect a fifteen-page handwritten letter of advice. Harrison was allegedly ready to revitalize the Republican Party in the state by supporting an Independent Republican movement through the appointment of independents to federal office, and Murray tried to talk him out of it. He played on Harrison's emotions by describing black voter loyalty to the Republican cause despite personal danger and tremendous electoral obstacles. He urged the president not to punish this loyalty by supporting non-Republicans for federal offices in the Palmetto State.[36]

Murray's letter was one part of a concerted South Carolina Republican campaign to mend fences with Harrison. In early January 1889, the Republican state chairman, Ellery M. Brayton, a white Harvard-educated lawyer, published a twenty-four-page pamphlet publicly repeating the arguments Murray had made in his personal letter. Murray was now included in the highest echelon of state politics—the Palmetto State's relationship with a Republican president.[37]

This rumored 1889 movement to remake the South Carolina Republican Party was nothing new or unexpected. Republicans were a sectional party and, after the war, the national GOP feared that a revitalized, nationally based Democratic organization would push them permanently out of power. Therefore they believed they had to gain many converts in the South to survive politically. Obvious targets were newly freed and enfranchised blacks and former white southern Whigs. Blacks became Republicans, but only a limited number of southern whites joined them. As Reconstruction ended, most southern Republican parties, like South Carolina's, were predominately black and weak in the face of an unremitting white racism.[38]

National Republicans had tried to compromise with southern Democrats in 1876. They had ceased contesting white Democratic control of southern state political life in return for southern acquiescence in Rutherford B. Hayes's election to the presidency and a promise of fairness to black voters. Persuasion, not continued military force, would settle the turmoil in the South, national

Republicans believed. They would convince white southerners that Republicans were worthy of support. Unfortunately for them, this policy failed. During the 1880 presidential canvass that elected James A. Garfield, Republicans realized that many of their black southern adherents had been eliminated from the political process, and they had gained only a few white converts.

James Garfield's presidency was the time when Republicans implemented elements of all the basic policies that they were to follow well into the twentieth century to try to strengthen their party in the South. Garfield wavered from "bloody shirt" anti-Democratic Party polemics, to talk of educating black voters, to an attempted alliance with dissident white Democrats. Republicans faced a formidable problem: they had to build up the white membership in the southern Republican parties without sacrificing blacks and thereby alienating black voters in pivotal northern states. The result was a recurring appeal to dissident whites, then support for blacks, then back to whites, all the while insisting that this activity was being done to ensure continued black participation in politics. Actually, the maneuvering was not altruistic. The national party was interested in the black voter to the extent that he could help the national party. As southern disfranchisement inexorably eliminated these voters, the national Republican hierarchy became increasingly interested in white converts and decreasingly concerned for blacks. National Democrats had no interest at all in the black franchise, so the weak Republican interest was the black man's only hope. He had to live with repeated Republican appeals to white southerners and try to prevent them from resulting in his total electoral elimination.

The emergence of an 1889 South Carolina Independent movement, therefore, was nothing more than a repetition of events that had transpired in 1878 and 1882 (and would be repeated several times in the future). The victorious Harrison forces were unhappy with the depressed condition of Republicanism throughout the South, and, in South Carolina, they were particularly upset that the Palmetto State delegation had not supported the president-elect during the national convention. Inside the state, there were Republicans, Greenbackers, and dissident Democrats who, displeased with the racial composition and weakness of the state GOP, also supported change. These two attitudes, national and state, merged in early 1889; South Carolina Republicanism once more faced an involuntary transfusion of white blood. Economics, particularly the tariff, was touted as the way to gain GOP converts; the disastrous race issue was to be put aside.

A veteran of state Greenback and Independent politics, J. Hendrix McLane led the South Carolina movement. During the 1880s, McLane had been a congressional candidate several times, and, in 1882, he had been the Independent Republican candidate for governor. Frustrated at his lack of success, he had gone north in 1886 to enroll at Boston's Tufts College Theological School. He also married for the second time, and his new wife was the daughter of a Boston family with ties to Bay State reformers. Encouraged by these new acquaintances, McLane hoped to revitalize South Carolina Republicans with the help of New England money.[39]

This Independent resurgence stimulated the Regular Republicans, the established South Carolina GOP, to action, but their letters to Harrison took a strange tack. They called on the new president to name William Mahone of Virginia, a turncoat Democrat, the nation's postmaster general. They supported a white Republican movement and merger with fallen-away Democrats on the national level in their attempt to oppose similar individuals within their own state. Murray contributed to this contradictory policy. Although his earlier letter to Harrison had opposed South Carolina Independents, he now supported Mahone, arguing that the Virginian had "led out of the camp of one idea and death a sufficient number of white men to be felt as a party within the boundaries of a southern state." He left unsaid why McLane's activities in South Carolina should not receive equal support.[40]

South Carolina's restrictive electoral laws had all but eliminated any Republican hope for success in state elections and so both factions, the Independents and the Regulars, had to look to Washington to determine the outcome of their disagreement. The two sides thus fought over office to gain the national party's recognition. A political party without office holders had little appeal; South Carolina Republicans could gain only a few elective offices, so they had to look for patronage positions from Washington for their survival. But it was not this seeking of patronage that caused the factionalism in the first place. Patronage was the symbol of success in the intra-party strife, not the cause of it.

Harrison demonstrated his uncertainty on how to deal with South Carolina Republicans when he made his appointments to office. He named the Independent leader Dr. V. P. Clayton postmaster at Columbia, and he made another Independent the postmaster at Anderson, but his major 1889 South Carolina federal officer appointments were all long time Regulars, one black and three whites: Robert Smalls, the black Civil War naval hero and former congressman, as collector of customs at Beaufort; G. I. Cunningham, a longtime GOP politician and Charleston businessman, as U.S. marshall; E. A. Webster, the soon-to-be state party chairman, as internal revenue collector;

and T. B. Johnston of Sumter County as customs collector at Charleston. The Independents, to quote the press, had met their "Waterloo." McLane maintained his New England and Washington contacts, and he even tried to remain close to regular state chairman Ellery Brayton. The essential fact was, however, that the Regulars had survived the Independent assault and remained in control of the Republican Party in South Carolina.

The Regulars could not, however, claim personal credit for their victory; it resulted from national events. Harrison's national Republicans concentrated their revitalizing efforts on Alabama, Louisiana, and Virginia and decided to hold the line in South Carolina. Their efforts failed, most spectacularly with the defeat of Mahone in Virginia. They then returned to old-line Republican policies by trying unsuccessfully to pass a federal law protecting black suffrage, the so-called Force Bill. Had Mahone been successful in Virginia, however, McLane would eventually have won in South Carolina, too. Fortunately for Murray and other South Carolina Regular Republicans, their support of Virginia readjuster William Mahone had not paved the way for their own demise. The national Republican dalliance with the Independents and their unenthusiastic support for the Force Bill gave the South Carolina Regulars a new, though uncertain, lease on life.[41]

Murray had played a visible role in all this maneuvering, but he still remained outside the Republican leadership circle. His lack of clout was evident in his unsuccessful attempt in 1889 to gain the Sumter postmastership.[42] Yet, the Regulars' victory and his own widening activity augured well for his political future.

Murray added to his visibility through participation in the Colored Alliance. This organization, the black equivalent of the all-white Southern Alliance, aimed to improve the lot of the struggling black farmer. At times, such as at the Ocala, Florida meeting of 1890, the two organizations cooperated, but white farmers were usually unable to overcome their racism.[43]

The Colored Alliance apparently came to South Carolina with a Texas organizer in May 1888. In June 1889, representatives from twenty counties met in Columbia and established a state-wide organization. At this time the Colored Alliance claimed a membership of thirty to forty thousand farmers. Murray was one of Sumter County's representatives at the June meeting, and he played the major role at the first important Colored Alliance state-wide event, a barbecue near his farm. White Alliance men were invited to the festivity, and a few were conspicuously evident on the veranda of the old house from which the speakers boomed out their messages to the crowd of nine hundred listeners. Several leading white Alliance men presented addresses, but Murray gave the speech that received the most attention.[44]

Murray's oration echoed the central ideas of the Alliance movement: self-help, middle-class morality, education, obedience to law and order, and economic improvement. He urged his black listeners not to distrust their white brothers but to work with them for mutual benefit. He hoped, he said to the whites present, that in the future "they could meet on such friendly footing in all of their interest in life." He thought this was the first time Palmetto State blacks and whites had ever met together like this, and he believed "a new era had dawned in which white and colored farmers would pull together for the good of South Carolina." Recognizing the anti-black prejudice that was undeniably an integral part of South Carolina life, Murray tried to deal with it here by identifying with the oppressors of his race. Improve yourselves and trust whites, he told black farmers, and discrimination will go away. As if to underscore this desired unity, a black band played "Dixie," and three cheers were raised for "Dixie, the land of cotton." The whites courteously passed a resolution of thanks to their black hosts.[45]

Such euphoria was short-lived. The Colored Alliance held its next state convention in November 1889, and a resolution to withdraw from the national organization was introduced because many South Carolina black Alliance men were angry over an assessment to help finance a national exchange. The promise of a state exchange in Charleston quickly appeased the dissidents, but the debate and the subsequent failure of such a state exchange produced hard feelings. At various times, too, there was talk of starting a Colored Alliance newspaper (*Alliance Light*), once supposedly at Sumter and another time in Columbia. Like the discussion about the exchange, this debate produced more frustration than benefit. The rumor that a Colored Alliance bank with capital of $100,000 was being planned in Charleston also raised hopes, but again nothing concrete resulted. When the South Carolina group was encouraged to cooperate in a nationwide Colored Alliance cotton picker's strike, and it never really materialized, the result caused conflict within the organization and between it and its white counterpart. A March 1889 local boycott in Kershaw County, South Carolina was summarily squelched by white landowners.[46]

These failures were not the Colored Alliance's major problems. The movement encountered its major difficulty when it attempted to cooperate politically with the state's white farmers. In 1890, the Shiloh Colored Farmers Alliance of Marlboro endorsed Benjamin Tillman, the dissident white Democrat farmer, in his race for the governorship against the Conservative Democrats; the incumbents became furious. They demanded to know: "What have the Colored Alliances to do with our present 'purely family fight'?" They applied enormous pressure on the white farmer Democrats to explain their cooperation with blacks. In response, the white farmers angrily replied that they had not asked for black support, nor did they want it. The ever present racial animosity replaced the momentary friendly tone of the barbecue and the fact of common economic problems.[47] The Colored Alliance's attempt to make a political linkage with white farmers and the resulting shrill rejection soon completed its demise.

Murray's role in all this turmoil was shadowy. His Republican fealty was strengthening during these years, but, at the same time, the Colored Alliance was booming him for Congress. When the state organization met in 1892 in what was apparently its last session, Murray was one of the mere fifteen delegates present. This convention reported a membership decline from forty thousand to twenty-five thousand, and debate once more displayed the fatal weakness: uncertainty as to its role in state politics. The handful of delegates voted to remain politically uncommitted, and the white alliance later approved. But it was too late. The South Carolina Colored Alliance, like its national parent organization, slipped from existence, and its death in South Carolina was largely the result of white supremacy ideals.[48]

Even though he was a leading Alliance men, Murray had little time to think about his organization's demise. He had cast his lot with the Republican Party, and the 1890s were to see him move into a position of prominence in that organization. His decade of teaching, farming, membership in the Colored Alliance, and political experience had prepared him to become a leading figure in Palmetto State politics. The former slave was making his mark in the white man's world in education, agriculture, and, most importantly, in politics.

Murray's major occupation, the political arena, was fraught with problems. Republican uncertainty in the face of determined active white opposition had resulted in a steadily deteriorating position. While Murray's stock in the party had risen, the party's position had eroded. What was needed was new Republican leadership on the state level, stronger support from the national party, and a crack in Democratic solidarity. The early 1890s were to witness a split in the white political ranks to give hope to the floundering GOP. Murray's activities also contributed to the rising optimism.

2

# The 1890 Election

## Success and Failure

Every January 1 during the post–Civil War years, blacks celebrated Emancipation Day. There were parades, prayers, and other festivities with a leading black political or religious figure always presenting a major speech. To give an Emancipation address was a mark of distinction in the black community. When George W. Murray mounted a rostrum on January 1, 1890, therefore, this action demonstrated concretely his importance in South Carolina's black society. The location for the celebration was Charleston, the most important city in the state and the center of its black elite, so Murray's speech indicated clearly that he was now a major black figure in the Palmetto State.

He quickly demonstrated that he was an exponent of black pride in the midst of an anti-black society. Murray urged blacks not to continue to celebrate the fourth of July in preference to the first of January. The events of July 4 may have lifted tyranny from whites, but they had only intensified discrimination against blacks. Emancipation Day, not Independence Day, marked the true beginning of black freedom.

Blacks also had to recognize that real emancipation comprised freedom from two kinds of slavery, physical and mental.[1] Though blacks had gained freedom from physical slavery on January 1, 1863, they were still mentally enslaved in 1890. To rid themselves of this remaining slavery, black attitudes had to change. They had to stop imitating whites and had to "get down to work at once to create . . . race pride and self-respect." Black leaders had to show black people that it was not their skin color but "their condition" that caused discrimination. Blacks should not blame their subordination on white people, Murray insisted: "I would rather say we should blame ourselves."

Black pride alone was not enough, however. For a black parent to tell his child that he was as good as anyone else was meaningless when that child saw countless examples of black inferiority around him. Black pride required business success. "Around [the] business and commercial classes everywhere rotate and depend all other classes, as the satellites do around the sun." "In order to elevate ourselves," Murray exhorted, "*we must get control* of that portion of the business of this country resulting from our numbers and consumptions." "In the long run the influence of coppers, dimes, and dollars falling in the drawers of the businessmen outweigh all the eloquence and genius of the brilliant statesman in the halls of legislation." Black financial success was the true agent for black pride and mental emancipation.

For black businesses to be successful, however, black people had to spend their money wisely. There were about 750,000 blacks in South Carolina, Murray pointed out, and computing an average expenditure of $25 per year per person, this meant a potential reservoir of some $18,750,000 for black betterment. Unfortunately, blacks did not recognize their own economic power: they did not realize that a wealthy black man enriched the race while he was enriching himself. Consequently, blacks spent foolishly; they did not restrict their spending to black businesses. Whites in general and Jews in particular recognized the importance of group solidarity, so their establishments were successful and provided jobs for their children. Blacks had no such outlets. When black youth completed their educations and they found no jobs, they mistakenly blamed the educational system. Actually it was the lack of black patronage of black businessmen that caused the lack of jobs for talented young black people, Murray intoned. In Charleston, for example, if blacks controlled only one-fourth of the city's businesses, their stock would increase and whites would have to treat them better.[2]

Such group solidarity meant uplifting the black masses. "In order to elevate ourselves we must elevate the race," Murray said. The world blamed the entire race for the transgressions of any individual, so every black person had to perform with superiority and honesty for the good of all. Black overcrowding in the cities had to stop. Too many people were abandoning the country for the city, and this exodus was driving down wages. Black labor organizations should find work for the unemployed "or drive them out of the city." Blacks should even organize vigilante groups to help the police track down "every vagrant and loafer" on the streets.

Murray, who was a full-blooded black man, saved his harshest condemnations for the black exponents of status according to lightness of skin. "The idiotic attempt to found society upon color, especially that having its origin in questionable fountains is unreasonable and damaging beyond imagination and is really an encouragement in and invitation to, the destruction of all morality and virtue." To adhere to such an idea was "to make our boys representing the purity and nobility of the race ashamed of their dark faces." He urged his Charleston audience to ostracize anyone espousing such ideas whether that person be businessman, politician, or preacher. In conclusion, he appealed to black history, calling on the ancient African civilizations to "reanimate you to have more pride and respect for yourselves and to make greater efforts to regain your standing and heritage in the history of grandeur of earth and glory and crown of heaven."[3]

In the tradition of nineteenth-century oratory, Murray had spoken for over an hour, filling his speech with classical allusions and flowery overblown rhetoric. He ignored politics and spoke of black pride and economics. In his words could be heard the philosophy of the Colored Alliance, echoes of black thought since the Civil War, and the later more famous accommodationist words and philosophy of Booker T. Washington and his National Negro Business League.[4] The modern historian can also notice prophetic hints of "black is beautiful," salvation for the masses, and black separatist themes identified with later black rhetoric. In his speech, Murray was reflecting the thought of those black contemporaries who saw economics rather than politics as the solution to black problems. But, he was also reacting to the anti-black prejudice of South Carolina society by calling for a strengthening of in-group ties. Overcome discrimination by drawing closer together economically, he told his black audience.

Despite this rhetoric, politics remained important to him. He had already spent significant time and effort pursuing the aim of black political empowerment, and his own land ownership had shown him the importance of economics. His philosophy of life included both economics and politics. Black pride and progress came from a combination of both spheres, and he was determined to pursue each. The state's press, however, ignored his strong words. The Columbia *Register* noted the celebration, but commented only on another speaker's call for black emigration. Murray was snubbed because he obviously said things that whites did not want to hear. The black elite heard him in person, however, and this speech benefited his political future. Murray tried to take advantage of the situation by applying for a patronage position to shore up his political stock in another way. He asked his Sumter Republican colleague, T. B. Johnston, the recently appointed Charleston collector of customs, for the post of customs inspector. The Custom House in Charleston was *the* center of state Republican political activity, so a job here would enable Murray to be privy to most South Carolina GOP state activity. To his satisfaction, he gained the post.[5]

The same day he became a customs inspector, he participated in a meeting that demonstrated how precarious black life was in South Carolina. On

December 28, 1889, eight blacks in the Barnwell, South Carolina jail were lynched. Such violence was common in the state, but the multiple nature of the Barnwell murders was especially egregious. On seventy-two hours notice, four hundred blacks, including Murray, rushed to Columbia's Wesley Methodist Episcopal Church opposite State House Square to protest. The meeting voted to send a delegation to the governor with resolutions calling for law and order, and Murray was named to a committee drawing up the resolutions. The committee labeled the murder of the eight jailed blacks uncivilized and criticized white press sensationalism for stimulating the mob to action. It rejected rumors of a black insurrection as justification for the lynchings and called on whites to respect all black rights. In a weak display of militancy, the committee lamely threatened the departure of blacks from those areas of the state where such violence occurred. Murray signed the committee resolution, but he was not part of the delegation that met with the chief executive and received a cordial but noncommittal reception.[6] State authorities continued to stand idly by while blacks were murdered.

The simultaneous development of Democratic intra-party factionalism of the worst kind was an important reason why there was no favorable response to black appeals. In January 1890, Benjamin R. Tillman's Farmers Association issued its "Shell Manifesto," scheduling a March meeting for the purpose of capturing the later Democratic Party state convention. The shocked white Conservatives, the dominant political force in the state, could hardly afford to criticize black lynchings in the face of such a political threat.[7]

This split was a manifestation of the agrarian protest rocking the country during the 1880s and 1890s.[8] Every state with a large agricultural population was in turmoil, as the Alliance movement and the later Populist Party attempted to organize farmers to try to solve their economic problems. Benjamin Ryan Tillman began his South Carolina farmers' protest in the fall of 1885 because he too found the farmers' plight unpalatable. However, Tillman was not interested in the grand economic issues that the Alliance movement was thrusting forward. He railed against alleged corruption in the state government and called for state agricultural institutes and an agricultural college. Though a large plantation owner himself, he insisted on representing himself as the small farmers' champion.

Tillman's Democratic opponents, the Conservative Democrats, remained the state's old-line leaders, the officers in the Confederate Army during the Civil War, and the "redeemers" from alleged Radical and black rule during Reconstruction. Led by Wade Hampton, a Civil War general, later the governor, and finally a senator, the Conservative Democrats saw themselves as defenders of South Carolina's past. Most of them were also agrarians, but they had no program to deal with contemporary agricultural problems except to call for loyalty to the past, to all that had supposedly made South Carolina great—that is, to leadership by people like themselves.

The major difference between the Tillmanites and the Conservatives was not agrarian economics; it was who should rule in South Carolina. Tillman did not try to establish a new radical political organization; he simply wanted to capture the Democratic Party. He espoused no innovative programs to help the farmer. His success in having Clemson University established as a place for educating farmers was his major achievement. His campaigns were issue-less; personal attacks on his opponents and consolidation of his emotional hold on the electorate. He did not even mount a campaign of small versus large farmers because he was a large landowner himself. Tillman campaigned against what he called the corruption and the irrelevancy of the Conservatives and their political message. He wanted to replace these aging leaders with his young lawyers, politicians, and landowners, men who had previously gained office on the local level but had not held statewide positions before. An agricultural depression and Tillman's leadership gave them the opportunity to contest the old leaders, and they took full advantage of it.

It would be inaccurate to overemphasize the differences between the Conservatives and the Tillmanites. As Tillman's early biographer correctly put it, "both Hampton and Tillman were ever loyal Southerners who believed in the Confederate tradition, white supremacy, and the Democratic party."[9] The Conservatives believed in a white Democracy based on pre–Civil War leadership, while the Tillmanites believed in white Democracy based on the post–Civil War generation. Most importantly for Murray and the South Carolina Republican Party, both Democratic factions agreed that there must be no meaningful black participation in the state's political, social, or economic life. The Tillmanites promised action, and, ironically, their violent takeover of the Democratic Party meetings was reminiscent of the early Conservative conquering of the Reconstruction Republican Party.[10]

No matter the precise differences and similarities undergirding the Democratic split, it seemingly provided the first opportunity since the early 1880s for South Carolina Republicans to gain political office. The Democratic factions might be forced to ally with Republicans. The obstacles, however, remained formidable: widespread white support for lynching, legal and illegal discrimination against all Republicans but black Republicans in particular, uncertainty as to how to negate it, and continued Republican squabbling.

On March 18, 1890, party chairman Ellery M. Brayton, a white man, tried to take advantage of the Democratic split by calling on the state's Republican supporters to intensify their efforts to register. The 1882 registration law, he pointed out, required registrars to open their books on the first Monday of each month until July. He encouraged every precinct within the state to organize a registration effort. There was a good chance Congress would pass a national election law (Force Bill), he advised, so every Republican should be ready to take advantage of the law when it became a reality.[11]

This call only intensified the already existing criticism of Brayton within the state party. One South Carolina Republican called his statement a "piece of political imbecility or party treachery." Brayton had previously given little thought to registering voters, this Republican said, and suddenly he announced an action that stupidly threatened Thomas E. Miller's contest in the U.S. House of Representatives to gain the congressional seat denied him in the 1888 election. Miller, who was a leading black attorney, state legislator, and Republican party leader in Beaufort County, could hardly claim Republicans were being kept from the polls if the party chairman admitted that many of them had not even bothered to register. Another Republican surmised that Brayton had issued the address for the sole purpose of salvaging his waning influence in Washington. E. A. Webster, a white man who was hoping to unseat Brayton as state chairman, was even more critical. He wrote Miller that Brayton could not have issued his address at a worst time had he been an employee of the Democratic Party. Miller surprisingly defended Brayton and taunted Webster with his own inaction.[12] Republicans were responding to the feuding Democrats by fighting among themselves, thus lessening their slim hopes even further.

Brayton's registration address actually hurt Republican chances for a different reason. It frightened the Democrats, causing the shaky Conservatives to call for unity. The Conservative Charleston *News and Courier* warned its readers that Brayton's address was ominous because black Republicans did not normally try to register until the last moment. There was an obvious moral, the paper said; Democrats better stop feuding and unite against the black threat.[13]

GOP vitality seemed to bear out the Conservative concerns. Rumors spread that the Republicans would soon be convening a convention to nominate a full state ticket for the first time since Reconstruction. More significantly, blacks were flocking to registration sites all around the state. In Orangeburg, the largest number of blacks ever seen in the city during the summer months crowded in front of the registrar's office. In Union, more than five hundred blacks registered, and many more were turned away. In Columbia, Brayton personally directed registration activity.[14]

The determined Republican efforts produced few results, however. In Orangeburg, blacks were turned away because the registrar there said the law called for his books to be open on the first day of each month, not on the first Monday as Brayton had announced. In Columbia, a registrar closed his office rather that register blacks, and a grand jury refused to return an indictment against him that Brayton demanded.[15]

The 1890 census indicated that blacks made up approximately 60 percent of the state's population, yet the Republican vote in presidential elections had steadily dropped from an 1876 high of 50 percent of the total votes cast to a mere 17 percent in 1888. Some Republican voters were white (and no doubt some blacks voted for Democrats), but the Republican vote was still a reasonable indicator of black voting in the state. Clearly, black participation in the electoral process had deteriorated badly between 1876 and 1888. The registration law was proving to be effective against black voters despite Republican efforts to undermine it.

Beginning on March 1, Murray was in a perfect location to participate in all this Republican activity. He began his job as an inspector in the Charleston Custom House, the state Republican political headquarters. He moved to rented accommodations at 56 Nassau Street, his wife and family apparently remaining on his Sumter County farm. His duties as customs inspector consisted in boarding ships entering the port, inspecting the cargo to prevent smuggling, and determining correct tariff charges. Murray was not the first black man to hold such a position, but he still had problems because of his race. One of the first times he tried to inspect a ship, the captain of the vessel grew angry at his questions and refused to deal with him any longer, citing his black skin as the reason. After the two men came close to blows, the captain reluctantly backed down when someone from the main office told him that his ship would not be allowed to enter port without Murray's approval. Murray had no further problems.[16]

Murray also played a key role in the registration drive led by Brayton. In July, for example, he addressed a group of Sumter County blacks while they completed affidavits to try to obtain registration certificates. Such tasks were

routinely assigned to party functionaries, but Murray had decided to run for
Congress from the Seventh District, so this activity was part of his campaign
effort. Once more, he displayed political audacity. He was not only running
in the only district where Republicans had a chance to win, but he was also
willing to challenge party luminaries such as Miller and Brayton for the post.
His Sumter speech showed that the task did not awe him. He attacked State
Party Chairman Brayton, confident in his support from T. B. Johnston and
other Republican Custom House officials. Squabbling Democratic leaders
were convinced that the three way contest was a subterfuge to stimulate black
registration, and then rumors spread that both Democratic factions were plotting a fusion with the resurgent GOP.[17]

The Seventh District Republican battle was no sham; all three candidates
were serious. The campaign leading up to the August 12 nominating convention in that district was filled with speeches, county conventions, local meetings, and vilification. Speaker after speaker accused Brayton of running for
Congress only to boost his later candidacy for governor. He allegedly had
already declared his gubernatorial candidacy at a secret Sumter meeting. His
wife was accused of diverting into her husband's pocket funds she had solic-
ited for the families of the Barnwell lynch victims. Brayton's major problem,
however, appeared to be his white skin. Blacks in the Black District wanted a
black congressman.[18]

Murray ran a hard campaign. He appeared at his own rallies and in joint appearances with his opponents, benefiting from the district's pro-black attitude.
When he spoke on the same platform with Miller and Brayton in heavily black
Georgetown County, the crowd clearly showed its preference. Unfortunately
for him, Murray's full-blooded Negroid features were not preferred to Miller's
lighter hue. The "Canary," as the mulatto Miller was called, received the crowd's
support. In his own county, however, Murray was the beneficiary of pro-black
feeling. Brayton was heckled, and a slate of pro-Murray delegates was elected
in Stateburg, a town close to Murray's farm and the scene of his 1889 Colored
Alliance speech. A mulatto expressed the attitude of many district voters when
he demanded the nomination of a black man to demonstrate forthrightly that
there were qualified blacks available for public office. The Sumter County convention reflected this attitude. The supporters of T. B. Johnston withstood a
bolt of Braytonites and backed Murray, the candidate described as being "a
negro as black as they are made."[19]

The congressional district nominating convention was no less raucous,
and fellow Republican and U.S. Marshall G. I. Cunningham had to be sum-

moned to maintain order. Since Cunningham opposed Brayton as state chairman, the Braytonites demanded his departure. The Millerites demanded he stay. He remained, amid steady tumult. On the second day of the scheduled one-day meeting, the convention finally nominated Miller over Brayton and Murray, twenty-one to eleven to seven. The frustrated Braytonites, claiming fraud, bolted and nominated Brayton. Two Republicans (a white and a black) claimed the same nomination, but racial differences did not cause this fierce battle. The contest between two whites, Brayton and E. A. Webster, for the state chairmanship was the actual reason for the split. There were blacks, mulattos, and whites on both sides of the dispute.[20]

Despite the double nomination of Miller and Brayton in the district set aside for Republicans, the ever tightening registration and voting restrictions, and Congress's failure to pass the Force Bill, Republicans seemed undeterred when they issued their call for a September 17 state convention. They continued to focus on the Democratic split rather than on their own rifts. Registration and voting discrimination, internal discord, and disappointment over national government inaction were the usual fare for South Carolina Republicans. A massive Democratic split was not. Chairman-hopeful Webster told a reporter that the extent of the Democratic split at the time of the September convention would determine what action the gathering would take. He opposed a separate Republican state ticket and wanted instead to fuse with whatever Democratic faction offered the most in return.[21]

Even as they plotted to take advantage of the internecine Democratic feud, Republicans continued arguing among themselves. Their contemporaries and later historians have condemned the GOP for this feuding, ignoring the fact that rowdiness at Palmetto State political gatherings was commonplace. Whether one considers the all-too-frequent violence against Republicans or the shouting down of fellow Democrats because of the Tillman-Conservative split, it is clear that calm deliberation was not the norm in South Carolina politics. One hostile reporter, in discussing the shouting and arguing at one local Republican meeting, reminded his readers that Republicans "had precedent for this procedure in some of the recent Democratic conventions."[22] Republicans feuded among themselves because they could not strike back safely or effectively at their oppressors. By disputing among themselves, they were vicariously and, of course, unsuccessfully attacking the discriminatory system that was preventing them from any meaningful political participation.

One exception to this statewide Republican political din was a Sumter County meeting. Brayton's bolting supporters had either been ostracized or simply did not come to this conclave. Republicans thus were able to unify because of their common opposition to Brayton. Murray was a major beneficiary. He was reelected county chairman,[23] the victory demonstrating that his recent congressional nomination defeat had not cost him his home base. He continued to lead a unified local organization pledged to the rising state party leader E. A. Webster. In a time of political party turmoil in both parties, this achievement of unity made Murray look good indeed.

Unfortunately, the Sumter unity was not duplicated at the state convention. The state Executive Committee meeting the night before was so intense and long that it delayed the convention's opening session for ten hours, until 10 p.m. that evening. Even then, the convention's organization had not been decided. Just like the split Democrats, the Republicans disagreed not over policy but over personality. The dispute centered on the alleged corruption and incompetence of Brayton's leadership and whether or not a change was required.

Normally, the state chairman held the position of temporary chairman at any Republican convention, but the Webster forces refused to allow Brayton even this small honor. They nominated Robert Smalls, a black Civil War naval hero, instead, and Murray was openly vocal in his support. The ensuing vote demonstrated Brayton's weakness; Smalls beat him seventy-four to fifty-one. As the voting proceeded, a white delegate named Ball Hendrix walked around the hall causing shocked gasps wherever he went. He looked like Ben Tillman: he was a walking reminder in the midst of Republican bickering of the Democratic opposition.

Webster's strength and Brayton's weakness grew even more obvious when the Credentials Committee recommended the seating of all the Webster supporters except those from Berkeley County. Murray protested against giving Brayton even this tidbit. In rebuttal, several speakers accused Murray of having run for Congress on the color line and of now trying to punish Berkeley for not swallowing it. The Brayton delegation from Berkeley County was seated despite Murray's protest. It was a tiny island in a sea of Webster supporters.

Murray's steady rise in Republican politics now reached another pinnacle. He was named the state convention's permanent chairman. When Webster squashed Brayton ninety-six to twenty-four to become the new state chairman, Murray's status was insured. His leadership of a unified pro-Webster county delegate slate, his Custom House connections, his respectable showing in his first congressional race, and his decade of experience in Republican politics and the Colored Alliance had all brought him to this new prominence.

For the next fourteen years, he would remain at the center of Republican state politics. Henceforth, the rise and fall of his career would reflect South Carolina Republican fortunes as a whole.

Unfortunately for them, Murray and the Websterites had little time to savor their resounding victories. They were faced with the most crucial Republican Party decision since the days of Reconstruction: Should the GOP nominate its own state ticket or should it try to fuse with one of the Democratic factions? A week before, Ben Tillman had captured control of the state Democratic Party and had been nominated for governor. Many in the defeated Conservative Democrat faction, however, supported the former Confederate colonel Alexander C. Haskell to oppose Tillman in the general election. Edmund H. Deas, an important black Webster loyalist, made the motion that the Republicans back Haskell, but the convention hesitated at this bold step. Some Websterites urged the Executive Committee to make a decision at a later date. From the chair, Murray argued forcefully that the Democratic split gave Republicans their best opportunity since 1876, and they ought to make the most of it. "Let the matter be referred to the executive committee," he urged. "If advisable let the party unite with the Straightout Democrats [great applause] or with the Tillmanites [No! No!]." His statement spurred even more debate, and Murray let it proceed before arbitrarily cutting it off. He ignored a roll call demand and, over protest, sent Deas's motion to the Executive Committee. Murray served his new leader well, entrenching himself even further in the high command. E. A. Webster and his supporters were in full control of the South Carolina Republican Party, and Murray had played a key role in achieving this victory.[24]

Tillman's successful capture of the Democratic party at the September state Democratic meeting, the resultant Haskell bolt, and the new Republican leadership seemed to indicate that a realignment of Palmetto State politics was a dramatic possibility. Republicans seemed to be in a pivotal position between the two Democratic factions, and their new leadership provided hope that they would take full advantage of it. Although the Tillmanites expressed so much confidence in victory that they showed little interest in the Republicans, fusion with Haskell was a distinct possibility. As always, however, race was the major stumbling block. White South Carolinians would interpret any open appeal for Republican support as threatening continued white supremacy and any faction making such a gesture would lose as many white voters as it would gain black ones. Haskell was not yet even sure if he should run, so he refused comment on the Republican convention. Republicans also had decisions to make. Should they wait for Haskell to declare himself before they took further action, or should they strongly endorse him in the hope of helping him decide? Would their support hurt more than it helped? Should they instead make overtures to Tillman despite his apparent lack of interest? What about the Republican rank and file who could not vote despite the registration effort in the spring? Finally, how would those Republicans with the franchise react to an unpopular endorsement? Like Haskell, Republican politicians groped for answers to difficult questions.

On September 30, Haskell announced his decision. He issued a manifesto calling for a Democratic ticket in opposition to Ben Tillman, at the same time half-heartedly appealing to black voters, holding out as incentive the hackneyed Conservative promise of fairness. On October 9, in response to this "Haskell Manifesto," "Straightout Democrats" nominated Haskell to head a separate state ticket.[25] A group of Conservatives had formally split the Democratic party and were calling for Republican support—without actually mentioning fusion.

Race conditioned white Carolina's response to Haskell's candidacy. White solidarity had become such an ingrained part of the state's mentality that even many anti-Tillmanites (such as Wade Hampton himself) shied away from Haskell's candidacy because they viewed it as a threat to continued white dominance. The mild appeal to the black voter, which was really only a restatement of the traditional Conservative pledge going back to 1876, was condemned as excessive. Whites became concerned that blacks might indeed gain political leverage because of a falling out of whites.

Adding to the confusion was the convening in Columbia of an all-black conference on October 15, which was also attended by many black Republican politicians, including Murray. Eighty delegates from nineteen counties were present, with the main order of business being the formulation of a black reaction to the Democratic split. A motion called on the Republican Executive Committee to decide what to do, while another motion disavowed any black desire for social equality, black domination, or racial hatred. The first motion precipitated a long debate, a committee that had been considering support for the Haskell ticket then reaffirming the resolution. Murray praised Haskell as a fit representative of the educated white man who had always been friendly to blacks. Tillman, in contrast, represented the "ignorant rabble" (the same group Murray had praised just a year previously at the Alliance barbecue). Another delegate immediately retorted that Tillman deserved support because he was responsible for splitting the Democrats. He ridiculed Murray's contention of Conservative fairness, citing examples of Conservative anti-black violence. In response, Murray insisted that, if blacks used their power wisely, both Democrat factions would respect them. Finally, despite the earlier vote calling on Republican Party leadership, the meeting passed its own pro-Haskell resolution and attacked the state Republican Party. Murray tried to eliminate this last section, but his motion was tabled.

The attack on Republican leadership in a resolution expressing black response to the Tillman-Haskell contest became understandable when the convention suddenly decided to hear a speech from Ellery Brayton. Murray protested, but the chair ignored him, and when Murray refused to sit down and admirers gathered around in support, the chairman asked a guard to evict Murray. A scuffle ensued, and the Sumter politician was taken from the hall. Tempers quickly cooled, however, and Murray was allowed to resume his seat and listen indignantly to Brayton's speech. The white Republican leader innocuously said he believed blacks would benefit from the state's political turmoil but then refused to support either Haskell or Tillman. His real purpose was to embarrass Webster, regain status after his humiliating defeat at the Republican convention, and garner support for his congressional race.

As soon as Brayton sat down, Murray jumped up to accuse him of organizing this allegedly nonpolitical convention to wreck the state Republican Party. Shouts and hisses drowned Murray out, and he was ruled out of order, the convention ending on this chaotic note.[26] Whereas the Webster forces had captured the Republican convention, the Braytonites ruled the all-black convention. Like the splitting Democrats, the Republicans feuded and factionalized.

Eight days later, the Webster-controlled Republican State Executive Committee overcame the drag of this factionalism to issue a carefully worded response to the Democratic split. The committee advised Republicans that they "could consistently vote the Haskell ticket without violating your allegiance to the Republican party, and while not urging this course as a party measure we commend the ticket to your favorable consideration."[27] The hard decision resulted in Republicans offering guarded support to the Haskellites. Although the statement was intelligently conceived and wisely unprovocative, it helped neither Haskell nor the Republican Party. Outraged white allegations of "Black Republican support" hurt Haskell among white voters and forced him to disavow it. Republican rallies all over the state ignored his negative response and backed him anyway. Such activity only intensified Tillman's racist rhetoric, and he openly threatened blacks with violence.[28] The white response to a reasonable Republican action was to view it as a dangerous interference in South Carolina's white-only politics. It produced mounting pressure for further disfranchisement. Appropriate Republican behavior was rewarded with a vicious white backlash.

To make matters worse, Republicans backed the losing candidate. The election resulted in a landslide victory for Tillman and the destruction of the Straightout Democratic movement. Tillman gained 59,159 votes to Haskell's 14,828, while Republican congressional candidates all went down to defeat. In the Seventh Congressional District, Miller out-polled Brayton and the Democratic candidate William Elliott, but state election officials negated his victory on a technicality. In those days, candidates provided their supporters with ballots to cast on election day. Miller's ballots were found to be one-sixteenth of an inch narrower and one-eighth of an inch shorter than regulations allowed. The paper on which they were printed was also said to be darker than the regulation white, and the word "For" was illegally printed before "representative." At the Rafting Creek precinct, a heavily black area and Murray's home, Tillmanites conducted a raid and destroyed all the ballots, three ballot boxes, and a state registration book. With the aid of such chicanery, the Democratic candidate William Elliott was declared the winner. Miller could only appeal. The election of six black Republicans to the state legislature, an increase of three, produced the only slight ray of hope.[29]

In fact, the Republican Party had suffered another crushing defeat. Continued Democratic control of the registration process and the inability of the spring Republican campaign to surmount it meant that many Republicans had been unable to vote. The unwillingness and/or inability of Haskell and the Straightouts to appeal forthrightly for black votes prevented any hope for meaningful fusion. The Tillmanite threats of violence and their complete hostility precluded meaningful dialogue. Republicans were also in obvious disarray because of the Miller-Brayton congressional nomination split and the hard-fought Webster victory, but they had acted intelligently anyway. Their carefully worded statement of support for Haskell was a logical response to the state's political situation. Republicans suffered a crushing defeat not because of their own shortcomings but because of the unremitting white racism surrounding them.

This election showed once more that the continued existence of the South Carolina Republican Party depended less on the GOP's intelligent decisions and more on white Democratic action. No matter what Republicans might do or say, the white power structure saw them as an annoying and potentially dangerous disease in the body politic. They had to be eradicated, or the state would suffer a black political plague.

One of the few Republican victors in 1890 was George Washington Murray. During the year he had made a major speech, gained a patronage post, run for Congress, and participated visibly in major meetings. He was a member of a victorious GOP political faction and considered important enough to be its choice to chair a crucial state convention. Murray was now a major Republican politician. As his Emancipation Day speech and congressional campaign showed, he was also a bold proponent of his race. He was a bright new light who might in the future be able to pierce the growing racist darkness surrounding the Republicans as they struggled to find the path to political survival.

# White Republicans but One Black Victory

The 1890 election showed dramatically that a white Democratic split did not foreshadow GOP success in South Carolina. Republicans had selected what they hoped would be vibrant new leadership, and then they carefully and intelligently endorsed Haskell over Tillman. The result was just another crushing defeat. Thomas E. Miller was the only victorious Republican candidate in all that year's elections, but white officials counted him out on a suspicious technicality. The new governor, Benjamin Tillman, had threatened Republicans with bodily harm for supporting his opponent in the gubernatorial election, and he seemed ready to fulfill his threat. Everywhere they turned, Republicans saw hatred and animosity. Some GOP activists wondered, however, whether this hatred targeted all Republicans or only black ones. What if the state GOP purged itself of the Reconstruction-inspired accusation of black domination? Might it not then benefit from the continuing Democratic split? Was race not party the stumbling block for Republicans in South Carolina's politics? Some Republicans began trying to deal with the political suppression they were suffering by accepting their oppressors' white racist arguments and attempting to lessen if not purge the black role in the state GOP. The result was a new white Republican movement. Seemingly a casualty of President Harrison's 1889 patronage policy, white Republicanism again invited white Carolinians to become Republicans, this time as a white alternative to Tillmanite party rule. The dissidents, Reformers as they called themselves, mimicked the conservative Democrats and promised to be fair to intelligent black voters. Republicans had split into two factions again: the Regulars and the Reformers.

An important question surrounding this split and the others that had come before and would come later was whether or not such factionalism was proof of Republican corruption and incompetence, as its Democratic opponents and some later historians insisted. A closer look at the individuals most prominent in these splits may provide an answer. The available data on South Carolina's Republican leadership during these years consist of the birthdate, birthplace, residence, occupation (other than politics), education, and political positions of seven prominent Reformers and twelve leading Regulars. An analysis of this data is instructive.[1]

As a group, the Regular leaders were somewhat older than the Reformers. In 1895, the average age of the five Reformers whose birthdates are available was thirty-nine, while the average age of the eleven Regulars with available birthdates was nearly forty-nine. There was little difference in the places of birth, a roughly equal proportion of both factions' leaders having been born in South Carolina or out of state. Places of residence did not vary that much either. The few Reformers all resided up- country, while the Regulars lived in both the coastal and up-country areas. Persons attending both factions' conventions also came from every county within the state, so clearly there was no significant up-country versus seacoast split among either the leadership or the rank and file of the Republican Party. With one exception, all the leaders of both factions resided in counties that were overwhelmingly black. For example, Regular leaders T. B. Johnston and R. M. Wallace and Regular-turned-Reformer G. W. Murray all lived in Sumter County where the population was 73 percent black. Reformer L. W. C. Blaylock lived in Newberry County, which was 66 percent black. Republican leaders from both factions built their power on a foundation of black support.

The Reformers had an edge in the matter of education; more of their leaders had attended college. The Regulars, however, also had their share of college men. The presence of college graduates among both factions' leaders attests to their upper-class roots. Their occupations also indicate that they were not dependent on politics for their status or their economic welfare. There were among them bankers, lawyers, large farmers, physicians, and newspapermen. The Regular R. M. Wallace, for example, was a bank president and also an official of the Sumter Cotton Mills, the Sumter Telephone Company, and the local ice plant. The Reformer Lawson D. Melton was a member of an important Columbia law firm and, as will be shown later, Murray had substantial land holdings.

Reflecting the age difference, the Regulars had held more political positions at an earlier date than had the Reformers. Eight of the Regular leaders had been in Republican politics during Reconstruction; none of the Reformers had. The Reformers were comparative political newcomers, but they were hardly novices. They too had political experience within and without the Republican Party, but this political participation had occurred during the 1880s and 1890s, not in Reconstruction.

Rival convention platforms indicated little philosophical difference between the two Republican factions or its leaders. Both factions strongly supported national Republican administrations, and both simultaneously condemned South Carolina's electoral practices. The Reformers emphasized state issues slightly more and criticized their Regular Republican opponents more vociferously. The greatest Regular interest lay in electoral reform and lynching abolishment.

Both sets of leaders similarly did not disagree on the role blacks should play in contemporary society. During the late nineteenth century, the black community was split between adherents of a conservative policy based on vocational education and political silence espoused by Booker T. Washington, and those who believed in an activist political policy modeled after the ideas of Frederick Douglass. South Carolina contained supporters of both philosophies, but these differences were not reflected in Republican politics. Murray and his fellow Republicans (both black and white) firmly believed that blacks had to develop middle-class values, acquire property, patronize black businesses, and participate in politics. But, politics still came first. Black Republicans turned to a conservative approach only when politics failed. For example, George W. Murray and Thomas E. Miller both agreed on the need for a black role in politics. Later, both were to call on blacks to give up politics and follow an accommodationist route.

The always present tension over color distinctions within the black community was clearly manifested in Republican politics. Murray, for example, campaigned against the light skins of Miller and Smalls, and he heard his own dark features used against him. Murray's "Black Bold Eagle" and Miller's "Canary" nicknames indicate that skin hue was a factor in campaign rhetoric, though not a defining political factor. Of the seven Reform leaders discussed here, only Murray was black: of the thirteen Regulars, Crum, Deas, Miller, and Smalls were mulattos. Browns predominated over blacks among those African Americans considered to be Republican leaders, and this fact reflects the continuing mulatto significance in the black community. However, blacks and browns belonged to both factions, so this color issue was not a major cause of Republican factional division and conflict.

Analyzing all the available data results in several conclusions. There were no major differences between the two sets of GOP factional leaders over the black role in society, the issue of mulattos versus blacks, and support of the national party. Differences in birthplace, residence, and education were not significant enough to explain factional differences. Age and political experience seem to have been the only significant differences. The Regulars were older and had been involved in politics longer. They were the link to Republican Party failures and alleged transgressions during Reconstruction. The Reformers were the challengers, the new faces who promised a fresh start, free from the baggage of the past. The Regulars argued that they should maintain control of Republican Party activities in the state. There was no deep-seated disagreement over philosophy; the conflict was over who the leaders should be. The issue was not what, it was who.

Such a conclusion makes sense within the South Carolina context of that day. Republican factionalism duplicated the similar phenomenon in the state's Democratic Party. The rival Tillmanites and Conservatives also differed over who should rule. Here too, length of political participation was the crucial difference. Regular Republican leaders had been in politics since Reconstruction, and the Reformers were of more recent vintage. So too, the Conservative Democrats went back to the Civil War period, and many Tillmanites did not. Personality more than ideological differences split Republicans as they did Democrats.

Since the Regulars and the Reformers agreed on so much and were equally despised by the dominant South Carolina society, there was always hope for unity. Just a month before the Reformers began their reorganization, for example, they approached the Regulars, calling for a united front.[2] The Regulars saw no reason to accept these overtures, however. They still had President Harrison's blessing, while the Reformers, at this point calling themselves the White Republican League, were the same individuals whose organizing efforts had failed in the past. The Regulars knew that no Republican faction could become predominant until the 1892 presidential campaign, so there was no reason for an immediate response. Regular Republican inactivity expressed better than words the Republicans' inability to function outside the national party context. They correctly realized that, since their state party had no local electoral base, the national GOP leadership not local conditions would ultimately decide which faction would predominate.

The Regulars thus took no action of any kind until the election year arrived. Then they met in a secret session in early January 1892 to begin planning for a state gathering to elect delegates to the national nominating convention. After the meeting, reporters surrounded the chairman, E. A. Webster, asking him about the White Republican League. Webster flippantly passed the Reformers off as a dozen white men, but he wanted them to know, he patronizingly said, that they were always welcome to rejoin the true fold. Moreover, he no doubt still believed that Democratic feuding might prove beneficial to South Carolina's Republicans, despite their own disagreements. A March 1892 Conservative Democratic convention, though promising to abide by the later state Democratic convention, produced an anti-Tillman platform and candidates. In fact, Tillman controlled the Democratic Party, and his renomination was assured. His hold on the South Carolina political system remained secure, Democratic dissidents or Republican regulars and whites notwithstanding.[3]

The Reformers were not discouraged. Their Executive Committee met in late March, and the former Massachusetts governor William Claflin, one of their Boston patrons, arrived to offer moral and perhaps more negotiable support. In April, the Reformers met in general convention, with 150 delegates present: 70 blacks and 80 whites, former Conservatives and former Tillmanites, former Independents and former Regulars, and even the president of the Colored State Farmers' Alliance. J. Hendrix McLane, V. P. Clayton, W. W. Russell, Simeon Corley, and R. W. Memminger were particularly conspicuous.[4]

The opening speeches confidently spoke of the dawning of a new political age in South Carolina. The participants established a new state organization and selected two white and two black at-large delegates to the Republican national convention. Rumor had it that James G. Blaine was this gathering's favorite, though the conclave also passed a resolution praising the incumbent Harrison administration. Using code words that South Carolinian whites understood, the Reformers promised an honest state Republican Party with office holders of "moral worth and intellectual fitness." The Reformers were promising an all-white Republican Party, despite the fact that their convention was almost 50 percent black..

Suddenly, the smoothly running conclave was thrown into confusion. A black delegate demanded a roll call, but many white delegates wanted anonymity. Someone quickly made a motion to adjourn, but the convention only recessed. The roll call became public anyway. Viewing the list of names, neither the Regulars nor white newspapers were impressed. Except for leaders long associated with the movement, the convention delegates were political neophytes. The famous Republicans were not there, nor were there any major Democratic converts. Still, it was amazing to have eighty whites meet with seventy blacks anywhere in South Carolina. The White Republican League had talked about white Republicanism, but it seemed to have produced a thoroughly integrated party instead.[5]

The Regular Republican convention met one week later in the same House of Representatives chamber. All the well-known Republicans were present at this meeting, including a reconciled Ellery Brayton. Of the 125 delegates, only 15 to 20 were white, however, and these were the usual faces. Chairman

Webster opened the meeting with a speech supporting Harrison and praising the aborted Force Bill. When nominations for convention chairman were requested, Murray, then still a Regular stalwart, was unanimously elected to his second consecutive term at wielding the gavel. He was escorted to the podium and immediately implored the convention to work for the good of the party in an orderly manner. The GOP "had too many enemies—some in sheep's clothing—to come here and wrangle." The aim of the convention, he said, was to insure Regular Republican recognition at the national convention.

Murray quickly introduced a resolution to prohibit officeholders from becoming delegates to the national convention. Such a ruling was necessary, he said, to prevent the Reformers from charging the Regulars with trading convention votes for patronage jobs. Webster, as an office holder, could hardly have supported such an idea, yet Murray would hardly have introduced it without the party chair's authorization. Congressman Thomas E. Miller, another staunch black Webster lieutenant, supported Murray, while a number of other Websterites expressed opposition. The debate grew hot, so Murray arbitrarily called for a vote and ruled in favor of his side. He acted, a Charleston newspaper said, like a "colored Tom Reed," the tyrannical Speaker of the U.S. House of Representatives. The convention then began the delegate selection process and contradictingly repealed the anti-officeholder section of Murray's resolution. William D. Crum, Edmund Deas, E. A. Webster, and Ellery Brayton were elected delegates—two blacks and two whites, two office holders and two aspirants, three Websterites and the apparently reconciled Brayton. Webster had his way in the end.

The delegates rose to their feet and began to file out of the chambers when a Websterite suddenly introduced a resolution instructing the four newly chosen delegates to vote for Harrison. At first, Murray questioned the motion's validity, citing the fact that many delegates had already departed. Thinking better of it, however, he ruled the convention legally still in session. Webster personally seconded the resolution, and Murray ruled it passed. At 6:25 a.m. the eighteen-hour-long convention adjourned with Webster in firm command, and Brayton's election as a delegate indicating Regular unity in the face of the Reformer challenge and the Democratic split. Murray's performance as chairman had once again helped achieve a major Webster aim; Murray continued to demonstrate willingness to bend the rules on the party chairman's orders. Unlike his earlier years and what he would become in the future, he was no rebel; he was now a loyal party functionary.[6]

The newly formed unity faced a quick challenge. The day after the convention, Brayton amazingly wrote a letter to the Columbia *State* protesting the procedure for passing the pro-Harrison resolution. He supported the president, he said, and swore to it in a simultaneous private letter to Harrison, but he planned to go to the convention as an independent. Webster's attempt to present a united pro-Harrison front had failed. Brayton, supposedly back in the pack, continued to act like a lone wolf.[7]

The separate conventions of the Reformers and the Regulars had demonstrated yet again that, like the Conservatives and the Tillmanites, the Republicans did not disagree on basic policy but on the individuals who should carry out that policy. Neither policy nor leaders would determine the victors in the intra-party strife, however. National party leaders at the national convention would make this determination. Both sides worked hard to strengthen themselves by appealing to disgruntled Democrats. Webster confidently predicted that, if the Straightouts were shut out of the Democratic Party, they would fuse with his organization to oppose the Tillmanites. If the Tillmanites lost control of the Democratic Party machinery, their GOP supporters would then return to the fold. The Reform leader Virgil Clayton was similarly confident. He predicted that Tillmanites and supporters of the Farmers' Ocala platform would join his branch of the Republican Party.[8]

The rival delegations both went to the national Republican convention, the Regulars bound to Harrison and the Reformers uncommitted but allegedly leaning toward Blaine. Even Brayton expressed support for the president now, his anger dissipated by his public outcry and the promise of a position on the National Committee. The Credentials Committee heard arguments, then quickly voted to seat the Regulars, with Brayton to be the South Carolina representative on the National Committee. The Regulars had learned their 1888 lesson well. This time, they made sure they supported the most powerful candidate, Benjamin Harrison, and they were rewarded. The Reformers made the mistake of remaining uncommitted, and they were shut out.

Harrison's quest for convention votes was not the sole reason for the credentials decision in favor of the Regulars. The convention supported a suffrage plan that thwarted Harrison's desire to back away from the Force Bill and demonstrated that the GOP was not yet prepared to sacrifice southern black voters. Moreover, Republicans had high hopes of taking advantage of the Populist turmoil in the South, which was causing fissures in the Democratic Party. In South Carolina neither Republican faction could hope to fuse with Tillman farmers, however, so the national GOP decided to back the Regulars in the Palmetto State and concentrate its fusion efforts where hopes for success were more realistic. National Republican plans in other areas of the South once again aided South Carolina Regulars.[9]

The failure of the Reformers indicated once again their intrinsic weakness. Their major goal was to strengthen the party by adding white converts, and, if this had to be done at the expense of blacks, they seemed willing to do it. Yet, a white Republican party had to have some black representation to stay in the national party's good graces. The national hierarchy, however, chose the Regulars over the Reformers not for the good of the state's GOP or its black members but to aid the Republican presidential nominee. The needs of the national hierarchy, not the quality of local leadership or its cleverness, determined the future of the South Carolina GOP.

The Regulars spent no time analyzing their Pyrrhic victory. The national organization had eliminated their internal opponents, so they were excited about being a united party by default while Democratic wrangling continued. The growth of a Populist Party (or third party as it was always called in South Carolina) was also encouraging. Republicans were confident that the Populist presidential candidate James B. Weaver would take Palmetto State votes from the Democratic presidential candidate Grover Cleveland and thus aid the Republican Benjamin Harrison in the state. In both the state and presidential elections, then, the Democratic vote seemed destined to be a fractured one; South Carolina Republicans hoped to be the beneficiaries.[10]

Rumors spread that Republicans were planning to take advantage of this opportunity by running a full state ticket, with Judge Samuel W. Melton, a respected white Republican with GOP roots back to the Reconstruction years, as their gubernatorial choice. Webster, the state party chairman, went to Washington to secure funds for such an effort, but he came back empty-handed. Melton then denied any interest in the nomination. A fusion suggestion to the Populists was also rebuffed. When Republicans met in state convention on September 29, 1892, therefore, they decided against running a state ticket, determined to concentrate instead on the presidential and congressional races. They worried that a GOP state ticket might frighten the Democrats back into unity.[11]

This GOP decision had to have pleased the state party's rising star, G. W. Murray, because he had announced his candidacy for the Seventh District Congressional seat in mid-April 1892 and had been quietly campaigning ever since. The present congressman Thomas E. Miller and the former congressman Robert Smalls both wanted the Republican nomination, as did J. H. Ostendorff, a long-time white party functionary, and William W. Beckett, a young black political novice. Ellery Brayton was also a possible candidate. T. B. Johnston and the Customs House officials supported Murray, and he received an important boost from a shout-filled Sumter County gathering near the end of the campaign. When the district convention met at Summerville, he gained the nomination, shocking party professionals. He had defeated some of the party's best-known veterans. T. B. Johnston was accused of using Murray as a stalking horse for his own candidacy, but this accusation was false. Murray resigned his post immediately upon gaining the nomination, and Johnston, "desirous of aiding" him, asked him to suggest his replacement. The next day William W. Beckett, one of Murray's defeated opponents, applied, and two days later Johnston gave him Murray's old job.[12]

Having garnered the Republican nomination in the so-called black congressional district, Murray now had to face strong Democratic opposition in November. His rival was another Sumter County resident, the Conservative Democrat E. W. Moise, a Jew born in Charleston, South Carolina in 1832, a Confederate veteran, and a participant in the state's 1865 constitutional convention. In 1876 he had been elected state adjutant and inspector general on the original Conservative Democratic ticket of Wade Hampton. He had contested unsuccessfully for the Democratic Seventh District Congressional nomination in 1888, but this time he bucked the Tillman tide and secured it. He had a reputation for fairness that benefited his candidacy among those blacks who could vote, while the strong anti-Tillman attitude of his hometown gained him important white support there. As a white man and a Democrat (his Judaism playing no part in the campaign), he was also favored by the district's newspapers. The press described him as "a man of broad views, extended culture and a wide range of information, with a depth of patriotism such as is seldom seen." Even the Tillmanite Columbia *Register* called Moise a representative white man whose fairness to blacks had gained him their respect.[13]

Murray had no such easy ride. In late September/early October 1892, a convention met in Sumter County to name his replacement as county chairman, and Murray's faction lost control of the county's party machinery. In heavily black Beaufort County, the local party developed an even more serious split. Instead of continuing to support a local fusion ticket with white Conservative Democrats as had been the custom, a Republican faction fielded an Independent (Straightout) Republican ticket. Rumor had it that the Tillmanites had made a deal with these balking Republicans to defeat the Conservative-supported fusion ticket. This turmoil produced uncertainty for Murray in a crucial county.[14]

What had to hurt Murray the most was the formation of a black Harrison-Moise campaign club in his Stateburg, Sumter County neighborhood.[15] Endorsement of his opponent by his black neighbors signaled the softness of his black support. He could not expect to gain many white votes, so he had to keep defections among the dwindling number of black voters to an absolute minimum. If his neighbors abandoned him, what might other blacks do?

Murray tried to rally his black base by appealing to race solidarity, but he received some setbacks in this attempt. Once again, he experienced the lightness versus darkness criterion he had condemned in his 1890 Charleston speech. When he appeared at a rally in the coastal region of his district, some blacks left in disgust, "saying that if they couldn't have a colored man most like a white man they would rather have the white man, and they would vote for Moise." "Why we taut he [Murray] was a big fat man like Smalls, but he is a cornfield nigger just like we." Murray, appealing to black pride and unanimity, was repelled because his skin was too dark. He left as disgustedly as some of his listeners, but most had no such feelings and supported him.[16]

Undaunted, he pressed on, and most black audiences received him favorably. The white press, of course, reacted negatively. An appearance in Sumter on election eve elicited the newspaper accusation that his campaign speeches had all been "of an incendiary character, trying to array the negroes against the whites." Murray had ignored such attacks before, but now he publicly denied advocating the sword and the flame. In a stirring paragraph in which he justified not only his speeches, but also his candidacy and his race, he said: "Notwithstanding the hue of my skin, I am a South Carolinian in the manner born, and will yield to no one of her other sons regardless of color or condition, in love, devotion, and ardent wishes to see her outstrip every other state of this Union in everything that is honorable, progressive, grand and ennobling in the race of life." Whites remained unimpressed. On the eve of the election, the Sumter County Democratic chairman glumly warned that Murray and the Republicans were well on their way to establishing "negro domination."[17]

The Charleston *News and Courier* ridiculed such pessimism and predicted that black indifference toward Murray's candidacy guaranteed Moise's election. People whispered, however, that Republicans had consciously run a quiet campaign to avoid rousing the divided Democrats. Besides, the rumors continued, the Tillmanites were planning to stay home rather than vote for

Moise, a white Conservative. Despite all the difficulties Murray encountered in his campaign, he was the only Republican congressional candidate given a chance of victory.[18]

On election day, November 8, 1892, the polls in Sumter, Murray's home county, were not crowded, and, throughout the district, the number of black voters was smaller than ever before. Whites attributed the low turnout to black indifference toward Murray, but the discriminatory registration procedures and the ever-present intimidation were the real reasons for the electoral quiet. Those blacks who were able to cast their ballots for Murray did so because, as one expressed it, Moise "would not represent their color." In Stateburg, despite the existence of organized black support for Moise, the vast majority of black voters supported Murray. Early signs indicated that Murray's appeal to race solidarity was resonating.[19]

Unfortunately, election results were once again disappointing for Palmetto State Republicans. The Democratic presidential candidate Grover Cleveland gained more votes than the Republican Benjamin Harrison, and the Tillman-ites won another sweeping victory within the state. The number of blacks in the State House dropped from six to three, while in the congressional races, only the Murray-Moise contest was, according to the Tillman press, "un-pleasantly close." Moise confidently held victory celebrations in Beaufort and Sumter, and the Colored Moise Club of Stateburg Township met to ratify his election. On November 16, hard figures finally began to come in. The returns from Berkeley County showed that Murray had received 1,319 votes to Moise's 929, but Murray's votes had been thrown out because (as it had been alleged against Miller in 1890) his ballots were found to be one-eighth of an inch too short. When the official returns were published by the state on November 21, however, there were no results for the Seventh District. The Tillmanite State Board of Canvassers would have to decide the winner.[20]

Murray's supporters immediately cried foul. His Berkeley County manager insisted that the nullified ballots were not the ones Murray had passed out to his supporters. Murray's ballots had been printed on cheap off-white paper; the ones found in the voting boxes were made of better stock. Similarly, the ballots did not look crumpled and dirty as they should have been had voters handled them. The board met on November 25, 1892, and a Columbia news-paper warned it to obey the ballot size law and seat Moise. Grover Cleveland's ballots had been reprinted to meet the ballot requirements, so why should Murray receive a special favor denied the president-elect? "Gen. Moise is an accomplished Democrat, capable of representing ably the great and varied interests of the district. Murray is a negro Republican, utterly without capacity or influence."[21]

The State Board of Canvassers consisted of five state officials, all Tillmanites: W. T. C. Bates, the state treasurer; John McLaurin, later a U.S. senator but at the time attorney general and himself a successful 1892 congressional candidate; J. E. Tindal, secretary of state; H. C. Farley, adjutant and inspector general; and Cole L. Blease, chairman of the Committee on Privileges and Elections of the State House of Representatives and later the state's virulently racist governor. This was hardly a panel that could be expected to look kindly on a black man's candidacy. The board's first order of business was to publish the submitted returns, and these figures were hardly favorable to Murray's cause: Moise was credited with 4,937 votes, Murray with 2,695. All of Murray's 1,319 Berkeley County ballots and another 510 in Georgetown County were excluded because of their allegedly illegal size.

Two black lawyers ably represented Murray, ironically two of his old antagonists: General Sam Lee, then probably the most venerable black Republican in the state, and Thomas E. Miller, the sitting Seventh District congressman and a veteran of similar contests. Lee and Miller argued that Murray had provided legal ballots for his supporters, but someone had replaced them with the illegal ones found in the boxes. The two lawyers presented depositions from Murray supporters swearing that they had measured the ballots before the election and had found them to be of legal size. One of these individuals insisted that he had made a very careful measurement "being mindful of the fact that it was claimed that Congressman T. E. Miller's tickets were said to be short." Another said that the tabulated tickets were different from the ones voted, and he had come to the conclusion that they had been "in the hands of Cleptomanics [sic]."

Moise's respected white attorneys, Leroy Youmans, R. D. Lee, and J. T. Barron, argued his case with equal vigor. They cited precedent (the 1890 Miller contest) to contend that the ballot size law was stringent. They also argued that certain of Murray's other ballots were invalid because of illegal voting and staffing procedures in several precincts. Murray's lawyers responded by calling these so-called violations insignificant trivialities.

The board remained in session from early in the morning until 11:20 p.m. that night. The following day at 9:30 a.m. they heard closing arguments. In the midst of Miller's presentation, board member McLaurin, who had missed all the previous testimony because of official business, joined the deliberations for the first time. Despite his earlier absence, he took part in the last secret deliberations, but he did not cast a vote. At 4 p.m., State Treasurer Bates made a motion to accept most of Murray's votes, and Tindal and Blease supported the motion. Farley opposed it. The final certified election returns in the Seventh Congressional District were Murray, 4,995, Moise, 4,955, other candidates, 42. The State Board of Canvassers, close supporters of Ben Tillman and his openly anti-black movement, had chosen a black man to represent a South Carolina district in the U.S. House of Representatives.[22]

The news astounded the public. The Columbia *State*, a consistently anti-Tillman paper, headlined: "The Black Negro, Murray, Seated over Gen. Moise"; "Afro-Tillmanism Triumphs." The Charleston *News and Courier*, the Conservative stalwart, called Murray "a Congressman who will be black enough to suit the most exacting of the political moralists, nearly all of whom live in some other district." The perplexed hometown Sumter *Watchman and Southron* editorialized: "To us the decision appears inexplicable."[23]

Northern newspapers were pleasantly surprised at the electoral outcome. The Washington *Post* ridiculed the self-styled better element in South Carolina for being upset at the fair play of a group whom they had characterized as "Tillman boors." The Pittsburgh *Gazette* viewed the decision as a recognition that the black man's vote was now a factor in southern elections. Among black newspapers, only two, the Huntsville *Gazette* and the Washington *Bee*, announced the board decision, but neither made a substantial comment.[24]

All over South Carolina one newspaper after another repeated its surprise, its support of Moise, and its anger at the Tillmanite board. "As Tillmanism grows older its cloven foot grows longer and blacker," the Florence *Messenger* wrote. "A piece of political legerdemain," the Kingstree *Record* added. "Some people become monstrous fair, broad-minded and patriotic all of a sudden through self-interest and spite," the Cheraw *Reporter* insisted. "General Moise is a Conservative[;] Is there another negro in the woodpile?" asked the Newberry *Observer*. "'No quarter to Conservatives.' That is the cry," the Conservative press insisted. "Had they desired, they certainly could have found ground to have given Gen. Moise the certificate." Anti-Tillmanites also blamed themselves. Had sufficient numbers of Conservatives voted, Moise would have been elected easily, they said. In Sumter, for example, seven hundred Democrats had voted in the primary, but Moise's vote totaled only 369 in the general election.[25]

The Columbia *Register* was Tillman's only consistent press defender. It applauded the board's decision, calling it "absolute fair play," and proof to the rest of the country of just treatment for blacks in South Carolina. It even violated racial mores by headlining one editorial "Hon. Mr. Murray, It Is." When others were critical, the *Register* called their attacks the "most ridiculous and false statements." It denied any Tillmanite bid for the black vote, insisting that the Conservatives had no one but themselves to blame for Moise's defeat. Instead of ensuring Moise's election, they had been preoccupied with plotting Tillman's overthrow. The ballot issue was clear-cut too. The same company had printed all of the ballots used in the election, so if Murray's tickets were illegal, all the others were too. Finally, the Seventh District had been established to concentrate the black vote in one district in order to insure white control in the other six. It had not been created to elect a white, so it was unfair to demand one now.[26]

The day after the board's decision, Murray was seen walking up and down Main Street in Columbia. According to a hostile description, he was "about the happiest looking 'nigger' that ever walked the streets" of that city. A friend was said to remark jokingly that his head would soon grow too large for the stovepipe hat he customarily wore. A week later, Murray publicly said that the Board of Canvassers' decision had substantially improved race relations in the state, and he was sure that all whites would sustain the decision. Although he was not scheduled to take his seat in Congress until December 1893, he announced plans to visit Washington immediately to familiarize himself with the capital.[27]

The defeated Democratic candidate, E. W. Moise, did not want to contest the election in the House of Representatives, but he said he might have to at his friends' insistence. A week later he changed his mind. He had found no unanimity among his supporters, so he dropped the idea for a contest. His decision removed the last barrier to Murray's election. He became the nation's highest ranking black public official. Something amazing had happened. A board of elections controlled by followers of a man whom history identifies as one of America's leading racists had certified the election of a black Republican. Leading the opposition were Conservative Democrats, individuals who had conspicuously and often called for fairness to the black man. A Republican dream had been fulfilled; Republicans were the beneficiaries of the Democratic split. For the first and only time, their wishes came true. Tillman's acquiescence elected Murray. Everywhere else in the state, he had not been as kind, and Republicans had lost. Perhaps, however, Murray's success was a harbinger of future fusion. Perhaps Republicans might yet gain a foothold in Palmetto State politics because of the continued Democratic feuding.[28]

The reason for the Tillmanite board's decision long remained controversial, the issue amazingly debated as late as a 1930 political campaign. A later historian argued that Tillman supported Murray because the black politician was a silverite, while Moise was a Cleveland Democrat. Silver was a national political issue at this time, but it played no role in the Murray-Moise race or in the state campaign as a whole. Moreover, Tillman supported Cleveland until the coming of the Panic of 1893. Perhaps then, Murray's Alliance background appealed to Tillman. But, Murray was always more of a Republican than he was an Alliance man, and Tillman had less love for black farmers than he had for any other kind of black man. Perhaps then, the Board of Canvassers was concerned about Murray appealing to Congress and successfully contesting the rejection of allegedly small ballots, something that had already been used against Thomas C. Miller in a previous election. But the new House of Representatives would have a Democratic majority, so the chances of Murray making a successful appeal were nonexistent.[29]

The board's decision in favor of Murray resulted from a combination of factors. Of these, however, Democratic factionalism was the predominant cause. Tillman had conquered the Conservative Democrats to gain control of the state Democratic organization, but his victory had inflamed animosities. He wanted to destroy the Conservatives. In 1894, therefore, he personally took the Conservative hero Wade Hampton's Senate seat, while seating a black man over a white Conservative in an 1892 congressional election. Murray became a congressman because of a falling out among whites; Tillman allowed him to hold office in order to humiliate his Democratic factional opponents. He had no plans to form a new political alignment based on silver or any other issue, although some six months after the 1892 election, he invited Murray to meet with him, a meeting that apparently never took place.[30]

While defending Murray's seating, the pro-Tillmanite Columbia *Register* had flippantly commented that "If our party desires to control this district also, let a new apportionment be made by the Legislature." This was precisely what Tillman planned to do. A bill in the state legislature, whose sponsorship was murky, called for dismemberment of the Black District and the linking of most of its black voters to Charleston. Charlestonians immediately saw this action as punishment for their city's opposition to Tillman, and the Columbia *Register* hinted that they were correct.[31] The Tillmanites were attempting one more humiliation of their opposition and the simultaneous elimination of the last center of black power. Though the bill was postponed until the following legislative session, it demonstrated Tillman's attitude toward Murray. Even before the Sumter politician took his House seat, his alleged benefactors were plotting to prevent his reelection. Murray had benefited from a momentary crack in white solidarity, but later events demonstrated that this success was an exception. Tillman Democrats had not changed their racist attitudes. They had seated a black man to punish Conservative opponents, not to fuse with Republicans. Democrat split or not, Republican unity or not, the South Carolina GOP remained at the mercy of the state's white power structure.

Election year activities also demonstrated again that the national Republicans were willing to sacrifice their Palmetto State brethren if it served their purposes. The GOP's Washington-based hierarchy lamented the weakness of the existing South Carolina party, yet it summarily rejected a reform group that promised improvement. Instead of enforcing a compromise fusion of Reformers and Regulars, the national Republicans took the easier route of backing the loyal established organization. Palmetto State Republicanism suffered not only from determined and powerful in-state opposition, but also from weak national party direction. Even the most astute state GOP leadership would have floundered under such circumstances. And, South Carolina Republicans were hardly political supermen. Diminishing strength and continuing failure seemed the future for South Carolina Republicans in the face of Tillman's reelection and the presidential victory of Democratic Grover Cleveland. With a Democrat in the White House, state Republicans could hope for no national support, and, with Tillman further entrenched, they could foresee more electoral discrimination.

Murray was their only bright spot. In the excitement over his victory, Murray probably had few thoughts of grand political strategy, however. The redistricting threat had seemingly passed for the present, so the new congressman could concentrate on two years of service in the nation's capitol. He was now the state's leading black and Republican political figure and the highest ranking black politician in the country. How he had reached this pinnacle of success was probably less important to him than the fact that he was there. A black congressman elected with Tillman's acquiescence had the right to be happy and hope he had personally benefited from the beginning of a new political day in South Carolina.

# 4

# Congressman

Elections for Congress are always held in November of even years. For much of American history, however, the newly elected Congress did not convene until December of the following year, thirteen months later. On rare occasions this timetable was altered when the president called a special congressional session to meet a specific emergency. The Panic of 1893 provided such a calamity. The newly inaugurated president, Grover Cleveland, summoned Congress to meet in special session in August 1893. George W. Murray, South Carolina's Seventh District representative, thus began his congressional duties earlier than usual. Still, it was nine months from the time of his election until he entered the House of Representatives.

Murray gained instant fame as the nation's only black congressman. He went to the White House to meet the president, and according to newspaper reports of the meeting, he reminded Grover Cleveland of black apprehension over the election of a Democrat. He urged the president to allay these fears by appointing blacks to political office. Such action would create a political revolution in the South; parties would become based on principal not race. The current practice of refusing offices to blacks caused many to think "that they are less than other classes of citizens and may be maltreated and outraged with impunity, just as lust might crave, prejudice dictate, or selfish greed demand."[1] If the president paid any attention to Murray's recommendation, his actions did not demonstrate it. He did not appoint any appreciable number of blacks to public office.

In addition to his visit to the White House, Murray sat for an interview with a Washington newspaper. A reporter asked him about the recurring proposal to reduce southern representation at Republican national nominating conventions. Like the other black luminaries questioned (Frederick Douglass, former Virginia congressman John Mercer Langston, and former Mississippi legislative member John R. Lynch), Murray called the proposal "out of harmony with the principles of the Republican party." It was unfair to base national convention representation on the number of votes cast in elections. Discrimination in the South meant vote totals there were not "a fair measure of Southern Republicans."[2]

Murray's first days in Washington clearly boosted his new stature. His conversation with the president and his linkage with three major black leaders illustrated his growth to national political importance. He probably also made other contacts in the nation's capital, perhaps through his former classmate at the University of South Carolina, Whitefield McKinlay, an important Washington black figure. He probably did not stay long in the nation's capital, however, because a spate of lynchings in South Carolina forced him to hurry home. As the highest ranking black politician in the state, he had to return to deal with the crisis.

A complex of reasons helped bring on the increase of lynchings throughout South Carolina, and among these was the governor's attitude. During his first administration, Ben Tillman had taken a strong public stand against the crime, but early in his second term he reversed himself when a black man, accused of attempted rape, asked for the protection of the state government. Tillman handed the accused man over to local officials, and the man was soon lynched. Instead of condemning the crime, Tillman gave it his approval. The absence of capital punishment for attempted rape meant that lynching was the only available justice, he said. Conservative Democrats, hardly blameless themselves when it came to anti-black violence, reacted with shock. At a mass meeting, they accused Tillman of complicity in the murder. For their efforts, they were accused of seeking black votes and encouraging the black rape of white women. The anti-Tillman editor N. G. Gonzales of the Columbia *State* responded with similarly harsh language. The debate quickly evolved into an argument over what constituted a true South Carolina Democrat. Democrats debated the nature of their party over the dead body of a lynched black man.[3]

On May 18, 1893, South Carolina blacks held a mass meeting in Columbia to protest Tillman's position with sixty to seventy representatives from twenty-nine counties present. Murray was named to the committee drafting the convention's address, and he was clearly the major author of the statement, which revealingly was written on congressional stationery. He read it aloud for the convention's approval. One delegate immediately called the address too weak. Winchester rifles, not blank words, were the answer to lynching. "When they come to take our rights shoot them like dogs," the delegate insisted. The convention hooted such militancy down, however, and voted to endorse Murray's milder words.

The Murray statement was accommodating almost to the point of obsequiousness. The address reminded white South Carolinians how black slaves had protected white women during the Civil War. In return for such loyalty, these "matrons," "their daughters," "Confederate veterans and their sons" should now raise their voices against lynching. The address appealed to Governor Tillman, whom the address called "the most aggressive pioneer against lynch law." It also asked a "defenseless race, some of whom are charged with participating in the savage crimes which are disgracing our state and shocking the civilized world, to abstain from all crime and violence—and shun the plantation and business places of all who maltreat them." The press was urged to be fair, and blacks were encouraged to establish "protective societies" in every town, to provide sufficient capital to pay for legal talent when emergencies arose.[4]

Murray's address demonstrated black fright and his own determination not to antagonize those who had given him his congressional seat. Murray was clearly trying to maintain a good relationship with the Tillmanites. Tillman said nothing, however, therefore showing his unwillingness to moderate his anti-black position even for a black congressman his supporters had sent to Washington.

Murray's accommodating attitude was also evident in another action he took in June 1893; he appointed a white youngster to the United States Military Academy at West Point. The young man's name was Rembert, the same name as a town near Murray's farm. Chances are that the new black congressman had appointed a relative of the leading white man in his community. A newspaper praised the black congressman, pointing out that he had chosen the white Rembert over several black applicants. Obviously Murray was using the prerogatives of his new position to try to broaden his political base. He did not allow his advocacy of black solidarity to stand in the way of pragmatic politics.[5]

In August 1893, Murray returned to Washington to join his congressional colleagues in the heat and humidity of the Washington summer for the special session of the Fifty-third Congress. He lived alone at 1924 Tenth Street, N.W., his wife and family remaining in the South. According to law, he had become a member of Congress on Grover Cleveland's inauguration day in March 1893, so he had been drawing his $5,000 per year salary at the rate of $416 per month since then. He had also begun using his 20¢ per mile traveling allowance and the $125 per year allowance for postage, stationery, and newspapers. He was enjoying the financial benefits of his position, even before he actually took on its major duties.[6]

He was the only black man in the body and the only Republican from

South Carolina. The other six members of the Palmetto State congressional delegation were white Democrats, and, on the surface, they were totally different from their black Republican colleague. A closer look, however, indicates a number of similarities.[7]

William H. Brawley, the First District representative and the delegation's only Conservative Democrat, was a former Confederate army officer and a postwar state legislator. He was serving his second term in the House of Representatives. On February 12, 1894, he would resign his office to become U.S. district judge for South Carolina.[8] He served in that post until 1914 and was, during Theodore Roosevelt's presidential administration, one of Roosevelt's advisors on Palmetto State affairs.

The Second South Carolina District was represented by the Tillmanite, W. Jasper Talbert. Another Confederate veteran, Talbert had also served in the State House and Senate and had been superintendent of the state penitentiary. One of the founders of the South Carolina Farmers' Alliance, he had helped draft the Alliance's famous national Ocala Platform. He became Ben Tillman's close lieutenant even though he had defeated the governor's brother to gain his House seat. This was to be the first of his five terms in Congress. In 1902 he lost in a bid to become governor, and in 1912 he ran unsuccessfully against Tillman for the Senate.

Asbury C. Latimer, another Tillmanite farmer, represented the Third District for five terms, and, from 1903 until his death in 1908 in Washington he was a U.S. senator. While in the Senate, he was named a member of the U.S. Immigration Commission. He was the least known of all these representatives.

The representative from South Carolina's Fourth District was George W. Shell. He was a veteran of the Confederate Army, a farmer, and from 1888 to 1896 a local clerk of court. He served in the House during the 52nd and 53rd Congresses, but he did not run for reelection in 1894. As president of the State Farmers' Association, he had issued the 1890 Shell Manifesto, the call for Tillman's farmer forces to take control of the South Carolina Democratic Party.

Thomas Jefferson Strait was the Fifth District's representative. Another Confederate Army veteran and Tillmanite, he was a physician by profession. He was first elected to Congress in 1892 and served a total of six years. Later he served two terms in the State Senate.

The Sixth District representative was John L. McLaurin, the man destined to become one of the most controversial figures in Palmetto State politics. He was educated at the University of Virginia Law School, where he knew Woodrow Wilson. He was a lawyer, briefly a member of the State House, and the attorney general of South Carolina (in which capacity he had been a member of the Board of Canvassers, which had certified Murray's election). McLaurin was a member of the House for five years, but in 1897 he was appointed to the U.S. Senate. He served in the Senate from 1897 to 1903, not running for reelection because of political differences with Ben Tillman. McLaurin was originally one of Tillman's closest lieutenants, but the turn of the century found him literally wrestling with his former mentor on the Senate floor. By that time, McLaurin was working with Theodore Roosevelt to try to develop a white Republican Party in South Carolina.[9]

With the exception of the Conservative Democrat Brawley, then, Murray's South Carolina colleagues were all products of Tillman's farmers' movement.[10] McLaurin, who was thirty-three, was the only one younger than the forty-year-old Murray; the others ranged in age from forty-seven to sixty-two. Furthermore, the others all had office-holding experience, unlike Murray. However, Murray's service to the state GOP as party worker, county chairman, and patronage recipient meant that he was no political novice. His similar farmer background (albeit in the Colored Alliance) and his certification by a Tillman board that had included McLaurin gave the seven men something in common. Yet, their contacts were minimal. Murray was a Republican, they were Democrats—in a state where that difference was crucial. More significantly he was black and they were white, and this difference was even more fundamental.

Murray had the misfortune of serving in Washington during a period when for the first time since 1853, Democrats controlled both the presidency and the Congress. In the House, there were 231 Democrats, 133 Republicans, and 13 Populists and members of other political groups. One-third of the representatives were Civil War veterans, fifty-six having been Confederates and sixty-four Federals. Of more importance, twenty-two ex-Confederates and only four former Federal soldiers were committee chairman, indicating yet another problem for the former slave. Murray was a racial and a party minority in his state's delegation and in the House as a whole. Champ Clark, a fellow freshman and later Speaker of the House, characterized the 53rd Congress as "unharmonious, quarrelsome and factional."[11] Murray had no easy road to travel.

The House was called to order that August 7 and the president's plan for dealing with the Panic of 1893 was presented. It consisted of a call for repeal of the 1890 Sherman Silver Purchase Act and the lowering of the tariff rate.

Charles Crisp of Georgia was elected Speaker of the House over the Republican candidate Thomas "Czar" Reed, and the House proceeded to select assigned seats in the chamber. Each member received a number based on his alphabetical ranking, and, when a marble with his number was selected from a container, he was able to choose a seat. Murray was lucky enough to have his number drawn early. Standing erect as always, fitted out in the conservative dress of his day, the six-foot-tall black man answered the call in his deep resonant voice and took seat number 120 in the Republican section of the House, the left side, six rows from the bottom, the third row down from the top. South Carolina newspapers were quick to point out that, though he chose a good seat, other Republicans avoided selecting places near him. It was not until almost all of the other seats were occupied that his colleagues chose the seats next to his. As the chart was finally constructed, he had a Republican congressman from Iowa and another from Wisconsin sitting on either side of him.[12]

When committee assignments were announced, Murray, along with fellow South Carolinian John L. McLaurin, received a place on the Education Committee. Nineteenth-century Americans considered education to be a function of local government; the 1890 Blair Education Bill, for example, was attacked as federal government interference in local affairs. Murray's committee assignment, therefore, was insignificant. The committee seldom met (it was not even listed with other committees as having a regular meeting day). During the Fifty-third Congress, for example, the main order of committee business was to try to force a retraction from the commissioner of Education for his statements about the poor quality of education in Tennessee. The committee chairman represented the Volunteer State.[13]

The main item of congressional business during the special session was H.R.1., the repeal of the Sherman Silver Purchase Act. This 1890 law required the federal government to buy 4.5 million ounces of silver each month and issue legal tender Treasury notes redeemable in gold and silver at the Treasury Department's discretion. Grover Cleveland and hard-money exponents argued that this law placed a strain on the gold standard and that its repeal would ease the depression ravaging the country. Opponents disagreed. Eliminating this law would only worsen an already desperate economic situation.

House debate began on August 11, 1893 and continued until the repeal was passed on November 1. Considering the Republican Party's anti-silver philosophy and the Democratic president's strong hard-money stand, repeal should have come easily. But there was a solid block of silver Democrats, silver Republicans, and a handful of Populists who were adamant in their support of silver and their opposition to Cleveland's hard-money policy. The president's agent in the Congress conducted a tally of how congressmen were leaning when the debate began and matters looked grim for Cleveland. (Murray was listed in the doubtful column.)[14]

Murray quickly let it be known that he held no such doubt. Like his Tillmanite colleagues, he opposed the repeal. He publicly supported Missouri's Richard "Silver Dick" Bland, the leading silver Republican in the House. When Bland called a caucus of silver supporters, Murray visited South Carolina colleagues Strait and Latimer to ask them to inform Bland of his support. Without saying why, though fear of a racial rebuff was no doubt the reason, he said he would be unable to attend the caucus. However, he did defend his position: "My constituents need money and I am going to give it to them if I can. As Mr. Cleveland said, this matter rises above party politics."[15]

The Columbia *State* ridiculed Murray sarcastically, congratulating him for the "faithfulness with which he carries out the bargain, tacit or otherwise, by which he was given his seat over a Cleveland Democrat. Blifil and Black George are quite harmonious." This was hardly fair. The Tillman forces supported silver, but silver had not been an issue in Murray's congressional campaign nor in state politics generally. Murray's stand was aimed at improving his popularity with black and white farmers in his state, but there is no proof that he was fulfilling any bargain with the Tillmanites. Political and personal considerations motivate any politician, and Murray was no different. His personal convictions and political considerations, not any illicit bargain, pointed him toward the pro-silver position.[16]

The silver debate wore on day after day, and, despite impressive orations like that of the then little-known William Jennings Bryan, it was obvious that most minds were already made up. The Republican representative Horace H. Powers of Vermont expressed this fact well when he asserted: "Mr. Speaker, I am not vain enough to suppose that anything I may say, nor credulous enough to believe that anything anyone else has said, touching the pending proposition, will change any single member's vote or shade his belief. But animated by that common impulse of mankind which prompts us to talk of those blessings we do not enjoy, I propose to talk a few moments about money. . . ." Hoping to expedite debate, the House leadership assigned members specific times to deliver their orations. Murray's scheduled time was an inauspicious 10 p.m. on August 24, the last time slot for that evening. That afternoon, he announced his time in the Washington papers and, since he was the only black man in

Congress and a silver Republican besides, his announcement attracted a large curious crowd to hear his speech.[17]

Murray was closely observed when he stood up to speak. A newspaper reporter noted that "judging by his face, there is not a drop of white blood running in his veins, but his voice did not show his African origin."[18] The novice congressman began in standard pro-silver form. He divided the American people into three classes: (1) "capitalists, bankers and commercial men who want to keep currency as dear as possible;" (2) owners of silver mines; and (3) "the toiling and producing millions." "To the last-named class nearly all of my constituents, and the whole race of which I am the sole representative, belong." In fact, Murray said, he had the largest constituency of anyone in the House: his district and black people all over the country.

Applause interrupted Murray's speech several times, and two of his facetious remarks were greeted with appropriate laughter. He made the usual silver arguments, the speech filled with statistics to show that the per capita amount of money in circulation was declining, and this decline was particularly hurtful to southern and western Americans. He denied the Sherman Act's responsibility for the depression and warned against repealing it and increasing the common man's suffering. If the Democratic Party did not act in favor of silver, it would be swept by a "political cyclone." As for the Republicans, he urged them to support the metal in the tradition of its long defense of human rights. "I shall vote for the free and unlimited coinage of silver, because I am for the betterment of the miserable condition of my countrymen, and for America first and all of the world afterwards."

All these arguments were familiar silverite rhetoric. Murray's oration was unique, however, because of his use of racial references. He cited the long tradition of black participation in American wars to help justify black desires for silver. Later in the speech, he compared the plight of silver vis-à-vis gold to the plight of blacks vis-à-vis whites. "The little, yellow, gold man . . . is spitefully driving this large useful, humane philanthropic white man [silver] from nearly every place of honor, usefulness, and amusement." Later, he compared the physical slavery blacks had once suffered with the financial slavery so many Americans were presently experiencing. He ended dramatically: "Standing before you today, the lone spokesman for my race, I hear voices which you do not hear, I see faces which you cannot see."[19]

When Murray finished, he sat down to the sound of "Prolonged applause." He had shown conclusively that he was not afraid to oppose party leaders in order to improve his own political standing. The nation's black press did not mention this speech, however, while newspapers in Charleston and Sumter mentioned it only in passing. A devastating cyclone did severe damage to the seacoast region of Murray's congressional district and took attention away from his oratory. Beaufort County, where all but two thousand of thirty-four thousand people were black, suffered heavy casualties and a property loss of two million dollars. Murray's silver concerns gave way to worry for the homeless storm-tossed people he represented. He personally appealed for contributions from members of the House and urged any interested parties to send money to designated banks. He contributed fifty dollars himself.[20]

On September 11, after the former congressman William Elliott had conspicuously received promises of support from the president and the surgeon general, Murray introduced a joint resolution to provide storm victims with necessary food and medicine to fight the threatened "starvation and pestilence." He needed unanimous consent to get immediate consideration for his resolution, but he failed. C. B. Kilgore, a Democrat from Texas, objected, and Samuel M. Robertson, a Republican from New York, argued that the resolution should first be sent to committee. The Texas Democrat Joseph D. Sayers moved that the motion go to the Committee on Appropriations. The chair so ruled, and Murray's effort was thwarted. The resolution was never heard of again.[21]

Murray was ahead of his time. Federal relief in time of catastrophe was not an accepted nineteenth-century practice; each state was expected to take care of its own crises. The Charleston *News and Courier* said as much in answering a Boston newspaper's accusation that South Carolina was surrendering its constitutional scruples by asking for federal help. Four days before Murray's resolution, the Charleston newspaper insisted that no congressional aid had been requested; the state was doing everything possible on its own to aid sufferers. Yet, when the national Red Cross offered its help, Governor Tillman and the state's two senators cordially welcomed Clara Barton to the state. Tillman discouraged any relief for blacks, however, because, he said, they could not "be treated as we would white people." Murray's call for federal aid made sense, but his efforts were peripheral to the meager relief activity.[22]

In the House, meanwhile, the Sherman Act was repealed on November 1. The next major order of business was the repeal of all federal laws relating to federal election supervisors and special deputy marshals (HR 2331). This issue did not have the broad public interest of the silver debate, but to Murray it was a key issue. As the nation's only black congressman, he felt a special responsibility to support a continuation of the remaining limited federal protections of black voting rights passed during Reconstruction. Thus, he played a conspicuous role in the debate simply because he was black. Representative Talbert of South Carolina singled him out as proof that the Palmetto State was fair to black people, while Representative John F. Lacey, a Republican from Iowa, referred to him in an attempt to soften his allusion to South Carolina as a reason for retaining the federal election law. Both sides used Murray's mere presence to try to prove opposing arguments.[23]

Murray remained silent, even when his name was mentioned and he was pointed to. When the freshman representative and future House Speaker Champ Clark of Missouri called for the election law's repeal because of corruption, however, Murray interrupted him. He asked Clark if the Missouri representative really believed that U.S. marshals and supervisors had cheated congressional candidates. As someone who had worked elections, he knew this was impossible. Clark insisted it had happened. When Clark called on blacks to split their votes between Republicans and Democrats to end southern political problems, Murray interrupted again. He asked Clark whether he thought such a split could happen or would be beneficial if whites continued to vote a straight ticket. Clark responded that whites would never divide until blacks did. Murray answered that because of Democratic factionalism blacks in South Carolina had split their votes in a recent election. They were ready to do so again wherever or whenever whites split.[24]

The next day, Murray spoke up even more forcefully. Representative John C. Kyle, a Democrat from Mississippi, was debating "Uncle Joe" Cannon, a Republican, and, to clinch his home rule argument, Kyle quoted someone he identified only as a leading Mississippi Republican. He said this black Republican had accepted the 1890 Mississippi Constitution, which disenfranchised blacks, and opposed the 1890 Force Bill. Murray interjected that if that Republican was Isaiah Montgomery[25] he had also said in the speech Kyle was quoting "that he laid upon the altar of sacrifice the suffrage of a hundred and twenty-five thousand of his race, and that he knew it." Kyle answered: "Suppose he did, what of it?" Murray responded with his own question: "Do you believe that in a government constituted like ours, the suffrage should be one of manhood, inasmuch as the ballot is the only weapon of protection that a poor man has?" Kyle brusquely refused to answer the question because, he said insultingly, he did not understand it. Representative Charles A. Boutelle, a Maine Republican, twitted him that Murray would be happy to repeat the question. Kyle answered: "You can do it better than he can. You put the question. I want you to put it." Boutelle refused, and Murray pressed for an answer, repeating the question two more times without receiving a satisfactory reply. Murray had made his point. Kyle had also expressed his feelings; the Mississippi representative would not dignify his black colleague by debating him directly.[26]

Finally, Murray stood up to make his own election law speech. His statement was so long that it ran into a second day and required an extension of time. Murray must have shocked his listeners when he openly defended Tillmanism. He said that no one could find an administration "more honest and true to the principles of right than that which accorded my certificate of election and still controls in my State." Despite his own Republicanism, he expressed willingness to join the Democratic Party immediately if such action would reestablish a two-party system in his state "upon economy and morality, rather than race." White supremacy prevented nonracial politics, however, so blacks had no choice but to band together and be Republicans. Here, not in the silver speech, was Murray's repayment for his election, but neither contemporaries nor later historians ever noticed it.[27]

His own "self-interest and self-preservation" was reason enough for him to remain silent, Murray continued, but, as the "sole representative" of people "who are slandered and misrepresented in the remarks of almost every other man who speaks upon this subject," he had to speak out. He would explain the electoral situation in his home state, South Carolina, to show the continued need for election laws. He chose South Carolina not because it was the worst example, but because he knew more about it than he knew about any other state. His praise for Tillmanism notwithstanding, Murray castigated voting discrimination in the Palmetto State. His pro-Tillman words were clever politics, but he offered them only within the context of continued support for black political participation.

In order to vote in South Carolina, Murray explained, a person had to have a registration certificate, and the procurement of such a document was nearly an impossible task. Each registrar served a large area, and he opened his books only on the first Monday of the seven months before an election (despite the fact that the law required him to do so each month every year). The result was chaos: "Men massed themselves in such numbers around the doors of the houses in which the registration was carried on that they became a solid block of humanity, in some instances covering acres of ground, from 8 in the morning till 4 or 5 in the afternoon, yielding for nothing, not even the rays of the summer's sun nor the showers of heaven. . . ."

As Murray finished this point, Representative Talbert of South Carolina jumped up to offer an insulting denial. "I want to say that on the first Monday in every month the registration books are open all day, and you ought to know it, if you know anything, and you ought to have asked those who helped you to get up that statement to put that in." Murray, ignoring Talbert's personal attack, asked his Palmetto State colleague if he was saying that elections were absolutely fair everywhere in South Carolina. Talbert answered: "Absolutely fair and untrammeled." "Well, I am surprised at that statement," Murray replied to House laughter. As the hour was late, however, he agreed to continue his remarks the next day.

When he resumed, Murray denied Talbert's charge that someone had written his speech for him. It was a strange comment from a man who only recently had been accused of plagiarism himself, Murray said. Talbert did not answer, and Murray once more praised the Tillman administration but again insisted on the necessity of election laws to protect black voters. He compared voting statistics for the North and the South to show that southern voters were being kept from the polls; he denied that blacks had any interest in black domination; and he accused southern Democrats of reneging on their 1876 promises to protect blacks in their voting rights. He appealed to the House and to the nation not to permit the repeal of any election laws because "every man who votes for this bill has entered into a conspiracy with ballot-box stuffers, perjurers, and murderers, whom he has promised to shield by destroying the light by which their deeds are exposed." He closed on a moving religious note. "The same omnipotent power that heard the prayers and groans of black fathers and mothers away down in the valleys of cotton and rice fields and brought awful retribution upon you for the wrongs committed upon a helpless people, by arraying one section of this country against the other in a disastrous war, is not asleep, and those suffering people are still praying."

"Prolonged applause on the Republican side" and the congratulations of some Republican members greeted the end of the speech. Representative Benjamin E. Russell, a Democrat of Georgia, was not impressed. Murray had been "loaded to the muzzle with the cast-off implements of war and the exploded ammunition of the Republican party, to fire upon the Democratic side of this House upon this question," he said. Republicans were only waving the bloody shirt (the "ensanguined garment" as he put it) through Murray. "I think the entire party has had a finger in the pie of which he delivered himself yesterday and today," he said mixing his metaphors. It was "eminently fitting that the requiem gun of a once great but reckless party should have been fired by a son of Ham." When it was Representative Talbert's chance to speak, he did not respond to Murray's remark about plagiarism, but once again he cited the black man's presence in the House as refutation of his own speech. Murray was proof, Talbert insisted, that South Carolina treated the black man fairly.[28]

Judging by the attempt to belittle Murray's speech, he had made a solid impression on House members. Press response was also favorable. The Republican New York *Tribune* said Murray's speech was by far the best one given on the issue. With a fine burst of hyperbole, it reported that "No man ever spoke in the House of Representatives who was listened to more attentively." The Washington *Star* did not comment on the speech but later in the month published an interview with Murray. In it, the black congressman boldly defended his race and, shockingly by the standards of the day, predicted future mixed marriages.[29]

South Carolina newspapers concentrated their comments on Murray's response to Talbert. Tillmanite journals attacked him, and Conservative papers found his statement pleasing. The Columbia *State* facetiously said Murray's intimation that Talbert had stolen words from a dead man, Henry Grady, the prophet of a "New South," "was an ungenerous thrust." It was equivalent to accusing Congressman Talbert of "grave-robbing." The Tillmanite Columbia *Register* called Murray "malignant" and quoted the Atlanta *Journal*'s remark that an "Uncle Remus" was needed as stenographer to record his speech correctly.[30]

The black press was enthusiastic. *The Freeman* of Indianapolis printed Murray's picture on its front page and, although it misspelled his name ("Murry"), said his silver and election speeches proved his "strong convictions and brilliant abilities." The New York *Age* said that during his tenure in Congress he had "proven himself the peer of any member of that body," his latest speech being even better than his silver one. The Cleveland *Gazette* said he was "strong, courageous and worthy of a grand following"; his election law speech was "pointed, statemanlike and well-given." Murray's oratory had again served him well. Unfortunately, the House voted for repeal, 210 to 102.[31]

When he was not involved in debate or in making speeches, Murray was a conspicuous figure around Congress. As a black man of the darkest hue, he was more noticeable than the earlier lighter-skinned black representatives. He was also one of the tallest members of the chamber and his mode of dress, consisting of long black broadcloth coats and light-colored vests and trousers, accentuated his height. The autobiography he furnished the *Congressional Directory* also brought him attention. It was longer than other congressmen's entries, and it was full of flowery prose: "emancipation found him a lad of eleven summers: bereft of both parents, thrown upon the rugged shores of early emancipation . . ."; "among the waifs of his neighborhood he acquired an imperfect and crude pronunciation of monosyllables." Reading these words, the Indianapolis *Sentinel*, a white newspaper, decided that Murray was "a natural born orator," but the home-standing Columbia *State* thought him pretentious.[32]

Murray was also conspicuous because, unlike some earlier black congressmen, he dared visit the Senate. On his first visit he had difficulty convincing the doorkeeper that he was a congressman and therefore permitted to enter the floor while the Senate was in session. After some discussion he was reluctantly allowed to walk in. No senator greeted him, so he quietly walked around the outside of the chamber, looked into the cloak room, and then left. Some weeks later, he reappeared looking for South Carolina senator J. L. M. Irby to discuss Palmetto State patronage. Irby was not on the floor at the time, so Murray sat down, listened to some of the debate, and then left.[33]

Murray frequently encountered open prejudice, sometimes in the most blatant form. One day he went to the Government Printing Office and was in conversation with the head printer when Senator Anselm J. McLaurin of Mississippi walked in. McLaurin had written to the printer soliciting a job for a black constituent. When the printer saw McLaurin walk in, he interrupted his conversation with Murray and said to the Mississippi senator: "By the way, you wrote to me recommending a negro for appointment did you not?" McLaurin, seeing Murray, thought the printer was referring to him. Stammering and pointing to Murray, who he suspected of passing himself off as that candidate, McLaurin yelled: "Yes, but that's not my nigger!" The printer, visibly shaken, quickly pulled the Mississippi senator aside and whispered: "Sh-h Sh-h That's Congressman Murray of South Carolina."[34]

Perhaps because of such incidents, Murray soon began dealing with government departments through notes carried by his secretary. This aide, R. H. Richardson, was also a black man, and no doubt he experienced plenty of slights. Murray never dwelt on the anti-black prejudice around him, and his family later remembered him laughing about his colleagues' attempts to avoid him. He displayed little anger, but he did withdraw from unnecessary contact with other congressmen.[35]

The day after his election law speech in early October, Murray took a two-week leave of absence "on account of personal business." On October 27, he took another week. Such absences were not unusual; the pages of the *Congressional Record* are full of absence requests and unauthorized truancy besides.

Why Murray took a leave of absence at this time is not clear, but several reasons are possible. In South Carolina, Thomas E. Miller announced the appointment of a state committee to prepare for a November 28 national black emigration convention. Murray opposed emigration, and, in the November 1893 issue of *The Freeman,* which was devoted to discussion of the back-to-Africa idea, he strongly refuted the concept. When black lawyers asked him to support colonization, he told them he favored education to advance blacks in business and diametrically opposed any "utopian scheme which would create false hopes in the minds of the simple masses, so poorly prepared to immigrate anywhere." Murray may have left Congress for South Carolina so he could fight an emigration movement in his home state. A later October emigration meeting in Sumter was postponed, perhaps because of his arrival home to battle it.[36]

Family matters, not colonization, may also have caused Murray to leave Washington. His family—wife, son, and daughter—did not live with him in the capital because his wife refused to leave the Palmetto State. Once, his son remembered, Murray asked the family to come to Washington, but they did not go at that or any other time.[37]

Whatever the reason for Murray's leave of absence, it marked the end of his first experience in Congress. He had made two major speeches (though he said nothing during the tariff debate), and he had introduced one unsuccessful resolution (relief for storm victims). The Charleston *News and Courier*'s Washington reporter praised him for his "reticence" and "unobtrusiveness" but saved most encomiums for the other South Carolina congressmen. Actually, Murray's South Carolina colleagues had not outperformed him during the session, neither in speech-making nor in legislation. The House passed only one of Brawley's bills, which then failed in the Senate. Latimer and McLaurin each introduced one unsuccessful bill or resolution, while Talbert introduced three. Strait and Shell offered only private relief bills, and all were unsuccessful.[38]

An analysis of Murray's votes shows that they were not that different from his South Carolina or his Republican colleagues, with the exception of his votes on silver. Murray was a pro-silverite, and his voting record during the first session indicates this fact clearly. He voted "Yes" on silver questions 71 percent of the time. In comparison, the Republican leadership, consisting of "Uncle Joe" Cannon and "Czar" Reed, voted "Yes" only 27 percent of the time. The Democratic leaders Williams Springer of Illinois and Joseph Baily of Texas voted "Yes" 68 percent of the time. The leading silverites, "Sockless"

Jerry Simpson, a Populist, William Jennings Bryan, a Democrat, and "Silver Dick" Bland, a Republican, voted "Yes" 60 percent of the time. The Democratic rank and file voted "Yes" only 48 percent of the time, and Murray's South Carolina colleagues voted "Yes" 30 percent of the time. Clearly, Murray had the temerity to deviate from the Republican position on the major issue of this first session; he voted his conviction rather than his party. Clearly too, his vote was no repayment for earlier Tillmanite support. His silver votes were clearly different from those of his Tillmanite congressional colleagues.

Votes on procedural questions, however, show that Murray's independence did not extend beyond silver. On procedural matters (for example, quorum calls) the key vote was not a "Yes" or a "No," rather it was a "No-Vote." The Democrats controlled the House, so the "No-Vote" was a partisan Republican weapon to stymie the Democratic legislative program. On procedural questions, Murray did not vote 66 percent of the time, and this percentage put him squarely into the Republican camp. The two Republican leaders did not vote 54 percent of the time, all Republicans did not vote 60 percent of the time, and a sampling of Republican freshmen shows they did not vote 72 percent of the time. The Democratic leadership did not vote only 22 percent of the time, the rank and file did not vote 30 percent of the time, and South Carolina representatives did not vote 27 percent of the time. Obviously, Murray voted the Republican line on this partisan issue.

A study of all the votes in all three sessions of the 53rd Congress indicates conclusively that Murray was a loyal Republican partisan, not a Tillmanite lackey. On procedural questions in all three sessions, his 77 percent nonvoting record was closer to the 62 percent of the Republican leaders and the 64 percent of the GOP rank and file than it was to the 18 percent of the South Carolina representatives and the 12 percent of the Democratic leaders. The same situation existed on the tariff question and on every other issue facing the House—except for silver. But even on the silver issue, Murray's three-session record differed from his first-session performance when silver dominated the House. His three-session silver record of 36 percent "Yes" voting was substantially higher than that of Republican leaders and the rank and file (12 percent and 19 percent respectively). But it was much lower than the 79 percent of the Democratic leaders, the 52 percent of the Democratic rank and file, and the 50 percent of South Carolina's representatives . Murray did not vote "No" more often in the second and third sessions; rather he was absent more frequently and did not vote at all.

Murray's first experience in the U.S. House of Representatives indicated that he was a capable congressman. He made two effective speeches; he rebutted other House members when he felt they were distorting the facts; he introduced a resolution to try to help his constituents recover from the devastation of a destructive wind storm; and he was not afraid to dissent from his normal party loyalty when he felt it would benefit his constituents.

His race presented him with problems of personal professional associations that no other congressman had. He could do little to temper congressional prejudice, but he had to try to develop a relationship with the Tillmanites, the political force that had placed him in office. He did not vote with them, nor did he change his beliefs to try to win their support. Instead, he cleverly used every opportunity to praise them. The result was the incongruity of a black congressman beginning a pro-federal election law speech by praising an anti-black leader and the movement that made such a law necessary. Murray tried to stay on good terms with the Tillmanites while at the same time maintaining his Republican faith and his duties to his district and to black people all over the country. The success of such a strategy would require continued cleverness and Tillmanite openness. Murray had shown political agility, but the Tillmanites remained as anti-black as ever. The future did not look promising—despite Murray's determined attempt to make it so.

# The Congressman Runs for Reelection

The special session of the 53rd Congress was scarcely over before it was time for the regular session to begin on December 4, 1893. Unfortunately, problems in South Carolina prevented Murray from giving the opening days his full attention. Talk about gerrymandering his congressional district, the Seventh or Black District, had resurfaced. The Tillmanites were again rumored to be planning to punish Charleston and the white Conservatives. The freshman black congressman was clearly worried and had to pay more attention to state politics than congressional duties.

The redistricting measure had a torturous run through the state legislature. It was killed once, only to be reborn and passed five days later. As predicted, Charleston was placed into a new black district. Redistricting proponents shunted aside the Conservative cries of protest and insisted that the new law's purpose was not to punish Charleston but to prevent the election of any more black congressmen. A Tillman state senator said "he expected Charleston to do what was being done throughout South Carolina" to insure white supremacy. Unconvinced Charlestonians pointed to the Board of Canvassers' selection of Murray over Moise.[1]

Clearly, the new law was designed to disfranchise the state's black population more than it was meant to punish Charleston. By the measure, the legislature split the Seventh District. All the heavily black seacoast counties were made part of the new First Congressional District, while Sumter and Orangeburg Counties, with their large black populations, became part of the new Seventh. The state's seven newly constituted congressional districts still each contained a black numerical majority, ranging from fourteen hundred to sixty-eight thousand, but this margin was not enough to overcome registration chicanery, voting frauds, and intimidation. Tillmanites were so confident of their power that they no longer felt the need, as the Conservatives had in 1882, to gerrymander most of the state's blacks into one district. But if in the course of redistricting, Charleston should be "humiliated," so much the better. The Tillmanites were willing to show up their Conservative opponents by allowing the election of a black congressman in 1892 and by preventing his reelection in 1894.

If Murray hoped to remain in Congress, he had to run from the new First District, not the new white-controlled Seventh where he maintained his home. He acted quickly. Two weeks into the new session of Congress, he took a leave of absence "on account of private business." He used the time to organize a so-called Murray's Association in Charleston and to attend a banquet the group held in his honor. His Washington congressional secretary, the association's vice-president, introduced him, and he delivered a speech before the two hundred persons in attendance. Then he delivered an Emancipation Day address at Beaufort, another important part of the new First District. Though he continued to maintain his residence in Sumter County, he formally moved to Charleston. He had lived there while working in the customs office, so he may simply have returned to the same lodgings. He never purchased any property in Charleston County, but the residency question was never an issue.[2]

Murray finally returned to Washington after the Christmas holidays and found the House of Representatives in disarray. The chamber's Democrats wanted to deal with the tariff issue, but growing dissatisfaction with Grover Cleveland and the congressional hierarchy made it difficult for them to maintain a quorum. Only Talbert of the South Carolina Democratic delegation was present. Representatives Strait and Shell and Senator Irby were feuding, and Tillman was forced to come to Washington to play conciliator. Both the national Democratic Party and the South Carolina Tillmanites were in turmoil, and, despite his own political problems, Murray must have felt encouraged. With Republican minority leader Thomas Reed's blessing, he and other Republicans stymied Democratic legislative plans by regularly not appearing and even taking extended leaves of absence.[3]

It was not until February 23, 1894, therefore, that Murray took his first substantive action of the 53rd Congress's second session. He introduced a bill (H.R. 5942) and a supporting petition "to exempt the Young Men's Christian Association of the District of Columbia from taxation." The measure was sent to the Committee on the District of Columbia, the House and Senate passed it, and it became law with the president's signature.[4]

Having gained a legislative victory and having received the plaudits of the black press, (the Washington *Bee* calling him "the best representative that has been in the House of Representatives"), Murray turned his attention once more to political affairs in South Carolina. He was drawn into the state's major social/political issue, the controversy surrounding the dispensary law. The Tillmanites had recently established a system of state-operated outlets for the sale of liquor, and both proponents and opponents of alcohol disliked the system. Infuriated prohibitionists joined those opposed to any government liquor regulation in fighting the law. An equally determined Tillman attempted to eliminate the remaining illegal private liquor sources. Opposition turned to violence, and several deaths occurred in Darlington in April 1894. Tillman called out the militia, but it refused to obey his orders. Thwarted and furious, he called on his farmer supporters, and they rallied to his aid. To his surprise, however, the highest judicial body in South Carolina declared prohibition permissible and the dispensary law unconstitutional. Even greater chaos then ensued. In October, a Tillman supporter replaced a Conservative on the bench, and the two to one April decision was overturned. The unpopular dispensary system was reestablished.[5]

The dispensary controversy was a volatile social issue and another manifestation of the Palmetto State's Democratic split. State Republicans tried to avoid the conflict, but, in Washington, Murray was drawn in. He was quoted as saying that "the best element of the State, including the negroes, supported the dispensary law." State law did not always protect blacks, he said, but they obeyed it anyway. In response, an anonymous letter to a Columbia newspaper expressed at least one black person's disdain of Murray's comment. "Every negro," this writer wrote, "that gets his certificate signed to a big job by the Tillmanish Legislature, as did the Hon. Murray, will speak in such friendly terms of the Governor; for the perpetuation of his job depends upon such a policy." The black masses, the letter continued, opposed the governor because of his support for lynchings. If Murray wanted ordinary blacks to continue obeying the law, he ought to guarantee them protection, "else a day will come when it will be a difficult task to know those in authority from the lynchers."[6]

Tillman showed his disdain for Murray's support in a more concrete way. He proposed a constitutional convention to disfranchise blacks. He had advocated such action before, but when he actually placed it on the 1894 ballot it came as a shock anyway. In response, Murray published a statement already circulating by hand in the First Congressional District. He called on all Republicans to register and vote en masse against this proposal. The national Republicans were again talking about basing representation in the national convention on the number of Republican votes cast in presidential and congressional elections, so a large Republican vote was doubly important. He had been waiting for state Republican leaders to do something, Murray said, but the state GOP seemed passive and withdrawn. "The present [Tillman] administration claims to be fair and honest," Murray said, "let the failure to live up to these professions be laid at their door and not upon your cowardly negligence."[7]

This attack on the Republican state hierarchy (of which it must be remembered he was a part) and the lack of a similar blast against Democratic electioneering tactics indicated that Murray was hoping to stimulate Republicans without alienating Tillmanites. He wanted to turn out a large number of Republican voters to help defeat the constitutional convention proposal, to protect the state party against Republican convention cutbacks, and to get himself reelected to Congress. He was walking a shaky tightrope made of fragile yarn.

He continued to stay away from a deadlocked U.S. House of Representatives and continued to concentrate on state politics. He took another leave of absence, this time "indefinitely on account of sickness." Operating out of his Charleston residence at 55 Drake Street, he demonstrated that his only illness was a reelection virus. He was on the stump every night, trying to combat what he called "a powerful combination" against him: amazingly not the Democrats, but the supporters of Robert Smalls, the black Civil War naval hero, former congressman, and former Beaufort collector of customs. Smalls had lost his customs position when Cleveland had become president in 1893, so he had decided to run for the new First District congressional seat instead. G. I. Cunningham, a Charleston businessman and a former U.S. marshall, reportedly supported him. It was similarly rumored that Ellery Brayton, the former state chairman, supported Murray. Smalls and Murray became involved in a heated issueless campaign highlighted by widespread accusations, name calling, racial innuendoes, and dirty tricks.[8]

Perhaps the most emotional campaign issue was the question of each man's support for the 1893 storm sufferers. Murray vigorously countered accusations of corruption and unconcern by referring accusers to Clara Barton of the American Red Cross, while Smalls talked of having distributed clothes provided by the same organization. Murray, a black, once again appealed to racial pride against the light-skinned Smalls, his mulatto faction, and their alleged tie to whites. He and his supporters argued that "a typical black man," not a mulatto, should be sent to Congress. Some inconsistently threatened that if they could not have a real black man they would prefer to vote for a white. The accusations grew increasingly caustic, and at times they were humorous. During a rally, a Murray supporter used Smalls's famous Civil War exploit of stealing a Confederate ship against him. "Bob Smalls, you know you teef de buckra big boat in de war, an' me fow one wouldn't trust you wid a canoe." Another time, a Murray supporter set up a street liquor stand near a Smalls rally. Inebriated Murray supporters tried to disrupt the rally, and the Smallsites were so angry that they swore out arrest warrants. The two men feuded angrily against one another in a manner they dared not use against white opponents.[9]

The failure of the state party to establish a clear nominating procedure also provided conditions for the dispute. In May 1894, the National Republican Executive Committee told the state party it supported Murray's continued presence in Congress. The State Executive Committee established an ad hoc committee to study the matter; it was made up of two national Republican committee members, state chairman Webster, his close black lieutenant E. H. Deas, and Ellery Brayton. Brayton and the national committee had already endorsed Murray, but Smalls had too much support in the district to be counted out. The local committee delayed a decision.[10]

Perhaps stung by Murray's call on blacks to register, the Executive Committee voted to challenge the 1882 registration law. It raised funds, hired the Columbia law firm of Obear and Melton, and, on June 4, appeared before the South Carolina Supreme Court to ask for a permanent injunction and a writ of mandamus against the registration law and its continued implementation. The Conservative press, worried that the law would be used against its white supporters, reluctantly, almost defensively, supported the court effort. The Tillman Columbia *Register* disagreed. The court case, it said, was part of a statewide effort to register blacks in the forlorn hope of causing a wider white split. Meanwhile, the state's supreme court refused the injunction but ordered the registrar of Richland County (the site of the state capital) to show cause on June 11 why a writ of mandamus should not be issued. Ellery Brayton applied further pressure by issuing a public warning that any new constitution adopted under the present illegal registration law would eventually be declared null and void.[11]

On June 11, South Carolina's attorney general appeared before the state supreme court to claim that he had not had enough time to prepare his case properly. Furthermore, W. W. Macon, the Richland registrar, was ill. Republican lawyers vehemently opposed any delay because they said it would postpone judgment until after the November elections. The judges reprimanded the Republicans for waiting until the last week of the court's spring session and then ordered the delay requested by the attorney general. The elections for Congress and for a constitutional convention would be held under the 1882 disfranchising rules. Republicans had suffered a significant setback.[12]

The Conservatives were also upset. The Columbia *State* accused the court of tolerating the continued disfranchisement of thousands of persons. The 1882 registration act had been passed to exclude black voters, the paper said, but the Tillmanite political monopoly had used it against white Conservatives too. Tillmanites ignored the accusation and tried to forestall further litigation by opening the Democratic primary to white Republicans and to Populists. Conservatives accused Tillmanites of willingness to do anything to solidify their political power.[13]

The Republicans decided to run candidates in the November elections, to keep a record of all those not allowed to vote, and then to contest any unfavorable results.[14] They said nothing about participating in the constitutional convention election. Perhaps they feared hampering the Conservatives' anti-Tillman campaign. Republicans had frightened off the Conservatives before; perhaps they feared doing it again.

Murray tried to stay clear of all the legal maneuvering and instead worked to solidify his black support for the congressional election by going to Alabama to give the commencement address at Tuskegee Institute. Booker T. Washington, that school's soon-to-be famous principal, regularly invited distinguished blacks to visit his school and, in that way, gained their support. Murray now joined the ranks of these prominent black figures. He had received his invitation in March 1894, and, in early May, Washington forwarded the details. He told Murray he would be addressing "a fine audience of both races" gathered there from "over the State and country." Commencement proved to be a gala week, and Murray enjoyed talking to school officials and viewing the pavilion of exhibits displaying the varied agricultural and manual skills of the institute's students. On commencement day he delivered a speech that pleased his host. He told his large audience that black people needed character, education, and wealth. Vocational training was particularly important because "the honest toil of skilled hands was their only road to wealth."[15]

His Tuskegee visit clearly impressed Murray. When he returned to the House soon after, it began debating H.R. 7095, a bill calling for the use of the unclaimed bounties, salaries, and moneys due the estates of Civil War black soldiers to finance the erection of a Washington home for "aged and infirmed colored persons." Murray said that blacks needed the type of training offered by Hampton and Tuskegee more than they needed housing for the elderly and the ill: "I believe that a people's training ought to be in keeping with their condition." Therefore, while he supported this bill, he intended to introduce another bill "to appropriate all unclaimed funds in the Treasury belonging to colored people, to establish industrial institutions for the education and training of the colored youth of the country." A month later Murray introduced H.R. 7689, which went to the Education Committee, to which he belonged, where it promptly died.[16]

Booker T. Washington's direct influence on this proposed legislation is uncertain. Murray and Washington corresponded briefly about it with Murray asking for further information on industrial education. Washington and Murray never became close, and Murray never became a part of Washington's Tuskegee machine. The two men shared some beliefs, but they differed widely on the politician's role in black life, Washington severely downplaying politics in favor of economics.[17]

The South Carolina press ignored the Tuskegee speech and the industrial school bill, so neither had any effect on Murray's reelection campaign. Several other events affected his canvass more directly. Lawyers for the South Carolina Republican committee appeared before the Richland County Board of Supervisors to protest again that Registrar W. W. Macon was refusing to register Republicans. Macon argued that the two claimants the Republicans had produced had never seriously attempted to register. The board, which consisted of Macon and his associates, not surprisingly agreed. The claimants immediately announced an appeal to the United States Court of Appeals for the Fourth Circuit. No litigation could take place before the November elections, however, so this appeal would have little immediate electoral effect.[18]

The increasing state of GOP factionalism affected Murray's reelection chances directly. His contest with Smalls was still unresolved, while in the new Seventh District Ellery Brayton and T. B. Johnston were involved in a bitter nomination struggle. Although Murray had his own campaign, he became involved in the Seventh District contest too. At a Sumter meeting to elect delegates to the Seventh District nominating convention, he supported the Brayton slate headed by his secretary, R. H. Richardson. But his former patron, T. B. Johnston, captured a majority of the delegates. The Brayton forces then decided to field a rival delegation. Murray showed bad political judgment. He was running for Congress from the Charleston district, but he was also trying to influence the nomination in the seventh. His support for the losing faction only compounded the problem. His attempt to try to maintain a political base in his hometown failed.[19]

Still, Murray's own electoral chances continued to look good. The *Freeman* quoted the *Colored American*'s earlier endorsement, headlining its story "Niggers' Attempting to Defeat Murray." The paper agreed that the black congressman was "a decent man" who stood up "for the interests of the race," while his opponents were nothing but "ambitious and jealous politicians." The Washington *Post*, an important white newspaper, quoted an unnamed Charlestonian in predicting that the Tillman Board of Canvassers would certify Murray over Smalls in any contest between them. The Tillmanites had "always felt friendly to Murray, whose elevation in life has not given him the big head and who is said to stand in with his white colleagues a great deal better than did Smalls." Murray, running a pro-black campaign, was allegedly deemed a more suitable candidate than his lighter-skinned opponent both by the black press and by a racist political movement. A subcommittee of the Republican National Committee agreed. It chose him as the "regular nominee of the Republican party in his district." Smalls publicly accepted the decision, so Murray had seemingly won a major victory.[20]

· Before he could conduct any serious campaigning, however, Murray still had some congressional business to complete as the second session of the 53rd Congress neared its weary conclusion. Murray made one final comment during the House debate over whether to appropriate funds to Atlanta's Cotton Exposition. (Booker T. Washington appeared before a congressional committee supporting the exposition, and later he made his famous "Atlanta Compromise" speech there.) As always, Murray spoke on behalf of all American blacks. He said he favored the exposition because it would allow blacks to show off their post-Emancipation progress. Such an exhibition would refute the "traducers and slanders" who called blacks inferior and no "part of the Adamic creation" because they had not produced any inventors. He appended a list of black inventors to document his remarks. Any congressman who cared to look discovered that George W. Murray himself was on this list as inventor of a farm implement. While conducting his congressional career and his reelection campaign that spring, he had also been busy registering seven agricultural patents.[21]

Congress adjourned on August 28, 1894, so Murray was able to concentrate exclusively on Palmetto State politics in the face of an increasingly fragmented Democratic Party. Sampson Pope, one of several thwarted Tillmanite gubernatorial candidates, decided to run as an independent candidate against the victorious Tillman nominee, John Gary Evans. The virulently anti-Tillman paper, the Columbia *State*, cautiously recommended Pope to those who opposed Tillman politics. The Conservatives also considered choosing their own state ticket, but their major worry was the constitutional convention election eliminating their influence in the state.[22]

The Republicans hesitated about doing anything that might reunite the feuding Democrats. In early September, their state Executive Committee issued a cautious address. Republicans should nominate congressional candidates in every district and keep accurate records of everyone kept from the polls. Nothing was said about presenting Republican candidates for state offices or about promulgating any concrete plan to fight the constitutional convention. In early October the party ratified this position. With Murray present (but his vote unknown) the Executive Committee decided, fifteen to seven, not to hold a convention to nominate candidates for state office. Then, instead of discussing how to deal with the constitutional convention election, the committee turned to the Seventh Congressional District contest between Brayton and Johnston. A national Republican subcommittee had already endorsed Brayton, but the state committee, by a vote of sixteen to six, supported Johnston instead. Murray and those voting in the negative argued that the state committee had no authority to overturn a national committee decision. This strange vote demonstrated the state committee's short-sighted vision. It discussed a settled matter, but never considered the more important danger of the constitutional convention. It was not even clear whether Republicans were going to print any negative ballots for their supporters to cast.[23]

Rank and file Republicans were outraged. A popularly called closed mass protest meeting of seven hundred persons issued an angry statement lambasting the Executive Committee's decision not to run a state ticket. This decision was "so disastrous," the meeting said, that it was impossible to rectify it now. Republicans should now go to the polls, vote for the best man, and oppose the constitutional convention in any way they could.[24] Republicans were clearly hesitant, fearful, divided, and uncertain. They could see no way to defeat their feuding but still powerful antagonists. In 1890 they had disastrously endorsed Haskell. Now, in 1894, they seemingly hoped to benefit from the Democratic split by keeping quiet. If openness had failed in 1890, perhaps silence would work in 1894.

Murray's candidacy reflected this turmoil. Robert Smalls had publicly accepted the pro-Murray decision of the Republican hierarchy, but he and his associate, Thomas E. Miller, were apparently still campaigning against the incumbent congressman. Murray told a friend that Smalls and Miller seemed "more desirous of accomplishing my defeat than even Elliott" [sic], and they were doing "every thing [*sic*] in their power, foul or fair, to accomplish their object." But, Murray was just as bad. He was continuing to do to Johnston what he accused Smalls and Miller of doing to him. At a turbulent meeting in early October in the Seventh Congressional District, he conspicuously supported Brayton against his former patron. He continued running his own race and interfering in another.[25]

In late September, Murray spoke at the ceremony to mark the laying of the cornerstone for the Charleston Industrial School and Home for Girls. In Booker T. Washington tones, he criticized traditional education and emphasized the need for black education "along the lines of industrial pursuits and useful occupations." The crowd of three thousand blacks received his address well. Immediately afterward, however, controversy surfaced. During his speech, Murray had justified industrial training by decrying the number of educated blacks waiting on tables, driving white men's carriages, or working in barbershops. Two barbers published a letter defending their work as a trade, and Murray, campaigning in Georgetown, responded bitterly. "The persons who try to distort my words . . . are either fools or rogues. I do not believe the parties taking such exception intend anything else than to create prejudice." Another person who had heard the speech then wrote in to support Murray. The Charleston *News and Courier*, clearly enjoying the disagreement, sarcastically noted that "a good barber, whatever the color of his skin, is really of more account than a poor congressman." The battle of the barber shop did not help Murray's campaign.[26]

Murray had another more serious problem. Ever since the Board of Canvassers had certified his 1892 election, he had been accused of supporting Tillman. Sampson Pope repeated this accusation as part of his gubernatorial campaign and seemed to be gaining votes as a result. The Tillmanites had generally ignored this charge in the past, but now State Treasurer Bates, a member of the Board of Canvassers, published a denial. Murray's selection had not been part of any conspiratorial appeal for black support. Murray had received the most legal votes, said Bates, and the board had simply certified him. Surely, he wrote (no doubt with a straight face), Conservatives were not suggesting that the board should have "violate[d] their oaths of office" and illegally given the election to Moise. In late October, a Seventh District Independent Democratic congressional candidate accused Tillman and Murray of holding a secret meeting in September so that Murray might deliver black votes to Tillman in return for a congressional victory. A few days before the election, a self-styled "Conservative Republican" charged the same thing.[27] Allegations of a Tillman-Murray understanding were coming from both the Democratic and the Republican sides, and Murray's reelection chances were being caught in the crossfire.

In Beaufort County, local politics also proved troublesome. On the eve of the November election, the Conservatives accused Tillman of trying to guarantee his own election to the U.S. Senate by destroying the present fusion system. Beaufort Democrats had held an August primary to choose their candidates for the fusion ticket, and the Conservatives had defeated the Tillmanites. They had then followed that area's custom and fused with black Republicans. The angry Tillmanites went to anti-fusion Republicans and formed their own unity ticket. In was, the Columbia *State* headlined, "DEAL WITH THE DARKIES, Tillman's Great Double-Faced Anglo-African Act." The Conservatives contended that Tillman was appealing to black votes to get elected to the Senate while simultaneously calling for a constitutional convention to disfranchise blacks. Tillman denied these charges. "My policy had been simply not to interfere in these local combinations. I have recognized that the white men living in those communities are peculiarly situated, and must do the best they can to prevent strife between the races and stop corruption in local affairs." He denied any link with any black politician. For example, he supported Elliott not Murray for Congress, and "if Haskellites [Conservatives] don't like it; I am sure I don't care, as I am not trying to please them."[28]

Tillman's denial, like the state treasurer's earlier statement, convinced few people. The Seventh District Independent Democratic candidate reported a deal between Murray and Tillman to give all Georgetown County's votes to Murray in return for black support of the Tillmanite gubernatorial candidate John Gary Evans and the constitutional convention. Another report linked Murray with the Tillmanite candidate for sheriff in Berkeley County. The alleged but unproven Murray-Tillman connection was an integral part of the Conservative attack on Ben Tillman. It was a strange note in Murray's pro-black campaign.[29]

Murray's campaign also continued suffering from Smalls's and Miller's opposition. Murray was conducting a "black is beautiful" campaign against Smalls, and, despite Tillman's strong denial, the black congressman was simultaneously being accused of selling out to a racist. Most dangerous of all, further disfranchisement of black voters, this time constitutional, seemed inevitable. Murray's chances of getting reelected appeared nonexistent.

Near the end of the campaign, his chances suddenly brightened. The Republican National Committee sent several emissaries from Washington to help in the canvass. In the Seventh District, Brayton decided to withdraw in favor of Johnston, thus relieving Murray of one of his difficulties. It was also heartening to know that, despite all his campaign problems, both the Democratic and Republican state party chairmen considered him a favorite in his race.[30]

On election day, November 6, the Tillmanite gubernatorial candidate John Gary Evans crushed the independent Sampson Pope 39,507 to 17,278, and the constitutional convention was supported by a narrow 31,402 to 29,523. Republicans lost everywhere; only two blacks were returned to the State House and, in the congressional races, only Murray's race was in doubt. Early reports told of many blacks in Murray's district going to the polls, being refused entry, and then signing printed notarized certificates attesting to their exclusion. Murray's effort was actually more elaborate than that. His poll watchers filled out one kind of certificate for persons who swore they had voted for Murray and a different one for those who had been kept from registering and thus were unable to vote. Murray was obviously preparing for a contest. He remained in Charleston throughout election day, voted in the first ward of that county's first precinct, and that night joined a large number of his constituents reading returns at the *News and Courier* bulletin board. The early Charleston returns were not encouraging; Elliott led Murray 2,739 to 379. The rumor persisted, however, that Tillman would insure Murray's reelection to humiliate Charleston.[31]

As the outlying Black District returns slowly trickled in, they wore away at Elliott's substantial Charleston lead. In Beaufort County, for example, 1,128 voted for Murray, 921 for Elliott, but a dispute arose over local Beaufort office results. Thomas E. Miller represented the Tillmanite fusion candidates before the local election board, while other blacks supported the Conservative candidates. Murray's votes were not among those being challenged, but anything could happen in the face of the controversy. Murray did challenge or attempt to challenge returns in other parts of the congressional district, and it quickly became apparent that the State Board of Canvassers would again have to make the final decision. The board took the matter up on November 21 with G. E. Wheeler, a Washington lawyer, representing the black congressman, while Elliott spoke for himself.[32]

Murray worked night and day on the contest Tillman was allegedly ready to support, but he expressed no confidence. "I do not expect the state Board to set a side [*sic*] the prearranged determination of the Democratic party to count me out." Still, he said, he wanted people "to know that I have man-

hood enough" to make the contest. He believed he had made "ample prepara-
tion prior to the election" and had "sufficient data to make even Democrats
ashamed of themselves, if that be possible."[33]

When the board met to hear the contest, Murray was unaccountably absent, a strange development considering his detailed preparations. His lawyer
argued that his voters had been kept from the polls by registration and suffrage restrictions or by the closing of the polls in their faces. Yet, improper
registration certificates had been accepted from Elliott supporters, and his
count had been inflated. Elliott responded the following day that Murray had
not made an appeal to the Charleston county board, and, since the state board
only had appellate jurisdiction, it had no legal right to deal with the issue.
Wheeler retorted that the county board had refused to hear Murray's petition.
Board member Cole Blease was agreeing with Elliott's position when Murray
walked in and was immediately asked for the facts. He said the Charleston
board had refused to accept his appeal because of alleged improper documen-
tation. He had then made a verbal appeal. By the time the paperwork had
been completed, the board had adjourned. Hearing this information, the state
board went into an immediate executive session and quickly ruled "that the
complaint has not been sustained, and the case is therefore dismissed." Elliott
was declared the First District's winner, 5,650 to 3,913, exactly as the county
boards had ruled.[34]

The board decision disappointed Murray, but he must have felt particular
bitterness over the defection of black Republicans during the campaign. The
Savannah *Tribune*, a black newspaper, commiserated with him. "With what
intelligence he [the black man] may have acquired since he became a citizen,
none he understood so well as how to cut throats politically of each other,
and incidentally of his race. This he accomplished in fine style in the black
district of South Carolina." Murray's hometown white newspaper was not so
solicitous. It blamed his defeat on his over-confidence and on his attempt to
maintain control in the Seventh District while running in the first.[35] No one
said anything about Murray's supporters being kept from voting by registration and polling place irregularities.

The sweeping Tillman victories all over the state and the voters' narrow
acceptance of the constitutional convention made Murray's defeat even more
bitter. In Charleston there were instances of blacks being allowed to vote in
the convention contest, which they, like the Conservative polling officials, opposed, but not being allowed to vote in the congressional race where they supported Murray over the Conservative Elliott. Tillmanites hoped to solidify

political power by eliminating black voters, while Conservatives wanted to regain power by utilizing black voters for their own uses. Republican survival seemed even less possible.[36]

Murray's only hope for returning to Congress lay in Washington. On December 19, 1894, he formally submitted notice of his intention to contest the election result in the House of Representatives.[37] There was some hope of success, since the 1894 elections had returned Republicans to a wide majority. Still, any contest was difficult for a black man. Murray's experiences in Congress during his first term indicated that racism was a fact of life there as much as it was in South Carolina.

Murray received a momentary lift in the state legislature. He received two votes in the election for U.S. Senator, Tillman defeating the Conservative Democrat Matthew Butler, 131 to 21. Black legislators from Beaufort and Georgetown voted for Murray. Thomas E. Miller, an open Tillman advocate in Beaufort, cast his vote for Dr. W. D. Crum, the black Charleston physician and politician.[38] Murray, the alleged pro-Tillmanite congressman, had been rejected by the Tillman Board of Canvassers and had then received anti-Tillman votes in the state legislature. If there had been any conspiracy between "Pitchfork Ben" and black politicians such as Murray, it was certainly not evident on the general election day or in the Senate election. Miller's continued opposition to Murray also indicated that the election day defeats had only widened the spreading cracks in the fragile vessel that was the Webster-led Republican Party.

These events of late 1894 marked yet another turning point in Murray's career and that of the South Carolina GOP. For several years Murray had avoided attacking the Tillman Democrats and, on several occasions, he had even cleverly praised them. This careful politicking had produced no favorable results; the Tillmanite board did not return him to Congress. A white Conservative won in the First District, while a new Tillmanite won in the new Seventh. Conservatives had insisted that redistricting was devised so as to punish Charleston, but that port city did not suffer any adverse effect. Blacks suffered; they lost their only representative, and the voter acceptance of a constitutional convention threatened to complete the decade-long efforts to eliminate black Republicans.

The events of 1894 demonstrated Murray's basic political powerlessness and that of his race and party. The year had been a hectic one for the black congressman as he had tried to juggle congressional and state responsibilities. Throughout this time, he had made a genuine effort to remain on friendly terms with the Tillmanites, but their summary dismissal of his election appeal demonstrated their disdain for him. He was no longer needed to punish Tillmanite political opposition, so he was rejected. The former Black District that he represented was split to prevent him or any other black from ever returning to Congress. The Tillmanite treatment of Murray, like the Charleston Conservative Democrats' use of black voters, showed that whites tolerated a black presence in politics only as it suited their needs. The constitutional convention was called so that whites would be relieved of having to continue such manipulation any longer.

The state Republican response to the events of 1894 gave little cause for hope. The GOP state hierarchy, so apparently energized by its unification under Webster, was lethargic before the Democratic juggernaut. Republicans entered 1895 in a passive and withdrawn state, hardly an effective way to face the problems of the new year.

# Fighting Constitutional Disfranchisement

Blacks in general and Republicans in particular feared the upcoming constitutional convention. South Carolina's "legal" assault on black voting, begun with the 1882 eight-box voting system and registration law, could now be completed. Palmetto State blacks outnumbered whites 688,934 to 462,008, and the state's rulers believed this fact alone required definitive action to insure white supremacy. Democratic factionalism also demanded the removal of any Republican and black electoral threat. The state legislature demonstrated this obvious anti-black motive when it passed a special registration law for the election of delegates to the convention. This law provided only fourteen days for new registrations and required all those not already registered under the 1882 law to submit a full life history sworn to by two reputable persons, that is, whites. Since all registration supervisors were white Democrats, black chances of registering for the election were slim.[1]

In early January 1895, Murray, who remained angry over Republican Party inaction concerning the upcoming constitutional convention and the vociferous opposition to his congressional candidacy by some of these leaders, joined Republican dissidents associated with the 1891 white Republican movement to issue a state convention call. Led by the perpetually contentious former state Republican chairman, Ellery M. Brayton, they argued that the present GOP chairman, E. A. Webster, had failed to summon a convention the previous year as party rules required, so there was no legal state party organization. Webster denied the need for a convention and urged instead a continued registration drive to qualify blacks to vote in the delegate election. The proposed constitutional convention brought forth, yet again, Republican disunity.[2]

Other blacks were as upset at the Republican withdrawal from active organizing as were the Republican dissidents. The state's black ministers, powerful local community leaders, scheduled a convention for the week following the Republican splinter meeting. There was no plot of black domination in South Carolina, a spokesman insisted; all the black man wanted was "the protection of those who will govern the State."[3]

Another black group also entered the fray. It held a meeting a few days before the Republican convention and issued an equally self-effacing statement.

Twenty blacks, led by Murray's congressional secretary, R. H. Richardson, issued a statement supporting the forthcoming Republican convention and appealing to South Carolina whites to join in the fight against black disfranchisement. Blacks did not want to control the state government, this statement read, they just wanted fair representation. Blacks should register and then support "that class of white men whom we know to be too proud, broad and humane to take advantage of the weak."[4]

By the end of January 1895, then, four separate groups were appealing for action against the constitutional convention. A Republican faction and a large number of black ministers called for separate conventions. The Regular Republicans called only for registration, while a splinter group of blacks without any specific identification supported both a convention and registration. The unifying note in this otherwise uncoordinated chorus was opposition to the constitutional convention and appeals to white fairness. It was, however, a fragmented response. The Regulars were passive; the dissidents were militant; and the ministers and the black splinter group tried to calm white fears of a threatened black take over.[5]

There was also confusion among black people over whom to consider friends and whom to consider enemies among the rival Democrats. Most blacks were favorable to the Conservative Democrats, but some gave their support to the Tillmanites. Thomas E. Miller, a leading black Republican and a member of the state legislature, was openly praising Tillman in that body. Sampson Pope, a former Tillmanite and the loser in the November 1894 gubernatorial race, pledged to continue fighting against the convention, while John J. Gargan, a white Conservative from Sumter, was similarly advocating fair play for blacks. Who should blacks trust? What was the best approach? No one was sure.[6]

Murray represented this dilemma better than anyone else. In 1892 he had gained his congressional seat from a Tillmanite state board; in 1894 he had lost it at the hands of the same group. He had watched his political antagonist, Thomas E. Miller, fuse with Tillmanites at the county level, and his opponents in both his congressional campaigns had been Conservatives. When he spoke at the Emancipation Day celebration in Mobile, Alabama, such thoughts must have been foremost in his mind. He reiterated to his three thousand listeners his usual litany of opposition to emigration schemes and support for race advancement. Unlike his campaign calls for black pride and group solidarity, however, now he advised cooperation with whites.[7]

On February 6, the Brayton faction of the Republican Party, the latest group of Reformers, met in the chambers of the state House of Representatives. More than one hundred persons attended the meeting, of whom twenty to twenty-five were white. Leading Republicans such as E. A. Webster, Robert Smalls, Thomas E. Miller, T. B. Johnston, and Edmund H. Deas were all absent, however. Murray was there, and he supported Brayton for temporary chairman. Brayton was quickly elected, while Murray was named to the committee on organization. The meeting's address echoed the conciliatory line adopted in the black community during the previous month: black acceptance of a reasonable white supremacy. The Brayton Republican reaction to the threat of more disfranchisement was acquiescence to the oppressor's determination to keep blacks subordinate.

The meeting's only controversy was the expected one: which whites should the Republicans support. One of the delegates expressed unhappiness with the convention address favoring the Conservatives over the Tillmanites because he thought that both factions contained good people. The Reverend R. E. Hart, a leader of the black minister's organization, disagreed. "It was no use to say we are not fighting the Tillmanites, for we are," he said. Murray, "resplendent in patent-leather, shiny beaver [hat] and clothes generally of the latest cut," disagreed and defended the Tillman Democrats. A delegate incredulously asked if Tillman had not plainly said that the convention's purpose was to disfranchise blacks, and Murray evaded the question by blaming Republican leadership for the present mess. Murray still defended the Tillmanites, continuing to identify himself with the man who had called for a disfranchising convention.

The Brayton convention then established a Republican organization parallel to the passive Regular one. Lawson W. Melton, a white lawyer long active in Republican politics, was elected party chairman. Brayton and Murray were elected to two of the memberships-at-large on the new state Executive Committee. This action precipitated harsh debate, and several delegates walked out in protest. The issue of delegate election to the constitutional convention was then finally considered. Murray offered a resolution denouncing registrars who refused to register blacks and urging careful record keeping of each refusal for use in future contests against the new constitution's legality. Clearly alluding to the penalty clause in the Fourteenth Amendment, his resolution encouraged the sending of a petition to the U.S. Senate asking for an investigation to determine "whether we have a republican form of government or not in this State." The resolution passed, but little else happened. Rather than run their own candidates for the constitutional convention, the Brayton faction supported unnamed sympathetic whites.[8]

Eight days later, the Ministerial Union met in Columbia, with only fifty individuals in attendance. Like the delegates at the convention of Reformers, they too recoiled from strong action, even hesitating to elect a permanent slate of officers. The Reverend J. C. Tobin of Columbia was amazed at such timidity "even while the throats of our children yet unborn are preparing to be cut." In a strong statement of defiance, he announced: "I for one, am here to shed my last drop of blood and have my body burned and the ashes thrown to the winds" if necessary. The ministers finally agreed on a board of officers and after urging ministers throughout the state to aid their people to register, they adjourned.[9]

These black meetings clearly accepted white supremacy, yet they were still frightening enough for Tillman to compromise with the Conservative Democrats on a statewide plan to allot delegates proportionally. The Charleston *News and Courier* bluntly called for "a whiteman's Convention out and out," while telling the black ministers: "Politics is not your Business." The Charleston *Post* agreed. The Columbia *State* cautiously urged cooperation with the Republican Party because "for the first time in the history of South Carolina . . . [it had] committed itself to the doctrine of white supremacy." This support for Republicans, however, should not be interpreted as "appealing to the Negro." The state press applauded black acceptance of white dominance but condemned initiatives even as innocuous as those expressed at the recent conventions. South Carolina whites wanted nothing short of the total removal of blacks from all political activity.[10]

Meanwhile, Murray had to return to Washington for the close of the 53rd Congress's third session. He offered no bills or resolutions, and he took little part in the deliberations. On February 1, 1895, he took a leave of absence, and on February 24 he unsuccessfully attempted to introduce a resolution to allow Frederick Douglass's body to lie in state in the capitol. He was so little in evidence that one black newspaper wondered whether he was "still alive."[11]

A month later he demonstrated that he still had a great deal of life left in him. On March 12, 1895, he announced a damage suit against the state of South Carolina on behalf of a black man named Daniel Wiley, who, in Murray's company, had attempted to vote in the 1894 House of Representatives election but had been turned away for lack of a registration certificate. Murray's suit asked the United States Circuit Court (South Carolina) to award

Wiley $2,500 damages against D. L. Sinkler, the offending election official for violations of the federal and state constitution.[12]

This was not the first such litigation, Republicans and Democrats having instituted legal action before. The previous spring, for example, Republicans had tried unsuccessfully to enjoin the Richmond County registrar. In November 1894, Matthew Butler, at that time a Conservative Democrat U.S. senator, had brought a case to the South Carolina Supreme Court to try to prevent the Tillmanites from packing the convention at Conservative expense. When Murray introduced his litigation in federal court, therefore, there was already an anti-registration case in the state's highest court.[13]

The state buzzed over Murray's action, and he sprang yet another surprise. Accompanied by two leaders of the newly formed Ministerial Union, he boldly met with Governor John Gary Evans to request an extension of the fourteen-day registration period set by the recent law. Murray and this delegation told the governor that the special period was almost over, and the few days remaining under the 1882 law were not enough to give everyone a chance to register. Evans had recently revoked a white Sumter lawyer's notary-public commission for registering blacks, but he received the delegation courteously nonetheless. He promised to consider their written request carefully. In fact he did nothing but continue his anti-black rhetoric, so the Ministerial Union announced its support for Murray's court case and urged that money for legal costs be sent to him. Neither Murray nor the ministers explained how a damage suit would help register blacks, however. This was not a class action suit; each black man refused registration would have to go to court individually to collect damages. Such proceedings would be time consuming and expensive and would not keep the constitutional convention from meeting and completing black disfranchisement. At least, however, Murray and the ministers were doing something concrete; Republican leaders were only talking. Meanwhile, the governor's animosity was vocal, and state officials were more discriminatory than ever. When E. A. Webster, the Republican chairman, attempted to obtain proper registration forms for his constituents, the state attorney general openly impeded him. All over the state, voting supervisors continued utilizing their patented methods of procrastination, deceit, and illegality when blacks made the physical and economic sacrifices to try to register.[14]

Meanwhile, the black ministers organized their flocks to assault the unfair system. In Beaufort, they raised thirty-four dollars for Murray's court case. Not surprisingly, however, an old dispute marred the meeting. Beaufort blacks could not decide whether to run their own delegates to the constitutional convention or attempt to cooperate with whites and, if so, with which ones? Murray insisted that the only real option blacks had was to press legal action. He talked about going to New York to raise the necessary legal funds, but then he decided "to canvass the state and educate and arouse our people up to a realization of the situation and what they can do to help themselves."[15]

From March 1895 to the end of the year, Murray led the militant black opposition to disfranchisement. He seemed ubiquitous, crisscrossing the state to rally people, to raise necessary legal funds, and to urge his listeners to register and vote if they could. He took few moments of rest—within one month's time he was in Columbia one night, in Winnsboro the next, then on to Chester, Rock Hill, Sumter, Orangeburg, Greenville, Spartanburg, and Newberry, and a host of other locales. After several weeks on this murderous schedule, he felt he was "meeting with much success." At some meetings, the Reverends W. D. Chapelle and R. E. Hart, the leaders of the Ministerial Union, accompanied him, since the union was providing financial support for the speaking tour, and the ministers' prestige in black communities undoubtedly helped Murray reach a wider audience.[16]

The speech Murray delivered at Columbia was typical of his efforts. Depending on the eavesdropping white listeners, this oration was seen as sensible and conservative or inflammatory and radical. He discussed the Fifteenth Amendment to the U.S. Constitution and said the 1882 registration law violated that amendment. He confided to the huge crowd of blacks how, four years previously, he had tried to convince E. A. Webster to fight the 1882 law in court, but the Republican leader had urged Murray to do so himself. Murray also told his listeners of his debate with Congressman Kyle of Mississippi, bragging how he and Representative Boutelle had taken "the wind out" of the Mississippi legislator's sails. He then came to his main point: Tillman's disfranchisement plan could be thwarted. If blacks made a concerted effort to register, the federal government would be forced to act on their behalf. Washington lawyers had assured him that court action, at the cost of $1,200, could eliminate the registration law. At the same time, he left the door open to compromise. "We merely want to assist with our votes white men who are our friends," he said, "but not the Conservatives who go down on their knees and crawl like Chinese mandarins before his Royal Highness, B. R. Tillman." Murray then announced a collection to raise Richland County's $100 share of the legal expenses. "The house is afire, get your buckets of water and put it out," he admonished. When the buckets were passed, however, only $9.47 of "water" flowed in, and observers felt that the crowd had been generous.

Murray had similar results all over the state; the poor black man simply did not have expendable money to contribute to the legal fund, and prosperous Republicans did not donate generously. Murray accused T. B. Johnston, his former Republican patron and now a Websterite, of refusing to donate even one cent.[17]

Murray's attack on Webster and Johnston indicated that his activities were exacerbating the split in the Republican Party. Regular Republican inaction had caused the break, but past animosities also simmered beneath the surface, notably Murray's recent conflicts with Thomas E. Miller. Miller responded to Murray's fund-raising activities with a public letter of his own. Why, Miller wondered, was Murray making blacks believe his court action would help them register to vote when he knew he was promising more than he could deliver? Why, too, raise $1,200 for legal representation when black lawyers like himself and Sam Lee were available? Murray responded that Miller's objections had been carefully considered before the commencement of the *Wiley v. Sinkler* case, and they had no validity. Besides, this litigation was only one of several cases in preparation. He only wished Miller, the black lawyers, and other Republican leaders had acted sooner. At the least, Miller should have consulted him before publishing his criticism.[18]

The pro-Tillman *Palmetto Post* viewed this spat with glee, predicting that "by the time the Canary gets through with the Blackbird, the latter will be willing to shed his feathers." Actually, the exchange of letters ended the controversy. Murray was busy touring the state and preparing for his congressional contest, while Miller was organizing the black delegate ticket in Beaufort.[19]

Murray did introduce another case before the United States Circuit Court (South Carolina). Lawrence P. Mills, a twenty-six-year-old Columbia black man, met all the voting requirements set forth in the South Carolina and U.S. constitutions, yet the Richland County registrar, W. Briggs Green, had refused to register him. Mills asked the court for an injunction against Green and for a decision voiding all discriminatory registration laws. Federal judge Nathan Goff, a native of West Virginia, shocked South Carolina's whites by issuing a temporary injunction. The harsh registration procedure, already hampered by the state court injunction in the white Conservative Butler case, was now further crippled.[20]

As if this double assault on the Tillman-planned convention was not enough, the former Tillmanite Sampson Pope led yet another attack. He took the case of *Pratt and Price v. Evans and McCoy, et al.* before U.S. Circuit Court judge C. H. Simonton (a native of South Carolina). Pope accused Governor

Evans and the rest of the Tillmanites of conspiring to win the constitutional convention election by eliminating most black voters.[21]

Conservative Democrats, Republicans, and dissident Tillmanites had thus each instituted legal action against Tillman's constitutional plans. Butler's case was in the state judicial system, so there was little cooperation between him and the other two plaintiffs whose cases were in federal court. Murray and the Washington lawyers representing him (Obear and Douglass) cooperated with Pope and his legal colleagues and argued their cases together when they came due in early May 1895.[22]

Judge Goff heard the arguments in Columbia on May 2, in a courtroom packed with Republican politicians from both factions. He quickly declared the 1882 registration law and the special 1893 and 1894 constitutional convention registration laws racially motivated and in violation of both the federal and state constitutions. He issued a permanent injunction against Green.[23]

The shocked state government immediately appealed the decision to the U.S. Court of Appeals for the Fourth Circuit in Richmond, with Senator Ben Tillman crudely reminding both black and white South Carolinians that the registration law might be gone, but "the shotgun has gone nowhere." Governor John Garry Evans told registrars to ignore Goff's injunction. He warned state residents that the fight was now clearly between blacks and whites, and "God save the white man that goes to the negro." The Tillmanite Columbia *Register* counseled white unity in the face of Goff's "abolition speech." The Conservative Charleston *News and Courier* called Goff's verdict an insult to the state's integrity and a misreading of previous Supreme Court decisions. It predicted white unity like that of 1876. The Conservative Charleston *Post* blamed Goff's decision on Tillman's disruption of the Democratic Party and his refusal to allow Conservatives fair play.[24]

Black reaction was conciliatory. The Ministerial Union announced its continued acceptance of the white doctrine "that intelligence and money must rule" and promised to "always prove true to the faction of white men who protected us." The ministers also promised not to "follow the defunct Republicans, hitherto styled leaders" and advised blacks "to vote only for our white friends among the Conservatives." They urged the election of delegates "independent of politics." They scheduled a mass meeting in Columbia and presented Murray as the main speaker. In a one-hour speech, which the Tillman press called "entirely devoid of bitterness," he called Goff's decision "more advanced and far-reaching on citizenship than any that had been rendered since the war." Unlike the ministers, however, he did not support the Conservatives over Tillman, urging instead that his listeners support any white man favorable to blacks. "The white race was in the majority in wealth and intelligence," he said, "and should have the controlling power"; blacks "should only ask a minority representation." Still, blacks should continue the fight and should continue to raise funds for future legal battles. The ensuing collection brought in $20.26. In Beaufort, the home of Robert Smalls and Thomas E. Miller, the most important black action was another accommodating meeting of the Ministerial Union. This gathering considered "race unity," business, education, and farming, but it made no mention of politics or the constitutional convention. The state Republican Party remained similarly passive. Webster was silent, and Melton simply expressed confidence that the court of appeals would sustain Goff's decision. When Murray made similar speeches in Charleston and Barnwell, one supporter, S. E. Smith of Aiken, rejected Murray's conciliatory approach and advised his listeners to vote with loaded guns. "You may get killed," he said, "but in that event, if the muskets are loaded, they will still be handy for use for the old women and children." A few blacks, at least, were not as accommodating and confident as Murray, the ministers, and the Republican Party.[25]

Overconfidence proved ludicrous. On June 11, the U.S. Court of Appeals in Richmond, with the chief justice of the United States, Melville W. Fuller, presiding, reversed Goff's decision. Fuller ruled that the court's only jurisdiction in political matters was to protect property rights. Since such rights were not at issue in the Mills case, Goff's decision was invalid. The registration laws stood, and the injunction against Green was lifted. The great victory had lasted only a month.[26]

This reversal was demoralizing. Ellery Brayton saw no hope for preventing the delegate election, while two leaders of the Ministerial Union were so upset that they called on blacks to migrate from the state. Murray was attending the National Republican League convention in Cleveland, as a member of the Resolution Committee, and even before the congressman had time to react to the Mills reversal, Judge Simonton, who at the behest of Judge Goff heard final arguments in Sampson Pope's case on June 19, ordered a dismissal, citing the *Mills v. Green* decision as precedent. The electoral cause had suffered another setback. The final legal disappointment came on July 6, 1895, when the South Carolina Supreme Court threw out the *Butler v. Ellerbe* case on a split decision, demonstrating once again the continuing factionalism in the Democratic Party. The chief justice of the court, a Conservative Democrat, had written his opinion before the Goff decision in *Mills v. Green* and had used the same arguments to declare the constitutional convention registration laws unconstitutional. The two Tillmanite judges outvoted him, however.[27]

This succession of setbacks did not end Murray's legal activity. Charles A. Douglass of the Washington law firm of Obear and Douglass arrived in Columbia for two weeks of consultation and announced that the *Mills v. Green* case was going to the Supreme Court on appeal. He admitted, however, that the Court would probably not hear the appeal before the convention met, and he did not know what effect a favorable decision would have on any new constitution. Murray displayed more optimism. He admonished his supporters not to be discouraged; lawyers were convinced that the Supreme Court would overturn the decision of the appeals court. But, the Supreme Court appeal would cost money. He had already paid Obear and Douglass $902.06, so all that remained to complete the payment of the revised fee of $1,000 was $98. He called on black ministers "to redouble their efforts" and on black politicians "to sink self out of sight in this direful moment." In Washington, D.C., he had formed the South Carolina Suffrage Aid Society, membership consisting of the city's black ministers. Each preacher devoted a Sunday sermon to the Palmetto State issue, and the organization's president promised a mass meeting and financial contributions.[28]

Black ministers, independent of the Ministerial Union, also continued in the forefront of the anti-convention movement in South Carolina. Seventy met in Columbia in July, and at Murray's reminder that Tillmanites and Conservatives generally met behind closed doors, they went into secret session. After eight hours of deliberations, they issued a strongly worded address that was a far cry from the tepid expressions of the recent past. They called on "the strong arm of the national government for a defense of rights granted and guaranteed by itself." They appealed to Conservatives to support unlimited universal manhood suffrage. They promised to "fight the flesh, the devil and all his imps through every court and power in the nation before . . . [being] robbed of our rights by anarchistic nullifiers." They blamed lynchings on the Tillman government, castigated the Tillmanites for preventing blacks from voting in the constitutional convention primary, and criticized the Conservatives for agreeing to an equal division of delegates. They called for the establishment of a state executive committee to direct the delegate campaign among blacks. If no "liberal whites" appeared, then the black ministers said they would recommend a separate black ticket. Finally, the ministers' address urged the establishment of more ministerial groups throughout the state to raise money for future court battles.[29]

The conservative press was incensed, particularly ridiculing the demand for federal government intervention and universal suffrage. The Columbia *State* claimed that unnamed politicians had stolen the convention from the preachers. The paper insisted that "The Conservatives are for 'White Supremacy by honest means.'" A restricted suffrage and honest elections were better for blacks than universal voting. The Charleston *News and Courier* labeled the ministers' address an attempt to bolster the congressional hopes of blacks such as Murray. When W. D. Chapelle and H. M. Raiford, respectively president and secretary of the Ministerial Union, repudiated the address, and when Chapelle called it "the selfish work of politicians," the white press saw this as proof that the address was meaningless.[30]

In truth, politicians had not captured the meeting. Four members of the seven-member Resolution Committee were politicians (Murray, S. E. Smith, R. E. Hart, and W. T. Andrews), but the entire convention accepted the address. It was not a conspiracy of four. Besides, state Republican politicians had actually been displaying less militancy than had the ministers. The Republican Executive Committee under Lawson D. Melton issued resolutions offering to cooperate "with and under" the Conservatives who favored "free and equal elections and equal justice for everyone" or not to vote at all. The Webster Regulars said nothing. Even in Beaufort where blacks remained adamant in their call for a black delegate ticket, Thomas E. Miller advised cooperation with the Tillmanites "for they are in command and if we break off from them our votes will not be counted." Politicians were hardly militant, so the accusation of political conspiracy at the ministers' conference is unconvincing. The ministers' convention address was, in reality, an understandable reaction to the frustration of the registration battle.[31]

Murray ignored all such criticism; he was back on the road soliciting funds in Beaufort and simultaneously excoriating both Democratic factions for their white supremacy attitudes. He also traveled to Savannah, Georgia, and, as in Washington, he instituted a fund-raising organization. He also began a new court case, *Gowdy v. Green*. Joseph H. Gowdy, a black minister, who had lived in several areas of South Carolina, had not been permitted to register on three separate occasions in three different localities. Murray and his lawyers believed that the facts in this case were sufficiently different from those in the Mills case to preclude any prior prejudice.[32]

Judge Goff received the new petition and immediately on July 26, 1895 issued a temporary injunction against the repeatedly enjoined Supervisor Green. Tillman and state officials expressed no concern, and their confidence was well taken. On August 7, Goff recalled the injunction and decided against Gowdy because this case was too similar to the earlier Mills litigation. He had no other choice, he said.[33]

Murray's lawyers expressed satisfaction with this decision, but their reasoning was tortured. If Goff had ruled in their favor and if the state had then refused to honor the injunction, the only recourse would have been to arrest the supervisor, the attorney said. But, South Carolina would then have had to go to the United States Circuit Court (South Carolina) for a writ of habeas corpus, and had the state obtained it, there would have been no appeal from a circuit court to the Supreme Court on a habeas corpus question.[34]

The lawyers also issued a revealing public disclaimer in answer to attacks by the Columbia *Register*. As lawyers, they said, they represented their clients, but they were still trying "to be true to the best interests of the race to which we belong, as well as loyal to the faith of our fathers." Murray's attorneys, supposedly battling for a greater black participation in South Carolina political life, expressed loyalty to their whiteness first and the law second. This was hardly a comforting thought to the thousands of black petitioners paying for their services. Even alleged friends were enemies.[35]

Murray ignored his lawyers' disclaimer and took part in a Sumter Republican meeting that fielded an all-black constitutional convention delegate ticket. He also became a candidate himself for a delegate spot from Charleston. Republicans in general were making some effort to field candidates, but the effort was spotty. Since only about ten thousand blacks had been able to register anyway, Murray's legal action seemed a more promising approach.[36]

The constitutional convention delegate election was held on August 20, 1895, and only 6 black Republicans were elected, compared to 112 Tillmanites and 42 Conservatives. Five of the blacks were from predominately black Beaufort County: Robert Smalls, Thomas E. Miller, William J. Whipper, James Wigg, and Isaiah R. Reed. The sixth, Robert B. Anderson, was from heavily black Georgetown. Smalls and Miller led this small delegation and, as Murray's political opponents, they did not seek his cooperation. When Miller presented a petition to the convention signed by 22 Sumter blacks, for example, Murray's name was not included on the list.[37]

The constitutional convention began on September 10 and lasted until December 4. On September 30, five of the six black delegates wrote a letter to the New York *World* demonstrating that, if the convention established a suffrage based on literacy, about 75,000 blacks and 90,000 whites would be eligible. Tillman would, therefore, never tolerate a fair literacy requirement, they predicted.. The following day they were proven right. The convention's Suffrage Committee, modeling its report on the Mississippi Plan of 1890, established as suffrage law stringent residency requirements, a poll tax, no conviction for certain crimes, the ability to understand a section of the state constitution, or tax on property assessed for $300. The black delegates fought this proposal valiantly, but it passed. Black protest all over the state intensified. At an October 12 Sumter meeting with Murray present, resolutions were passed condemning the suffrage provision as "an attempt to nullify the supreme law of the land, and a vile surrender of the Commonwealth as a prey to despotic demagogues."[38]

Meanwhile, the United States Supreme Court heard the case of *Mills v. Green* in early October. The state of South Carolina moved for dismissal on the grounds that the plaintiffs had no legal right to appeal. At the same time, it claimed, the disputed election was already over, so the court had only a "purely speculative" issue to comment on. In rebuttal, Murray's attorney, H. N. Obear, argued that there was indeed a right of appeal in this case. The Supreme Court had to decide the case because the circuit court had clearly overstepped its jurisdiction. This was a test case to help decide whether "in this free land" it was possible "for a faction [in a state] to effect the permanent disfranchisement of a large class of citizens of that State." The Court heard the arguments and reserved judgement.[39]

At this same time, Sampson Pope, the 1894 anti-Tillmanite gubernatorial candidate, announced his conversion to the Republican Party. He attacked the new constitution as a Tillmanite plot and predicted that fifteen thousand enraged whites would vote Republican in the next election. At the same time, the Melton Reform faction, publicly the only Republican Party in South Carolina, issued a statement opposing the new constitution and promising to battle it in Congress and in the courts. Without citing Pope by name, they urged all opponents to join together in the fight. No general rush ensued because most whites in South Carolina approved of the disfranchisement of blacks. The Columbia *State* even argued that the new constitution benefited blacks. The document outlawed lynching and established a black college. Half a loaf was better than none, the *State* advised.[40]

Totally lost in the excitement over the conclusion of the South Carolina constitutional convention and the almost simultaneous acceptance of black political subordination in the Atlanta Compromise speech of Booker T. Washington was the U.S. Supreme Court decision in the *Mills v. Green* case. On November 25, 1895, the Court ruled that the ability of Mills to vote for constitutional convention delegates was no longer pertinent, so the court could grant no relief and dismissed the case. "It necessarily follows that, when, pending an appeal from the judgement of a lower court, and without any fault of the defendant, an event occurs which renders it impossible for this court, if it should decide the case in favor of the plaintiff, to grant him any effectual relief whatever, the court will not proceed to a formal judgment, but will dismiss the appeal." After all, the opinion read (sounding like the South Carolina brief), the court's task was "not to give opinions upon moot questions or abstract propositions, or to declare principles or rules of law which cannot affect the matter in issue in the case before it."[41]

In quick succession, other court decisions finished off the Murray forces. In December, Judge Simonton took up the *Wiley v. Sinkler* case and predictably declared against Murray. In December 1899, the case was taken on a writ of error to the South Carolina Supreme Court, but, in October 1900, this court upheld Simonton's decision. The *Gowdy v. Green* case was also taken to the United States Supreme Court, but, like the Mills case, it too was dismissed. Murray and his supporters had tried to use judicial means to halt the disfranchisement of black voters in South Carolina, and they had failed in every effort.[42]

One wonders if Murray, in the midst of his harried battles to maintain black suffrage, noticed a statement attributed at this time to Booker T. Washington. The man who in May 1894 had invited the congressman as an honored guest to address the graduating class of his Tuskegee Institute, was now quoted as saying that "while the Negro was running after a seat in Congress he should have been learning how to cultivate a potato patch."[43] Washington's September 18, 1895 Atlanta Compromise speech had made him a white favorite and the acknowledged national black spokesman, so this statement was significant. In the South Carolina context, it meant that blacks should accept the new constitution. The document's provisions for a black college were more important than the restriction of black voting rights. Washington's attitude signaled the victory of accommodation over militancy, making black politicians such as Murray as irrelevant in the black community as they had always been in the white.

Despite all these setbacks, Murray could still look back on the past year with a great deal of personal pride. Angered by the lack of meaningful Republican activity, he had helped launch a new GOP organization. When that group had instituted legal action and then faltered, he had helped organize black ministers to battle disfranchisement. His temporary court victory was the only flash of light in the gloom of electoral defeat. Blacks were clearly at the mercy of the dominant whites, and no amount of activity could alter this fact. Even Republican unity or sagacity could not overcome the race issue; both white Democratic factions agreed that blacks should be disfranchised. The Democratic Party's fraternal debate revolved around how and which white group should benefit the most from the disfranchisement, not whether it should happen. Similarly, the failure of federal court action indicated that the national government agreed with white Carolinians that blacks could be politically excluded. Murray's activities and his continued hope for a return to Congress indicated his unfaltering belief in the political process, but his effective leadership had proven insufficient in the face of unbending prejudice. Murray was now the most visible Republican in the state; he had reached his political apex. Still, he was powerless. Like the political party and the race he belonged to, he was a legally defined cipher in his own land. He had tried various strategies, and he had failed at all of them; no one could have blamed him had he now given up, but he did not. Foiled in his judicial approach to winning fair treatment for blacks, he tried several other approaches, each time hoping he had found the road to the promised land of political equality.

# Reaction to Disfranchisement

The new South Carolina constitution blatantly disfranchised most Palmetto State Republicans, while simultaneously facilitating a rapprochement between Tillman and his Conservative rivals. Republicans were used to defeat, however, so they did not despair. Public dissatisfaction with President Grover Cleveland's handling of the Panic of 1893 remained high as the 1896 nominating convention season drew near. Democrats would be hard-pressed to retain control of the presidency, and restored Republican power in Washington could only benefit the South Carolina GOP, whose dependence on the national party was even more crucial now than it had ever been before.

This fact made the December 1895 meeting of the Republican National Committee especially important for the Palmetto State GOP. Both factions sent representatives. E. A. Webster, Robert Smalls, and Thomas Miller argued that the so-called Reform or Reorganized faction of Brayton, Melton, and Murray had no right to claim that it represented true Republicanism in South Carolina. In response, Ellery Brayton vociferously justified his faction's existence on Webster's negligence. The Websterite Regulars responded with a call for a joint debate before Thomas H. Carter, the Republican national chairman, and James S. Clarkson, the leader of the Republican National League. Brayton refused. The Republican committee issued no pronouncements, but its members could clearly see that disunion had been the South Carolina Republicans' response to Ben Tillman and his constitution.

When the two sets of contentious Republican leaders came home to South Carolina from the national Republican meeting, they immediately demonstrated their mutual animosity. They maneuvered so feverishly that one newspaper exaggeratedly surmised that "Not since '76 have the Republicans been as active in South Carolina as at present." The Reform/Reorganized faction issued twenty-one rules to govern its organization, and this codification showed how much previous white Republican movements influenced the participants. The bylaws called for a system of separate white and black clubs to give fallen away Democrats the chance to become Republicans without having to associate closely with blacks. The Regulars, meanwhile, held an Executive Committee meeting, called an April state convention, denounced the opposing faction, and urged everyone to register and vote, promising to issue an address of instructions in the near future. Like the Reformers, the Regulars invited all South Carolinians to join them, but they made no provisions to make such a move palatable for anti-black whites.[1]

After his year in the glare of publicity, Murray maintained a low profile. He was present at Reorganized Republican meetings in Sumter, but he sent a proxy to represent him at a state Executive Committee meeting. His major concern was his congressional seat contest against the Democrat William Elliott, and even here Republican factionalism reared its head. Murray suspected Robert Smalls, a member of the rival faction, of sabotaging his campaign. Smalls denied the charge, but their angry exchange once again dramatized the vehemence of the Republican split.[2]

House Election Committee #3 had begun holding meetings in January 1896, but the large number of contests kept it from making rapid progress, so Murray could only wait impatiently. Unlike Republican contestants in three other South Carolina districts, he did not base his appeal on the unconstitutionality of the state registration law. Instead, he argued that election supervisors had used the registration law fraudulently. Black voters had been kept from the polls, while Elliott's supporters had voted dead people and absentees. He presented reams of signed affidavits in support of his argument. Simultaneously, the Illinois Republican representative Robert R. Hitt presented pro-Murray petitions from Mississippi and Memphis, Tennessee. The majority of the members of the Election Committee were Republican, and these arguments convinced them. In April they voted to declare Murray the winner of South Carolina's First District congressional seat.[3]

The committee's decision was, however, not unanimous; three Democratic members (all southerners) appended a strongly worded demurrer. They agreed with Elliott that significant black opposition, not fraud, had defeated Murray. "Unless the presumption is indulged," the minority report concluded, "that every man who has a dark skin is a Republican and votes the Republican ticket at all times and under all conditions and circumstances, even when he swears that he voted otherwise, it will be impossible to give the contestant the seat which he claims."[4]

The entire House of Representatives, not the committee, made the final determination, but Republican control of the House by a wide margin assured Murray's victory. There were other factors, however. If Republicans hoped to make an appeal to border or southern states, they might vote for Elliott. If the party leadership was concerned about the black vote in the pivotal northern states, Republicans might vote for Murray. The sheer bulk let alone the validity of the evidence favored Murray, but national Republican politics rather than evidence usually determined such contests. The House committee's decision had hardly settled the issue. The Ohio Republican representative Charles H. Grosvenor, a McKinley backer, said that "Czar" Reed and his backers had pressured the Election Committee to vote for Murray in return for the black congressman's promise of black support for the "Czar's" presidential bid. If this fact became widely known, Grosvenor warned, Murray would lose on the House floor. The Charleston *News and Courier* titled the accusation, "The Speaker's Conspiracy with a South Carolina Coon," and it soon became the conventional wisdom.[5]

Newspapers ignored Grosvenor's comment and treated the committee's statement as final, nonetheless. Most South Carolina newspapers agreed with the Sumter *Watchman and Southron* that "an able and efficient officer" such as Elliott had been defeated by a person such as Murray, who had "never done anything for his constituents." The black press, in contrast, called the decision "justice." *The Freeman*, which published the most favorable report, called Murray "a man of sterling character, of high intelligence, a forcible speaker, and a clear thinker." The Washington *Bee* expressed similar satisfaction with the decision, though it called Murray "too silvery in his views" and urged him to "get on the sound money platform."[6]

Fresh from his triumph in Washington, Murray played a leading role at his faction's state convention in South Carolina. He was a member of the Reform Republican Platform Committee and introduced an important compromise section on silver. Saying he had "learned better" (though his election contest was no doubt the real reason), he now opposed free silver except under an international agreement. In the election for national convention delegates at-large, he received the highest number of votes of the four individuals chosen. He went along with a compromise resolution expressing willingness to support any of the leading Republican presidential candidates. (This action later caused him to be accused of complicity with an effort, led by Speaker of the House "Czar" Reed, to block McKinley.) He pushed through a resolution (like the one he had introduced in an earlier convention) calling on the federal government to determine whether South Carolina really had a republican government. Finally, he enthusiastically supported the passage of a resolution opposing his old antagonist Thomas E. Miller's candidacy to become president of the new black state college set to be established under the new constitution.[7]

Like the Regulars who had met earlier, the Reorganized Republicans, as the Reformers now increasingly called themselves, supported basic Republican policy and only differed with their rivals on the presidential candidate to be supported. Actually, both sides were ready to support whomever the party nominated. The Reorganized faction had enticed a large number of whites into their convention, but the less successful Regulars were not discouraging white converts either. The major difference continued to be one of personality. Both sides argued over who were the true Republicans and who were the interlopers. They battled each other because they could not effectively attack their real enemies, the state's Democrats.

It was clear, too, that Murray was still a leading Reorganized Republican. His time-consuming battle for a congressional seat had not kept him from continuing his active party role.[8] But the contest had changed his silver views. In 1892 he had followed his farmer instincts and supported silver. Now that he needed national Republican votes, he supported the GOP position on the metal. Murray was flexible enough to alter a political stand when he thought it necessary.

When the Election Committee reports were debated before the entire House on June 3 and 4, it became immediately evident that Murray was in no trouble. On June 5, 1896, he was seated by a vote of 153 to 33 with 168 not voting. Disappointed Carolinians, including the defeated Elliott, were sure that Republican corruption explained this vote. The Charleston *Post* blamed the Tillmanites; they had allowed Murray to become the First District congressman to gain "sweet revenge" against Charleston. Murray remained a center of controversy, but he was back in the House.[9]

Murray was in attendance during the congressional debate on his election. The Indiana Republican representative Jesse Overstreet, a member of the Election Committee, presented Murray's case. Once the vote was over, Overstreet escorted Murray to the Speaker's desk where, to Republican applause, he was sworn in. This ceremony was his first and last House appearance that session. The following day he received a leave of absence for ten days "on account of sickness in the family." Before that time was over, Congress adjourned. Murray had missed the entire first session. Actually he had missed little. As the *Review of Reviews* evaluated it, this congressional session was "noteworthy" for little else "but its 'brevity.'"[10]

The Republican national convention took place in St. Louis soon after, and the Reorganized Republican delegates must have been shocked to see the strength of the McKinley candidacy. Mark Hanna, the chief McKinley operative, talked to the leaders of both South Carolina factions about McKinley's candidacy and received the promise of all eighteen Regular votes and only six of eighteen of the Reorganized votes. From that point on, the Regulars were clearly predominant. The national committee gave its blessing to them without alluding to activity or lack of activity during battle over the South Carolina constitutional convention.[11]

The Reorganized Republicans now were being called the Lily Whites despite the presence of Murray and other blacks. They were bitterly disappointed over their convention defeat.[12] How could they claim to be Republicans after the national party had rejected them? How could McKinley, should he win the presidency, give them any patronage? Without recognition and patronage, how could they overcome the Regular Republicans, let alone the Democrats, and survive in the hostile South Carolina political climate?

Murray did as badly at the convention as did his faction. Being the nation's only black congressman provided him with no special favors from the McKinley staff. His suspected ties to "Czar" Reed were hardly the credentials to win him a warm McKinley welcome. In South Carolina, his supporters recognized his waning strength and began to drift toward Robert Smalls of the victorious Regulars. Murray took swift corrective action. He participated in meetings all over the state ratifying the McKinley-Hobart ticket to demonstrate his faction's continued GOP loyalty. In mid-July 1896, he was one of the main speakers at a large gathering in Beaufort.[13]

Murray also continued to insist that he was the Republican nominee in the First Congressional District election coming up that November, having gained the post at an earlier Reorganized Republican convention. When the Regulars defiantly scheduled their own district nominating convention, Murray refused to participate. A former supporter, E. C. Frierson, accused him of having used "the doctrine of colorphobia" to gain his House seat in 1894 and of now attempting to maintain that seat by appealing to whites, who were "once the object of his hatred." The sparsely attended Regular convention gave its nomination to Cecil Cohen, a white Charleston railway mail clerk. The Regular Republicans, the majority of whom were black, had chosen a white man to run for Congress from the Black District, while the so-called Lily Whites had nominated an exponent of black pride. Could Republican politics become any more confused?[14]

The two Republican factions gathered in state convention simultaneously on September 17 in the South Carolina State House.[15] Webster's Regulars met in the chambers of the House of Representatives; the Brayton/Melton Reorganized faction met in the chambers of the Senate. The Reorganized Republican proceedings indicated a genuine desire for compromise, those of the Regulars showed interest in reunification only in terms of the other side's capitulation. The Braytonites sent an emissary to the Websterites and then established a Negotiating Committee. The Regulars set up a parallel group but continued playing hard to get. The factions nominated separate state tickets. Sampson Pope, the former Tillmanite who was now the apostle of Lily White unity, was the Braytonite candidate for governor; a long-time Republican, R. M. Wallace, a white businessman from Sumter, was the Regular candidate. Webster was reelected his faction's chairman, but Melton, declining another term, was replaced by Dr. V. P. Clayton, a leader in the 1891 Lily White movement. Both factions supported national Republican policy and candidate McKinley, and both ignored blacks. The Reorganized Republicans had a lily white chairman and a lily white gubernatorial candidate, though a majority of its members were black like Murray. The mass of Regulars was similarly black, and its leadership was also primarily white.

Murray was highly visible at the Reorganized Republican meeting. He was a member of the Negotiating Committee and the committee that selected presidential electors. He escorted convention officials to the platform, and he offered the major orations of the day. In his first speech, he warned his listeners against the folly of the Democratic fiscal policy being espoused by the presidential candidate William Jennings Bryan. He now totally embraced the Republican hard-money position. He warned that free silver would drive out of circulation $600 million worth of gold and would rob the working man of 48¢ out of every dollar he earned. In his 1893 congressional speech he had called silver the salvation of the working class; now he called that white metal its ruination.

Near the end of the convention, Murray electrified his listeners with his second speech. He read from a volume of the *U.S. Statutes at Large* to show that southern states had only been allowed back into the Union after ratifying the Fourteenth Amendment and promising not to disfranchise any class of citizens.[16] His listeners, in excitement, drowned out his voice and forced him to repeat himself. He explained that the U.S. Constitution contained protection against disfranchisement like the kind written into the new South Carolina constitution. He urged immediate court action to implement this protection. Three hundred dollars would begin litigation, and he was willing to donate the first hundred. A delegate interrupted to ask about the earlier court case. Murray did not mention the Mills case defeat but replied that there was then still a case on the Supreme Court docket, obviously referring to the Gowdy case. Several delegates immediately offered money, and Murray called for the establishment of a subcommittee of the state Executive Committee. Melton, as a lawyer, expressed willingness to begin the case at minimum expense, but he cautioned against expecting too much. Murray reported a collection of $115, and Dr. V. P. Clayton, the new state chairman, promised to take action immediately.

The Lily Whites had made no progress toward reuniting South Carolina Republicans, but one of their black members had created the greatest sensation of either convention. His call for another court battle, this one based on the ultimate weapon, the Fourteenth Amendment, moved the spotlight away from factional reunification. Murray still hoped to thwart the disfranchisers by beating them in court, but the state's white leadership was unconcerned. The Columbia *State* pointed out that, according to the Fourteenth Amendment, the penalty for a state violating its conditions for returning to the Union (and the paper admitted South Carolina was violating these conditions) was a reduction in representation. The South would happily accept such a reduction, the newspaper said, and then openly disfranchise every black man within its boundaries. Surely Republicans did not want that. Apparently they did not because there is no record of any new case in federal court. Melton did take a case to the state judiciary, but there it predictably failed. Any constitutional attack on black disfranchisement was doomed to failure as the Supreme Court was to make clear in several other later cases.[17] Murray and his Lily White Republicans should have realized this hopelessness, but they seemed willing to continue battling for black voting rights. The Regulars, supposedly the black champions, continued to remain passive.

Murray also had his bitter congressional election race to worry about. He wrote angrily to a friend that the convention that had nominated Cohen had been composed primarily of persons who had supported Elliott during the House Election Committee hearings. Cohen was nothing but "a little insignificant, hypocritical Jew" controlled by Webster and Smalls, Murray said. He would be "very roughly handled" in the campaign. Murray felt confident of victory particularly if Republican factionalism could be healed.[18]

Unfortunately, E. A. Webster's stubbornness doomed such hopes. Standing with a number of his supporters in the lobby of a Columbia hotel, he told a reporter: "We don't propose to run an electric car for the benefit of the other party." Reunification depended on the Lily Whites' willingness to surrender.

The national party had refused to recognize them, yet they had held an illegal convention anyway. Webster's statements chilled any hopes for a Republican rapprochement. Negotiating committees failed to reach an agreement.[19]

The continued intra-party battle now revolved around the gubernatorial election and the Murray/Cohen/Elliott congressional race. The Regular candidate for governor, R. M. Wallace, limited his appearances to rallies in Columbia and Charleston. He attacked the other faction and the Tillmanites, while supporting national Republican policy. Lily White Sampson Pope made a more thorough canvass and spoke to large crowds all over the state. As a new Republican inexperienced in the long line of frustrating defeats, he retained hope of attracting dissident whites and pulling off an upset. He ignored Wallace and concentrated his attacks on his former Tillmanite colleagues.

Other dignitaries from their faction usually accompanied both gubernatorial candidates. In Charleston, for example, when Pope spoke to a crowd of about twelve hundred persons, Murray joined him. The black congressman did not mention Cohen or Elliott, but he did stir the crowd by recalling how, during the Civil War, blacks had protected the American flag from those who had tried to trample it. In Darlington, Pope spoke inside the courthouse while Edmund H. Deas, representing the Regulars, debated a heckler on the courthouse steps.[20]

Both Murray and Cohen appeared before the Republican Congressional Committee in Washington. After Cohen spoke to Representative J. W. Babcock, the head of the Republican Congressional Committee, he resigned his job at the post office on his return and began his campaign in earnest. Murray not only talked to Babcock, but he also asked for arbitration of the nomination deadlock. Babcock was angry at Webster for his inept handling of the entire South Carolina Republican nominating process, and he found Cohen's tardy resignation from his federal job at the post office similarly irritating. Murray's blackness was also critical to Babcock because the Republican official was concerned about the black vote in the North. He told a reporter: "Why your district belongs to a colored man. Did not the legislature set aside a district for negroes?" The 1894 redistricting notwithstanding, Babcock certainly thought so, and his mistaken belief helped Murray.[21]

Cohen and Murray toured the state in a campaign of mutual recriminations. The press accused Murray of bribing Beaufort County Republicans and using smear and scare tactics. Murray's supporters allegedly threatened Cohen and assaulted a minister on the grounds that "he was no Christian because he was helping a man whose forefathers [had] crucified Christ." They also accused Cohen of running a sham race, that is, he was preparing to drop out as soon as he was offered a postmastership.[22]

In late October, the national Congressional Committee endorsed Murray's candidacy. The Reverend R. C. Browne, Cohen's black campaign manager, harshly attacked the decision, calling Murray's candidacy illegal. The June 1896 national convention had refused to recognize the Reorganized Republicans, so the convention that had nominated Murray was illegal, and he was no GOP candidate. Cohen's supporters also whispered that, despite the Congressional Committee's decision, their man had the confidential support of the Republican National Committee's executive group. Murray countered this claim by publishing strong letters of support from both the national and the congressional committees. He kept up his torrid campaign, but he began to show the strain. In Beaufort he was hoarse and exhausted. He still had enough energy left, however, to defend the tariff, attack his old nemesis, Robert Smalls, travel to Georgetown to speak before more than a thousand people, and take part in an enormous barbecue dinner.[23]

On election day, McKinley easily won the White House, and the Republicans retained control of the House and the Senate. In South Carolina, however, the Democrats swept everything. William H. Ellerbe won the governorship over Pope and Wallace, 59,924 to 4,402 to 2,780 respectively, and Democratic presidential electors polled 58,801 out of the 63,900 votes cast. Only one black man, the last one until modern times, was elected to the State House. In the First District, Murray defeated Cohen 2,478 to 173, but Elliott's 4,652 votes easily won him the congressional seat.[24]

The South Carolina GOP had so thoroughly displaced its anger that Republicans spent little time discussing their trouncing at the hands of the Democrats. The Reorganized/Lily White victory over the Regulars was deemed more important than the loss to the Democrats. Republicans had lost track of who their real enemy was, and Murray clearly shared the loss of reality. He expressed happiness because, he said, it had been "years since our people showed the bold, determined and enthusiastic front that they presented at this election and if they could have voted I would have secured one of the largest majorities of any Congressional candidate in the United States." He had defeated Cohen, so his loss to Elliott seemed not nearly as significant.[25]

Murray's statement contained elements of the truth, however. Had blacks been able to approach the polls freely, Murray's election results and those of the entire Republican ticket would have been different. In the six counties comprising Murray's congressional district, the population was overwhelmingly black. According to the 1900 census, the black population ranged from Beaufort County's 90 percent black to Williamsburg County's 63 percent black. Despite such preponderance, Murray received only about 35 percent of the votes cast in his congressional race. In the presidential election, though South Carolina as a whole was 58 percent black, William McKinley, the Republican candidate, received only 8 percent of the votes cast. Some whites stayed away from the polls to protest William Jennings Bryan's candidacy, while other whites voted Republican, so the extent of black disfranchisement was even greater. A comparison with the 1892 election shows this fact even more clearly. In 1892 a much less popular Republican presidential candidate, Benjamin Harrison, had received 21 percent of the votes cast that year. The 1895 constitution was doing its disfranchising work well.

Murray quickly appealed his loss. The supervisors in Charleston County, however, adjourned before his representatives could appear. He then went to the state board on the basis of fraud, improper electoral procedures, and an "unjust, unconstitutional and void" registration law. When his lawyer appeared before the board on November 23, 1896, however, Murray unexpectedly had him withdraw the statement concerning registration law and concentrate on the fraud instead. The board was not impressed. They certified Elliott and Democratic candidates in all congressional districts.[26]

Murray was determined to carry his appeal to Congress, but he had one more session of the 54th Congress to attend first. He did not take an active part in the few congressional sessions left before the Christmas recess. He introduced H.R. 9757, a bill "to insure minority representation in Federal elections" through the use of federal machinery and penalties within individual states. It was sent to the Committee on Election of President, Vice President, and Representatives of Congress, and it received little notice.[27]

Murray gave no indication of what was to come during the Christmas recess and a ten-day leave of absence that followed. When he returned to the capital, however, he boldly announced his intention to stop the presidential electoral count. He was determined to force an investigation of South Carolina's election laws and new constitution. He had with him, the Charleston *News and Courier* said, "a monster petition signed by thousands of Republicans."

Murray's announcement was viewed in South Carolina as part of a Republican conspiracy, endorsed by McKinley and Hanna, to gain southern votes. (Why McKinley would delay or endanger his own election was not explained.) Senator Ben Tillman blamed Murray's threat on the Republican National

Committee and declared that it was only a scare tactic that would quickly be withdrawn. Senator George F. Hoar, the powerful pro-black Republican from Massachusetts, said Murray's threatened action came under the purview of an 1887 law, which, unfortunately for him, did not give Congress the power to investigate the returns to determine the legality of the elections or of the state's certifying procedure. Samuel W. McCall, a Republican congressman from Massachusetts, put Murray down less elegantly. Agreeing with Ben Tillman, he said that Republicans would not tolerate any delay in McKinley's election. While it was true that many South Carolinians were disfranchised, these were the illiterates who did not deserve to vote anyway. "A full generation has passed since the colored men were enfranchised, and I do not know how long they can expect us to coddle them and fight to secure their electoral rights, while they neglect to learn to read and write." McCall was expressing white America's disdain for black voting rights, so his inaccurate racism was not challenged. Murray's scheme was futile.[28]

Republicans tried to convince Murray that his action might cause a longer interruption of the electoral count than he wanted. He responded that he planned to consult with "friends in the House" and then act accordingly. On four separate days he submitted not one but fifteen petitions to the House, and these were all referred to the Committee on the Election of President, Vice President, and Representatives of Congress. He then capitulated to the pressure; he announced he would not interrupt the electoral count. "No good will be accomplished by it and much harm might result," he said. His aim had always been to get South Carolina's election procedure before the nation, and he had accomplished that. There would not be what one newspaper had feared in a headline, "Another Hayes Tilden Affair."[29]

When the electoral count was made on February 11 and the tally came to South Carolina, "an expectant silence" fell over the assembled salons. "Not a whisper of protest was heard." South Carolina's vote was accepted, and the count went on; Murray did not interrupt the tally. Quickly, however, he made some face-saving gestures. He introduced House Resolution No. 543, which called on the Speaker of the House to set up a five-member committee "to investigate the political affairs of the State of South Carolina." This resolution was sent to committee, and hearings were immediately called. Murray had apparently been bought off with the promise of other House action.[30]

On February 18, Murray appeared before the committee, but he found no quorum present; even the Republican chairman Newton M. Curtis of New York was absent.[31] Representative Henry M. Baker of New Hampshire chaired a brief informal meeting. When the committee met again on February 25, members had to be hunted up to form a quorum. Murray, Ellery Brayton, and Robert Smalls, representing both factions, spoke in favor of the petitioners, and South Carolina representative Stanyarne Wilson defended the state. Wilson insisted that Murray had never planned to interrupt the electoral count; his purpose had always been to aid Republican congressional contestants. Murray disagreed strongly. The issue was not congressional seats but the existence in South Carolina of a conspiracy to disfranchise black voters.[32]

When the committee next met on February 26, Sampson Pope joined Murray. South Carolina representative W. Jasper Talbert took great pains to depict Pope as untrustworthy, but his insults were irrelevant. House leaders had obviously agreed to hold the meetings only to prevent any disruption of the electoral vote. In the Senate, William E. Chandler, a Republican of New Hampshire, talked about supporting Murray, but he quickly backed off when Tillman threatened to talk any resolution to death. On March 2, 1897, with the congressional session almost over and a new president about to be inaugurated, Republican representative Harrison H. Atwood of Massachusetts submitted the committee's decision to the House. Murray's questions were "of grave importance," he said, but because the present Congress did not have sufficient time to deal with them, the committee presented "the statement of the charges and allegations under the resolution without findings" and recommended referral to the 55th Congress. The matter was dead. Another attempt by Murray to overturn South Carolina's biased electoral system had failed.[33]

Black response to Murray's latest unsuccessful thrust against Palmetto State disfranchisement was mixed. The Savannah *Tribune* said Murray's "manly stand" had caused the issue to receive "a proper airing," while *The Freeman* accepted his reasoning for its failure. Murray's long-time political antagonist Thomas E. Miller, now the president of a newly established South Carolina state college for blacks, did not agree. He called Murray "a heartless traitor" who bragged about his plans while "cowardly deserting them before the battle was on."[34]

Murray was stung by what he called Miller's "malevolent remarks." He compared his old rival to Judas Iscariot and Benedict Arnold and called him a "miserable vampire" for good measure. He said Miller, who ostentatiously had opposed the new constitution during the convention, had later toured the state praising it in order to obtain his college presidency. As a lawyer, Miller should know, Murray said, that the 1887 law only allowed a protest when there were two sets of electors contesting each other's validity. The law did not give

Congress the power to investigate a state's electoral system. (Murray did not indicate why he had taken his action if he had always known this.) Though a lawyer, Miller had never personally undertaken any litigation to aid black voters. "I have done my full duty," Murray said.[35]

This exchange was so bitter that one black newspaper worried about a duel. But the anger soon dissipated: Miller was busy with his college presidency, and Murray was completing his term and making plans for the future. His last congressional action was to introduce H.R. 10377 (the penultimate bill submitted in the session) calling for the erection of a public building in Georgetown. This bill did not emerge from committee before Congress adjourned.[36]

Murray completed his abbreviated second congressional term more sensationally than he had finished his first. Two of his three bills and resolutions, though they were unsuccessful, were among the most dramatic measures of the session. His threat to stop the electoral count had briefly worried Washington and forced an unconcerned Congress to consider, if only in passing, his state's unfair election practices.

Murray's plan to stop the electoral count and his attempt to utilize the Fourteenth Amendment were further manifestations of his determination to use all available means to overcome South Carolina's anti-black election laws. The unsuccessful court battles against the state constitution, his wish to return to Congress, and his support of a new Republican faction demonstrated his continued belief that politics remained the main hope for black salvation. He held this view despite recurring defeats, increased disfranchisement, and continued Republican disunity in the face of ever worsening suppression.

The prejudice experienced by the South Carolina Republican Party continued to frustrate its members as they battled one another as a way of coping with it. The prospect of patronage from the Republican president McKinley did not mitigate this animosity; it sharpened it. Patronage might keep one of the factions alive, and thus Republicans of all stripes pursued political favors. No other kind of political victory was possible for Republicans in the Palmetto State. The South Carolina GOP did not factionalize so they could gain federal patronage. Its members were not venal office seekers. They sought patronage as the only remaining method of surviving the crushing prejudice they were facing.

# 8

# Political Nadir

When William McKinley took office in March 1897, he had Republican majorities in both houses of Congress. Like all new presidents, however, McKinley was overwhelmed with patronage problems; he brought six steamer trunks full of job applications with him when he arrived in Washington.[1] Republicans hungered for the positions held by Grover Cleveland's Democrats, and the president and his advisers had to decide which of the faithful to reward. There were campaign debts to be paid, opponents to be punished, and factions to be rewarded, encouraged, or destroyed. McKinley had to deal with these issues for better than a year. Even the trauma of the February 1898 sinking of the U.S. battleship the *Maine* and the April 1898 advent of the Spanish-American War did not defer the problems. McKinley remained under constant pressure to make patronage decisions.

South Carolina Republicans were conspicuously present in this jostling at the federal trough. Their desperate situation at home made patronage even more important to them than it was to northern Republicans. They had no chance of winning local office, and congressional seats were becoming equally unattainable. The only state GOP hope for political office (and thus for continued existence) resided with the Republican administration in Washington. Southern delegates controlled approximately one-third of the delegate seats at the quadrennial national conventions, so, despite their inability to deliver election votes, southern Republicans remained important to national political leaders.

In South Carolina, McKinley's patronage did not create Republican factionalism, but his decisions on federal officeholders in the state might finally determine a definitive victor in the already existing Republican factional feud. Would President McKinley continue to support Webster and the Regulars as candidate McKinley had done at the St. Louis convention? Or, would the stronger showing of Reorganized Republicans in the November elections convince the president to recognize them? South Carolina Republicans of all persuasions realized that McKinley's decision was central to their futures, and they scurried harder for the spoils of Republican victory. McKinley took his time, and by the time he had finished making all the major appointments, his

decision seemed clear. Except for appointing Lawson Melton of the Reform/
Reorganized/Lily White group to the post of U.S. marshall, McKinley recognized the Regulars. E. A. Webster was made collector of the Internal Revenue;
Abial Lathrop became a U.S. district attorney; John R. Tolbert was named
the collector of customs at Charleston; Robert Smalls became the collector
of customs at Beaufort; and George I. Cunningham became the postmaster
of Charleston. McKinley rewarded those who had supported his candidacy at
the national convention. He ignored the issue of in-state vitality.[2]

Murray not only suffered with his faction, but he also experienced several
personal defeats. He strongly supported the lawyer Julius I. Washington for
the Beaufort post office, but the national administration appointed Samuel G. Bampfield, the son-in-law of his political foe Robert Smalls. Murray's
candidate for the Charleston post office was similarly ignored. Despite his
major role in the battle of the constitutional convention, Murray's hope for
continued leadership seemed futile, and his failure reflected the problems of
his fellow blacks. A few here and there received minor South Carolina post
offices, but, as a general rule, they were ignored. "The McKinley administration doesn't seem inclined to do very much for the colored brother," a state
newspaper said. "He is all very well in his way when it comes to voting, but
when the plums are to be distributed, the ones which fall to his lot are very
small and are liable to be worm-eaten." In fact, McKinley appointed the white
leaders of the predominantly black faction of the party. Were he pursuing a
true Lily White policy, he would have recognized the Reorganized Republicans, the state's whiter faction. McKinley rewarded the whites in the black and
tan faction that had supported his nomination.[3]

This was not the worst of it. Those blacks who did obtain patronage, notably post offices in small towns, were in danger of harassment and even death.
Frazier B. Baker became the postmaster of Lake City, Williamsburg County, South Carolina, at the behest of the Regular leaders E. A. Webster and
Edmund H. Deas. In February 1898, a mob of three to four hundred people
killed him, and the manner of the slaying shocked the nation. The Baker house
was set on fire, and when the father, mother, son, two daughters, and twelve-
month-old baby tried to escape, the mob fired on them from nearby woods.
Baker and the baby in his arms were killed, and the rest of the family were
seriously wounded.[4]

This murder took place in February about the same time that the *Maine*
was sunk in Havana harbor, so the nation's attention was quickly diverted.
Still, both houses of Congress discussed the incident; McKinley held cabi-

net meetings; he sent inspectors to investigate; and he closed the Lake City post office. He commiserated with a delegation of protesting South Carolina Republicans that included Murray, Smalls, Crum, Deas, and Wallace, but he focused primarily on matters in Cuba, not South Carolina. Palmetto State authorities arrested several people, two gave state's evidence, and a Charleston federal grand jury brought forth a strong indictment, but the May 1899 trial resulted in a hung jury. Meanwhile, voluntary charity established the Baker family in a new home in Boston. In 1901, authorities decided not to retry the case, so the perpetrators were never punished. The lesson was clear; it was not safe to be a black officeholder in South Carolina. A black newspaper, the Washington *Bee*, lectured Republicans on their betrayal. "The republican [*sic*] press is devoting a lot of space to Dreyfus and the hypocrisy of the French government. We would advise it to clean the Augean stables of our own government before taking the contract to teach civilization to the French."[5]

Black officeholders were not alone in facing violence; those blacks who tried to vote and whites who attempted to help them were also in peril. On election day in November 1898, the Phoenix/Greenwood County area in the Third Congressional District witnessed a four-day riot, resulting in the lynching of numerous black voters and the injury and banishment of several white Republicans who had been aiding them.

R. R. Tolbert, who had recently become the Regular Republican state chairman, was also a candidate for the Third District congressional seat. He encouraged disfranchised blacks to come to the polls, try to vote, and, when rejected, sign an affidavit for use in a later contest. Such activities were not unusual; Murray and others had followed the same procedure in previous contests. This time, however, there was a violent white backlash. In Phoenix, a white man overturned the Republican table manned by T. P. Tolbert, the candidate's brother, while a crowd of whites fired into a nearby group of blacks who fired right back. Numerous people were wounded, and the white table spiller was killed. Whites denied starting the fracas, insisting that blacks had ambushed Democratic voters. They responded with an orgy of lynchings, drove out the Tolbert family, and charged the candidate's uncle, John R. Tolbert, the Charleston customs collector, with inciting the riot, even though he had not arrived on the scene until after the violence was at its peak. At the behest of leading state Republicans, President McKinley reluctantly sent federal officials into the state to try to prevent further bloodshed. In March 1899, the South Carolina governor issued a proclamation calling on Phoenix residents to let the Tolberts come home, but as late as August anti-black feeling remained so intense that whippings and rape were common. The Lake City and Phoenix incidents demonstrated clearly that it was unsafe for a South Carolina black man to vote or to hold office or for a white man to encourage him. The state's Conservative Democrats and a Republican president protested such violence, but they did nothing to prevent it or to bring the guilty parties to justice.[6]

In fact, conditions were deteriorating for the black man all over the nation. He was being disfranchised through constitution and law throughout the South. The United States Supreme Court in *Plessy vs. Ferguson* (1896) gave its blessings to segregation, and, in *Williams vs. Mississippi* (1898), the Court accepted literacy tests for voting. A Republican administration provided neither patronage nor protection against anti-black violence. Everywhere he turned, the black man saw hostility. There was an obvious need for a unified effort to fight the growing proscription and violence, of which incidents such as the Baker murder, the Phoenix riots, and a major disturbance at Wilmington, North Carolina were only the most obvious manifestations. Murray tried to provide leadership to battle such terror. In May 1897, he helped found the Negro National Protective Association in Washington.

Murray was this shadowy organization's president, and he apparently toured the country on the group's behalf. Its headquarters was located in Washington; an elementary school principal in that city, John W. Cromwell, was the national secretary; and auxiliary committees with vice-presidents in each state (for example, the newsmen T. Thomas Fortune in New York and John Mitchell, Jr., of the Richmond *Planet* in Virginia) promulgated its philosophy. Dr. J. N. Johnson, the group's financial secretary, indicated that Murray and his organization opposed migration to Africa or within the country and supported no particular political party. They believed in money, homes, businesses, and professions for blacks. Johnson said Murray was preparing blacks to live in the South through "home-buying movements on a large scale."[7] Murray regretted lynchings and rape, Johnson said, and he opposed whiskey and lewdness. In short, Johnson argued, "There is nothing in our plans that any good American citizen could object to." W. Calvin Chase, the editor of the *Bee*, was equally favorable (he was listed as president of the Washington branch). He also said, however, that "Making speeches and nothing else has been the order. Lets [*sic*] do something."[8]

Murray and his group apparently planned to prevent anti-black violence by convincing whites that blacks agreed with their anti-black criticism. Blacks indeed had to improve themselves, Murray said, and they were working to do so; violence against them should, therefore, cease. Though there is no evidence that Booker T. Washington was associated with this organization, he must certainly have approved of its approach.

In December 1898 and the early months of 1899, the constitution and by-laws of what was now being called a "National Racial Protective Association" appeared in the Washington *Bee*. The high point of the association's existence was probably an inconclusive December 1898 meeting when it passed an anti-McKinley resolution based on T. Thomas Fortune's castigation of the president and urged black retaliatory violence. Like many other such organizations, however, it became part of the 1898 revival of the old Afro-American League, now titled the Afro-American Council. Murray's organization sank permanently from sight.[9]

The Afro-American Council had a fitful existence itself. In many ways it was a forerunner of the later Niagara Movement and the more successful NAACP. It attempted to establish a black national organization to protest the increasing racial injustice of American society. It never was very significant because of the internal conflicts frequently revolving around Booker T. Washington. The head of the Tuskegee Institute founded the Negro Business League at the turn of the century partially to undercut the council's influence and criticism, but he also gained control of the council itself. Washington was concerned about the council's militancy, so he did all he could to temper it.[10]

The organizational meeting of the new council took place in Rochester, New York, on September 15, 1898.[11] Only a few people attended this gathering, so the group met again on December 29, 1898 in the Metropolitan Baptist Church in Washington, D.C. This time a large crowd was present. Bishop Alexander Walters, its president, chaired the meeting; the Ida Wells-Barnett, who was famous for her anti-lynching activities, was the secretary. Booker T. Washington sent his regrets, but North Carolina congressman George H. White and former congressmen Henry P. Cheatham and John R. Lynch were among the black dignitaries in attendance.

Murray presented one of the conference's major speeches: "Our Progress in Business." It sounded very much like his 1890 Charleston speech and like the more famous Booker T. Washington orations. Murray talked about the need for blacks to go into business and to support each other if they wanted whites to respect them. "A white tramp with good clothes is at present better off than a Negro millionaire. When we show a disposition to aid ourselves, the white people will aid us," he said. Other speakers that evening talked about self-protection, but Murray, the founder of a protective league, spoke about economics and black deficiencies. His speech was a clear reflection of the accommodationist attitude of the southerners at the meeting in contrast to the more militant attitude of the delegates from the North.[12]

The convention's Executive Committee met with President McKinley. Bishop Walters, Murray, the ex-Louisiana lieutenant governor P. B. S. Pinchback, Congressman White, the register of the U.S. Treasury Judson Lyons, and twenty-two others of their caliber had a fifteen minute interview with the president. They presented him with a memorial requesting a congressional investigation of the many recent lynchings throughout the South. They also expressed disappointment over McKinley's silence on the subject in his recent annual message. The president expressed a vague determination to help, and the meeting ended on this inconclusive note. The council meeting similarly adjourned with little resolved. It published a strong statement by T. Thomas Fortune demanding an end to violence, established an Executive Committee (Murray and Crum representing South Carolina), and talked of beginning a newspaper. Murray remained on the executive board for the next several years, but he never played much of a role after his significant involvement at the first gathering. The council itself passed out of existence in 1908.[13]

In addition to his activities on the national stage, Murray also continued a busy schedule in South Carolina. He made major addresses at the January 1, 1898 Sumter Emancipation Day celebration and at the August organizational meeting of the State Colored Teachers' Association. At the teachers' meeting he was an honored guest, the delegates viewing him, a former teacher himself and a person well known all over the state, as a key recruiting force for their organization.[14]

Murray spent most of 1897 preparing for his appeal to Congress, appearing before the appropriate congressional committee in early 1898. There were many contests that term, so Murray received no immediate word. The Washington *Bee* lamented that the Republican House seemed "to be very dilatory in deciding his case." It was only later that Congress's intent became clear.[15] It did not plan to take any action. The national government joined South Carolina in refusing to consider evidence of disfranchisement and fraud against black people. Congressional unconcern was now added to the disfranchising constitution, registration frauds, voter intimidation, and violence to doom any Republican's election chances. The existing South Carolina Republican Party fracture only added to an already impossible situation. In truth, however, even a solidly united party could not have changed matters; a harmonious Republican organization would not have been able to overcome the ever-increasing disfranchisement movement.

The outlook was so discouraging that the Regulars decided not to hold a state convention in 1898, while the Reorganized/Lily Whites were too dispirited even to consider the question. In Charleston County, the two factions merged long enough to nominate Murray unanimously over Dr. Crum and Robert Smalls for the U.S. Congress. Unfortunately, this consensus lasted only briefly. A white Republican named T. Barker Jones, though not a delegate, was allowed to announce his intention to run against Murray, justifying his candidacy on the allegedly illegal nature of the convention. He denied any racial prejudice. He supported hard money, while Murray, he mistakenly said, was a silverite. Finally, he boasted, he could attract more than two thousand white Democrats to the Republican Party, something Murray could never do.[16]

Jones withdrew just before the election, but the perennial Democratic candidate Congressman William Elliott was the real opponent anyway. Murray apparently decided that to win he had to unite the few remaining black voters. He tried a "dirty trick." He had a Washington printer prepare a thousand copies of a circular letter fraudulently signed by "A Disgusted Democrat." He explained to his Washington friend Whitefield McKinlay: "I used the word 'nigger' so as to make the language as contemptible and as much like that of the most prejudiced Democrat as possible." To gain maximum effect, he planned to release the letter in Columbia on the eve of the election. Unfortunately, one of his Beaufort County supporters handled the material so clumsily that the plot was exposed. It was of no consequence anyway. Black voters had been so systematically eliminated that even had Murray's ill-conceived plot succeeded it would have made no difference. The *Palmetto Post*'s comment was accurate: "George stands as much chance as the proverbial cat did in sheol."[17]

The election results were expectedly disappointing. Murray and the entire Republican ticket lost badly. Murray was the leading Republican vote getter, but Elliott still defeated him 3,030 to 1,529. The next highest number for a Republican congressional candidate in the state was only 505 votes. The extent of this decline can be seen by recalling that in 1892 Murray had gained 4,995 votes and as late as 1896 he had gained 2,478. Black disfranchisement was destroying the South Carolina Republican Party and Murray's political chances with it.[18]

Murray had missed the last three weeks of the campaign because of a fever, and on election day he was home in bed, his physical health an accurate barometer of his political fortunes. He tried to maintain his optimism, however. He protested the count in all his district's counties, and this time he attacked the suffrage section of the state constitution as "illegal." He also argued a point previously used against him—illegal printing of ballots. He did not, however, take the contest to the State Board of Canvassers. He simply forwarded his county letters of protest. The state board skimmed these letters and voted to certify Elliott's victory.[19] Murray could still appeal to Congress, but his failure to pursue his cause actively on the state level weakened his argument. Besides, his 1896 contest was still officially pending. He took no further action. His optimism gave way to the realities of his political life. He had reached his political nadir, his desperate straits mirroring those of his party.

In early 1900, with the presidential election on the horizon, the Republican Party scheduled a state convention to nominate delegates to the June national gathering. Republicans had no chance of winning any local victories so the choice of delegates to the national convention was the only meaningful political duty left to them. Webster's Regulars were in full control, the Lily Whites nowhere to be seen. Murray was the only Reorganized leader to serve as a delegate at the Regular gathering, and he played but a minor role. He made one of his fiery speeches calling on Republicans "to go forward a solid phalanx to meet Democracy which like a demon was overriding the liberty of the people," but he said little else. The election of delegates resulted in a solid Regular slate: Webster, Smalls, Deas, and the controversial R. R. Tolbert. The platform condemned lynching and discriminatory election practices in South Carolina, but it suggested no concrete action against either. The meeting symbolized the party's lack of vitality, the result of the unremitting white discrimination. When district conventions elected the remainder of the delegate slate, the Regulars were again victorious. Murray did not even appear at the district convention in Sumter, and his name was not among those considered.[20]

Murray attended the fall state GOP convention where, to the state's shock, two blacks, Edmund H. Deas and Robert Smalls, were elected party chairman and vice-chairman respectively. The presence of two black men as titular heads of the South Carolina Republican Party jolted the state and the nation that had so openly vitiated basic black human rights. The Charleston *Post* headlined "Whites Given Rear Seats." The Sumter *Herald* editorialized: "The negroes seem to be running the State Republican party. It is probably a case of survival of the fittest." Behind such sarcasm was anger that blacks had been able to gain any political prominence in South Carolina despite the efforts to eliminate them and despite the 1900 success of Republican Lily Whitism in other southern states.[21]

At this fall meeting Murray was once more a visible delegate. He raised points of order; he was nominated but declined the convention's temporary chairmanship; he seconded the nomination of Deas for state chairman; and he devised a compromise proposal when the convention was on the verge of open disagreement over the method of choosing electors. Under his plan, Dr. Crum and the white Republican Loomis L. Blalock were elected to at-large posts, and during a subsequent district caucus Murray was named an elector for the Seventh Congressional District.[22] His election in the Seventh District indicated that he had given up all hope of ever recapturing his old congressional seat in the First District. He would never return to Congress again.

When the November 1900 election took place, neither unity nor new leadership helped; the Republicans again went down to crushing defeats at all levels—from the presidential ticket to the congressional races. The vote for president was 47,233 for the Democrat William Jennings Bryan and only 3,579 for the Republican William McKinley. In Murray's old congressional district, the Republican candidate W. W. Beckett received only 1,378 votes to William Elliott's 3,666. In the other congressional races, the highest Republican vote was 534. Black control of the South Carolina Republican Party was an empty honor.[23]

The 1900 election seemed finally to exhaust black Carolinian stamina. Robert Smalls continued writing letters to protest the state's franchise system, but two other black leaders offered conciliatory, almost obsequious, statements at Emancipation Day 1901 celebrations. Thomas E. Miller, once a fiery politician but now the subdued president of the recently established state black college, identified with those who were oppressing his brethren. He told a Beaufort audience that the best friends blacks had were whites. The state was generously providing education for blacks, while the Republican Party was responsible for the harsh disfranchisement. At Laurens, Murray expressed a similar attitude. He had once sped all across the state and from one court to another trying to preserve the black franchise, but now he insisted that premature civil and political rights had hurt blacks. He told his applauding audience, as Miller had told his, that the state provided marvelous educational opportunities; black progress depended on blacks. Migration to Africa was a mistake because, he said in Booker T. Washington tones, "This is as good a place as you can find on earth." Blacks should purchase property and, in that way, secure their place in southern society.[24]

Murray followed his own advice—he expanded his property holdings and withdrew from South Carolina Republican politics. During the previous four years, he had run for Congress twice, he had become involved in national protest societies, and he had watched national GOP leaders make crucial choices for state Republicanism without recourse to local conditions. He had also seen the continued increase of anti-black violence. These years had witnessed the culmination of the long process of black disfranchisement and subordination, yet it had also seen GOP reunification and the first all-black South Carolina GOP leadership since Reconstruction. But the party was weaker than ever; leading it was a meaningless honor. Murray lost hope in politics. He had tried to find political solutions to black problems, and he had failed. He now undertook a new approach. He continued his battle against disfranchisement and subordination through economic, not political, means.

# Economic Success and Political Failure

Murray had long held that blacks needed economic success to improve their place in American society, but, unlike Booker T. Washington, who was the most famous exponent of that view, he had always emphasized political solutions to black problems. Now, having failed in his battle against disfranchisement on the stump, in the courts, and in the halls of Congress, he came over to Washington's view. He determined to fight on economically. The South Carolina Constitution granted the vote to any person who owned property assessed at $300. In the late 1890s, Murray instituted a land purchase plan to allow blacks to meet this constitutional provision. At the same time, he began building agricultural machines he had patented to help mechanize these small farms at an affordable cost.

Murray had operated his own small farm since the 1870s. The first expansion came in the fall of 1888 when he spent $100 to make two separate purchases, which netted him 327 acres in Sumter County's sand hill region near his original Rafting Creek farm. His next major purchase came in February 1894 when, under his wife's name, he purchased 1,536 acres for $4,000. From 1897 through 1901 he continued making purchases, so that by the end of the period, his total land accumulation was 9,418 acres at an investment of approximately $58,700. Almost all of this land was mortgaged. His December 1901 purchase of 1,144 acres, for example, was mortgaged to the seller, a leading Sumter white businessman and landowner named Henry J. Harby, for the full $11,000, payable in seven yearly payments at 8 percent.[1]

Murray never owned all of these acres at the same time, although several black newspapers and at least one modern book insist he did.[2] He steadily sold his land in packets of 17 to 100 acres for prices ranging from $153 to $976.05. All purchases were made under eight-year lease provisions with yearly payments as low as $76.50 or as high as $204 per year. At one time Murray had some two hundred tenant families working his properties.[3]

Murray had established an intricate system that he hoped would make him wealthy and, at the same time, provide other blacks with land and thereby the legal qualification to vote. He purchased large tracts of land, mortgaged them heavily, and filled them with tenants who signed promissory notes to make yearly payments until they had completed purchasing the land. The promissory notes were a lien on the crop and land until the final purchase payment was made, and the land was legally transferred. The yearly payments served a dual purpose; they purchased land for the tenants, while also paying Murray's mortgage. Unlike the usual southern sharecropping/tenant system, Murray's plan provided a way out; a tenant could eventually become a landowner. The economic viability of the small land plots was debatable, and default procedure was unclear. Still, the system gave blacks hope. Like Booker T. Washington, Murray developed a program to lift blacks up from poverty and gain the respect of whites; but unlike that of the Tuskegee Wizard, Murray's program did not necessitate the acquisition of new skills.

Judging by the available records and Murray's few surviving comments, his system worked. In May 1899, he told a friend about his collections that year of $4,000, with a total business profit of $20,000. In September 1900, he hoped to collect $10,000 to $12,000 despite poor growing conditions throughout the cotton belt. His tenants, he said, were so determined to purchase their lands as quickly as possible that they would produce 600 to 700 bales. His business ventures were becoming increasingly more complicated, but he hoped that, "without some unforeseen disaster," he would "be out of the wilderness within the next three or four years." In September 1901 he wrote to Judson W. Lyons, the black register of the U.S. Treasury, suggesting his "land scheme" for other areas of the country.[4]

Murray's true financial condition is difficult to calculate. The 1900 census indicates that he owned a house in Providence Township, South Carolina, and that he lived there with his wife, his twenty-year-old son, his seventeen-year-old daughter, his nine-year-old adopted son, and a fifteen-year-old boy he had taken in. County records show that he made approximately one hundred small land sales at a total price of approximately $40,000, and that he had ongoing leases worth nearly $9,000. The amount of additional money Murray was collecting from tenants not listed in the records is unknown. Simply by calculating the land sales that are documented, it is clear that Murray was a wealthy man by South Carolina standards and a very wealthy man by the standards of the black community of the same period.[5]

Murray's land business was not his only source of wealth during this time. He earned $5,000 per year plus expenses for the four years he was a member of the House of Representatives. His election contests were expensive, but the House reimbursed him. His other political offices also brought in money, but his extensive politicking was financially draining. He also ran his personal farm, but its size, the products, and the remuneration it produced are un-known. He was involved in several other financial ventures including a real estate company and a merchandizing concern, but detailed information about these undertakings is also unavailable.

A farm machine business was apparently his second most extensive finan-cial undertaking. In 1894, he gained eight separate patents on agricultural implements: a "Combined furrow-opener and stalk-knocker," a "planter," a "Combined cotton seed planter and fertilizer distribution," and a "reaper." Though eight separate patents were granted, Murray's invention was actually one farm machine adaptable to various uses. He had come onto the idea in the early 1880s while working on his farm. One day several of his farm machines broke down. Disgustedly he went home to collect himself and absent-mind-edly watched while his wife worked at her sewing machine. He noticed she used an attachment to do some hemming and then replaced it with a different part that allowed her to pleat. If interchangeable parts on a sewing machine were practicable, he thought, why not on a farm machine? Such technology would allow the farmer to supply all his mechanical needs at one-third the cost.[6]

Murray worked on this project for twelve years before he patented it in 1894. Sometime in 1897, he entered into an agreement with J. Milton Turner, a leading black lawyer and the former U.S. minister to Liberia. The two men established a manufacturing shop in St. Louis to produce a machine based on these patents. The J. Milton Turner Manufacturing Establishment was founded and staffed by six white mechanics and a stenographer. This shop was to complete a prototype machine in 1898, and the shop foreman was then to come to South Carolina for field testing.[7]

As it turned out, the Turner-Murray partnership was not productive. The prototype was not completed in 1898. In March 1899, Murray was still making arrangements to assign his patents to Turner, complaining that he had expect-ed a completed machine the previous month. Turner refused to send anything until he received the patent assignment. There were problems in transferring the rights, and Murray had to write several letters to Washington to try to expedite matters. The venture came to naught. Its cost to Murray and/or any profits are unknown. It cannot even be supposed that he ever saw a completed model.[8]

Murray's patents were not important contributions to agricultural technol-ogy. The correspondence he exchanged with his lawyer and the Patent Office indicates that his inventions were variations on earlier machines, and he had to make modifications of his claims in order to receive his patents. *Scientific American*, which during those years published lists of important patents, mentioned only his first one, "517960 Combined Furrow Opener and Stalk Knocker." Even in his home area, his inventions were not that unique. In 1890, a Sumter newspaper told of a black man who lived only about twenty miles from Murray's farm who had invented "a combined planter and cultivator" with removable attachments.[9]

Modern evaluations seem to buttress contemporary attitudes. Murray's inventions are not discussed in modern studies of black American inventors. A Smithsonian Institution authority on agricultural implements studied the patent documents and did not find them particularly significant. "The lack of any mention" of seven of Murray's inventions in *Scientific American* magazine "suggests, however, tentatively and imprecisely," he said, that the magazine was not impressed with them. The fact that his family never heard of them was yet additional "negative evidence" of the inventions' lack of importance.[10]

Murray's patents may not have been significant additions to American agriculture, but they are important to an understanding of his life. Despite his hard political career, he found the time and energy to think up an idea, develop it, take the expensive and involved path of gaining patents, and then attempt to manufacture the machines. Like so much of his life, Murray's inventions demonstrate his ambition, his drive, and his determination to overcome the anti-black prejudice around him.

Even though the totality of Murray's business ventures was making him a wealthy man, he could not resist the siren call of politics. Once more he was tempted to hope that participation in the political system, this time in a patronage post, could help the cause of Republicanism and his race in South Carolina. Even though he was an avowed advocate of black pride, his fate was once again tied to a white Republican movement, this one supported by the national Republican hierarchy. Perhaps this time an invigorated state GOP would emerge from the ashes of past failure.

Murray returned to politics because he and the Republican hierarchy in Washington believed his return would quiet the political turmoil once again surrounding the Republican Party in South Carolina. In one more attempt to revitalize the Palmetto State GOP, another white Republican movement had come to life. On April 15, 1901, President McKinley dumped the U.S. district attorney Abial Lathrop, the law partner of the South Carolina Republican boss E. A. Webster, and replaced him with a pro-McKinley Democrat, John G. Capers, who was the son of the state's Episcopal bishop and a close friend of the McKinley Democratic senator John McLaurin. Capers's and McLaurin's task was to make the Republican Party in South Carolina viable by eliminating blacks and replacing them with Gold and Commercial Democrats who were unhappy in the party of Cleveland and Bryan. McLaurin was to provide public leadership, while Capers would handle the organizational details.[11]

E. A. Webster died in the midst of these maneuverings, but his replacement, Edmund Deas, an experienced black leader, provided effective leadership for the Regular Republicans. McKinley died from an assassin's bullet before these plans could proceed very far, but Theodore Roosevelt, who succeeded him, continued the effort. He went so far as to violate the social mores of the day by inviting Booker T. Washington to dine with him at the White House in order to discuss the complicated South Carolina situation. The most pressing matter was Webster's replacement at the Internal Revenue office. Washington supported Dr. William D. Crum, the black physician and long-time Republican from Charleston, but McLaurin opposed any old-liners. Instead, he recommended a close white supporter, George R. Koester. Roosevelt took McLaurin's advice and appointed Koester.[12]

Deas was enraged at Koester's appointment and resigned his post as deputy Internal Revenue collector rather than serve under him. He said Koester had participated in an 1893 lynching in Gaston, South Carolina. Roosevelt, who was already reeling from the unexpected national furor over his dinner with Washington, now was accused of consorting with a lyncher. Roosevelt spoke to Koester and allowed himself to be convinced of his innocence, although the evidence indicated that Koester had indeed participated in a lynching.[13]

Koester took office on November 4, 1901 and tried to neutralize the furor by retaining a black man as his assistant and finding another one to take Deas's place. Ideally he wanted someone who would not alienate whites and would appease blacks. He chose George W. Murray. Murray's economic success, his status as a former congressman, his membership in an earlier white movement, and his recent rapprochement with the Regulars made him an ideal choice for this post. Murray would hopefully mute the lynching charge, though Koester insisted that politics had nothing to do with Murray's appointment. He chose the ex-congressman, he said, because he was a person acceptable to whites and would serve as "a rebuke to an obnoxious class of negro politicians and an incentive to the race." The choice of Murray was "simply . . . the appointment of the best and most available colored man for the place."[14]

To Koester's disappointment, Murray's appointment only intensified the swirling controversy. Neither Deas, northern blacks, nor southern whites found him acceptable. The white community was supposed to have accepted Murray because he fulfilled the Booker T. Washington criteria of wealth and success, but it attacked him because of his black skin. Blacks, meanwhile, were similarly upset. The Cleveland *Gazette* repeated Edmund Deas's accusation that Murray was guilty of accepting bribes from Capers and McLaurin. Deas pushed his battle against Koester's nomination in Congress, in the national black press, in the Republican National Committee, and in speeches all over the country.[15]

All this furor stunned Murray and the white politicians supporting him. He continued to back Koester, insisting that cooperation not confrontation was the best way for blacks to deal with McLaurin and Capers. He told a friend that he was actually conducting an undercover activity against the white leaders, and Deas was only spoiling it. He still sided with Deas, he wrote unconvincingly, but he found Koester "most kindly and respectful in his treatment of and association with colored men" and saw no reason to pull away from him now.[16]

These and similar such southern problems visibly discouraged the usually ebullient Theodore Roosevelt. In December 1901 he told Booker T. Washington that all the conflicting advice had him at his "wit's end to know what to do." He wished he could just "cast off all . . . [his] burdens." Instead he traveled to South Carolina to see the political battle ground itself. While ostensibly visiting the South Carolina Interstate and West Indian Exposition in Charleston, he conferred with local white leaders, all Democrats, and left the impression that all his future appointments would be whites. Then McLaurin announced he would not run for reelection, so Roosevelt appointed a white Rough Rider to replace Koester. Another white Republican movement bit the dust.[17]

When that Rough Rider, Micah Jenkins, replaced Koester in early summer 1902, his "first official act" was to fire Murray and replace him with a white deputy. Murray insisted he had not been fired, that he had resigned to go back to his businesses. His bitterness came out publicly, however, in a September 1902 letter to a national black newspaper. By encouraging blacks to own land and to develop commercial institutions, he said, he had done more for them "even politically than all such tramps, like McKinley and Roosevelt put together." Murray blasted the two presidents, but he said nothing about McLaurin, Capers, Koester, and the white Republican movement.[18]

There was little sympathy for Murray. One black newspaper said: "Apologists never succeed no matter how deserving they may be."[19] The black man of record in South Carolina was now Deas; it was not Murray. Deas had led the fight against Koester, and he had beaten him. McLaurin was dropping out, and Capers's time was running out because of Roosevelt's shift away from Republicans toward white Democrats. Deas was stronger than ever. He had eliminated all those he had set out to defeat even though, as a black man, there was no future for him in South Carolina. Deas's victory looked significant on the surface, but it only played into the hands of the real victors—the white Democrats. Meanwhile, a disgusted Murray went back to his Sumter County land and his varied activities. Politics had again served him badly. He was happy to leave public office behind and return to business.

In May 1899, Murray had signed an agreement with the Northwestern Railroad, then in the process of building a feeder line from Sumter and Camden to the expanding parent line, the Atlantic Coastline Railroad.[20] The deed granted a right of way through Murray's property and a one-acre site for a passenger and freight depot at Borden, a town Murray had founded. In early 1902, Murray and some of his tenants filed petitions with the Sumter County Circuit Court contending that the railroad had not fulfilled its part of the bargain. The railroad disagreed. It had constructed the depot as promised. Murray rebutted that the railroad had not built a depot equal to others on the line; it had constructed a covered platform. It had also removed the ticket agent and changed the station from a regular stop to a flag stop. These actions violated the railroad's agreement to maintain a station like others on the route. The court agreed and ordered the railroad to build a proper depot by May 1, 1902.

The railroad appealed the decision before the South Carolina Supreme Court. Its lawyers argued that the building at Borden fit one of the definitions of the term "depot." Full service was not warranted because business at Borden consisted of only one passenger a day. The court disagreed, and, on October 17, 1902, it concurred in the circuit court's decision. The railroad had to build a depot like those at other points along the same road. Murray had won a legal victory at a time when blacks seldom won in South Carolina courts, and railroads seemingly seldom lost in any court anywhere.[21]

Simultaneous local problems unfortunately took attention away from Murray's success in the state's highest court. He became embroiled in a heated argument and had a near fistfight with a white man, Magistrate Richard C. Folk, during some litigation in the Providence township court. Rumors spread that Folk was planning to settle scores. Black altercations with whites often led to lynching or whitecapping, the driving of a successful black out of a community, so Murray armed himself for protection. The following day four or five armed men accompanied him everywhere he went. At least once he kept watch all night on the front porch of his house.

The issue came to a climax when Murray's brother, seeing Folk talking to several white men at Borden Station, became suspicious that the magistrate was organizing a mob. He alerted Murray's tenants and sent someone on horseback to Sumter, where Murray was conducting business that day. A white man sent the same warning to Murray's Sumter lawyer. Murray immediately informed the sheriff. He then hurried home and barricaded himself in his house, while armed tenants patrolled the perimeter. In the meantime, Folk took the train from Borden Station to Sumter, where he denied any sinister plans. He convinced the sheriff of his innocence, so that official refused to honor Murray's request for protection.

County Supervisor W. H. Seale, another white man, lived near Murray and Folk in Borden. Returning from an out-of-town trip around midnight, he heard about the armed blacks surrounding Murray's house. He hurried there and found about a dozen armed men standing and lying in wait. (The Columbia *State* exaggeratingly set the number at 150.) Seale went to the door, and Murray's wife told him her husband was not at home. A few moments later, Murray appeared at the window. He told Seale that he was determined to defend himself and would kill the first hostile person who set foot in his yard. Seale supported Murray's right to defend his life and property and promised to guarantee Murray's safety personally. The ex-congressman accepted Seale's word and dispersed his armed defenders. The tense situation ended. The press twitted Murray for jumping to an erroneous conclusion and portrayed him as a coward hiding in a barricaded house behind the skirts of a woman and a legion of armed men. His son later remembered his father being courageously determined to defend himself, his family, and his property against any intruders. A contemporary black newspaper agreed. He had his "fighting clothes" on, it warned, and "When the 'gang' goes gunning for Brother Murray, they will find him in a receptive mood."[22]

Murray's concern had been justified. The lynching of blacks for reasons as trivial as arguing with a white man was not unusual. Similarly, Murray's financial success provided him with no special protection, black success sometimes actually stimulating white aggression. Magistrate Folk's own shocking death just two years later demonstrated the prevalence of violence in South Carolina during those years. Folk became involved in an argument with Supervisor Seale while the two men sat in a carriage about to leave for Sumter one August day in 1904. The argument grew increasingly heated until Folk pulled out a pistol. The supervisor grabbed for the gun, and the two men wrestled and fell out of the carriage. As they hit the ground, the gun went off, and a bullet passed through Seale's coat and into Folk's head.[23]

Murray's brush with violence, coming so soon after the political disappointment of the Koester case, dampened his surprising court victory over the railroad. In May 1903, he unaccountably gave up even this triumph. He and several of his tenants signed a new deed that reaffirmed the railroad's right of transit across their property, reaffirmed the $150 sale of one acre of land for a depot, and accepted $250 as payment to release the railroad from its obligation to construct the building. Murray had won two court cases to force the railroad to build a proper terminal, but, seven months later, he signed his victory away. Some sort of pressure forced his hand. Perhaps his simultaneous eviction proceeding against one of the tenants involved in the original railroad deal occasioned the new deed. Or, he may have compromised with the railroad in order to maintain at least minimum service to Borden. The railroad continued to serve the town far into the future, and the small shed-terminal was later used as a home well into the late 1960s. By the 1970s, the depot was gone and so was the railroad. By that time Borden was only a tiny community of a few houses and grocery stores. The railroad bed through town was still visible, but it was now a road to several homes and a small farm. Only a few people in Borden remembered Murray's name, and even that remembrance was cloudy.[24]

While Murray was busy with land sales, railroad litigation, and fears of violence, the Republican Party was embroiled in yet another patronage problem, this time over the Charleston customs collectorship. Collector R. M. Wallace's death had created a vacancy, and Roosevelt had to find a replacement acceptable to all elements of the local party, the national leadership, and South Carolina whites. His attempt to accomplish this by appointing Dr. W. D. Crum, the black Charleston physician, led him into the most sensational patronage battle in U.S. history. Murray took no part in the controversy; he tended to his business and let others fight this political battle. He knew now, without doubt, that there was no political future for a black man in South Carolina.

It was uncharacteristic of Murray to remain quiet long, however. Lynching was again on the increase, and when a black Presbyterian minister called a convention in late August 1903 to discuss the problem once more, Murray was one of the 150 mostly black delegates who came. He spoke on the explosive question of black social equality with whites. Repeating ideas expressed in past speeches, he called social equality a "relative term" that had "its foundation in mental, moral, commercial and financial equality . . . not color." In any case blacks had the right to political and civil equality. As usual, whites responded with ridicule of his speech and the convention. The Charleston *News and Courier* called Murray's attempt to discuss racial relationships in the abstract as farcical. Southern whites living among commonplace blacks—that was the milieu for race relations. Blacks were inferior to whites, the paper insisted, and lynching was the inevitable result, Murray's high-sounding words notwithstanding.[25]

In mid-January 1904, Murray had his last political hurrah. The Republican state Executive Committee met and endorsed Roosevelt for a second term, so pleased were they with his staunch support for Crum to be the Charleston customs collector. Deas and Capers, to quote a black newspaper, "buried the hatchet and smoked the cheroot of peace" at the "political love feast." The way now seemed clear for a united party at the February state convention.[26]

Only one obstacle remained. Ellery Brayton reiterated all of Deas's old charges against Capers to a Charleston black newspaper. At a county convention in Sumter, Murray came out of his political seclusion to carry the meeting for Brayton. The Capers forces then bolted and held what they called a "Roosevelt Administration, Deas-Capers Convention."[27] Sumter County, a major Republican stronghold, stood divided in the face of impending unity, and Murray was helping to orchestrate the split.

The state convention convened on February 24 in Columbia's Cooper and Taylor Hall. Brayton seconded the nomination of Deas as convention chairman to show at the start that he only opposed Capers. For an hour the two white Republicans debated each other, but, when Murray tried to join in, Deas broke his gravel in hammering him down. The convention was programmed to cement the Capers-Deas alliance, and there was no way Brayton, Murray, or anyone else could prevent it.

The debate ended with Brayton totally vanquished. When the election of delegates to the national convention was conducted, he received only 10 votes. Deas received 107 votes, Capers 102, and Blaylock 80. The dissident Murray was a surprising fourth with 47 votes, followed by Robert Smalls with 45 and Dr. Crum with an embarrassingly low 43. The black physician's poor showing could damage his confirmation hope in the Senate and might even convince Roosevelt to withdraw his support. Tears began to form in Crum's eyes. Another delegate rushed up to Murray asking for help. Murray agreed to withdraw in Crum's favor but only after extracting the usual favor; the black customs collector promised to pay Murray's convention expenses. Crum then captured the fourth delegate post on a recount.[28]

Lost in the euphoria over the regained state party unity was the fact that the McKinley-Hanna-Roosevelt-McLaurin-Capers plan to establish a white Republican Party in South Carolina had failed dismally. White faces were as rare as ever at the state convention; the South Carolina Republican Party continued to be predominantly black at a time when black voters were nearly extinct. The result of five years of turmoil was the nomination of one major black office holder (Dr. Crum), the nearly total disfranchisement of the black masses, no noticeable increase in white converts, and the obvious disdain of the national GOP organization. It was no wonder that blacks gave up on politics. It was, they had learned in so many hard ways, "the exclusive concern of white folks."[29]

Murray's political career had reached a similar low. Fortunately, his businesses were prospering, so his return to more lucrative pursuits in Sumter County seemed no great loss to him or his party. His latest foray into politics had convinced him once and for all that his place was on the farm and not in the forum. Lured from his business by the belief that he could have a moderating influence on the Koester imbroglio, he had quickly realized his mistake. He returned to his land when Roosevelt dropped Koester. He briefly returned to play a final conspicuous but quixotic role in the 1904 state Republican convention.

Murray's experience during these years indicated yet again the almost classical tragedy of his life. His political party was reunified yet impotent, and even the fragile reunification had been gained over his unwise opposition. There was no future in South Carolina Republicanism for any black man let alone a dissident like Murray. He had his successful land business, and he had won a court case against a railroad. Yet, he was the object of threatened violence, and his court victory was short-lived. His land scheme was a shaky financial pyramid in a state where black success was not relished. Whether in politics or business, South Carolina's anti-black prejudice made his future look bleak. As a black woman in South Carolina remembered years later, "Just generally, if you were black, you were not supposed to have either time or money, and if you did, you ought not to show it."[30]

# On Trial

After the disappointment of his latest foray into politics, Murray returned to the Borden region of Sumter County, to his tenants and lands. His life returned to its nonpolitical rhythm. He gave some local lectures in April 1904, but otherwise he stayed out of the limelight, still bitter about events at the recent Republican convention. He complained to his friend Whitefield McKinlay in early May that he had "sacrificed" himself "to save the cause of the race and prevent criticism of the President," a man who was "proving himself such a stalwart friend of ours," but William Crum did not seem to appreciate the efforts.[1]

In an offhand manner, Murray chatted with McKinlay about two recent Supreme Court decisions. According to Murray, these rulings invalidated the convictions of black men by all-white juries in areas where there was a large black population. He asked McKinlay to send him any information he could find on these cases. From the tone of the letter, Murray's interest was purely academic. It was not. On May 19, he appeared as a defendant in Sumter's Court of General Sessions; he needed the information for use in his own trial. (Since neither Murray nor his lawyer ever mentioned these cases in court, McKinlay must never have sent them.)[2]

The charges against Murray concerned his land sales.[3] The complaining parties were Scipio Chatman and his son, James, two poor black land purchasers. In 1897 the Chatmans made an oral agreement with Murray to acquire twenty-five acres of land under his standard eight-year installment plan. They took possession of the land in January 1898 and that year made the first payment, $50.14. On October 1, 1899, they made the second payment, $47.52, and, on November 4, 1899, they signed a written lease formalizing the eight-year term, the lien on the land and crops, and the eventual transfer. Waiting this long to formalize an oral contract was obviously legally dangerous, but it was not unusual. Verbal contracts between white land owners and black tenants were common during these years and were even protected by law.

Murray received no further payments after the execution of the signed lease. James Chatman deserted the farm, and three years later, on January 23, 1903, Murray instituted eviction proceedings. The Chatmans argued that they had not signed a lease; they had signed a contract of purchase. They wanted to pay off the entire cost immediately. Murray refused and demanded fulfillment of the contract's terms, so the Chatmans took him to court. In the May 1903 trial, the Chatmans admitted defaulting, but they expressed their willingness to make up all the arrears. Murray produced the contract to prove his point, and the court ruled in his favor. He then waited until December 29, 1903, to take eviction action. The Chatmans failed in their attempt to obtain a stay, so on March 4, 1904, Murray served notice that final eviction proceedings would commence on March 8. On March 7, Scipio Chatman charged Murray with forgery. The indictment read that during the earlier trial he "did willingly and falsely utter and publish as true, a certain false, forged and counterfeited writing, and instrument of writing, commonly called a Lease of Land." The key witness was a white man named Marion Cato who testified that he had seen Murray fill out the original Chatman contract in 1899, and the document that Murray had produced during the 1903 trial was not that same lease.

The entire trial focused on the contested piece of paper. The prosecution introduced what it maintained was the original contract, a printed blue piece of paper signed in blue ink by Scipio Chatman. The contract Murray had produced during the earlier trial was printed on white paper and signed in different colored ink by James Chatman. E. F. Miller of the Freeman Printing Company testified that he had not printed any white contract forms for Murray until late February 1900, almost four months after the November 1899 signing ceremony. Marion Cato was certain that the Chatman contract had been signed on the November date because he remembered going to see Murray on personal business. He produced as evidence a contract he had signed that day. He swore that the blue Chatman contract contained his signature as witness: the white contract signature that was supposedly his was not.

Murray's lawyer was Marion Moise (ironically the son of the man Murray had defeated in the 1892 congressional race). Moise made a motion for dismissal on the grounds of insufficient evidence. Judge R. O. Purdy refused the motion, so Moise immediately put his client on the stand. The community knew Murray well, but the local newspaper provided a detailed description that simultaneously expressed contemporary attitudes toward him and toward blacks in general. The editor wrote that Murray was "not an ordinary negro in appearance, intellectual ability, education or attainments in the fields of politics and business, in both of which he has won more than the ordinary . . . success and prominence. He is tall, well built, carries himself erectly, and possesses a dignity of manner that is not made ridiculous by the pomposity so frequently displayed by the negroes who regard themselves as better than their fellows."[4]

Murray explained to the court the details of his land operation. He said that he normally first made verbal agreements with prospective tenant-purchasers and then formalized these contracts in writing at a later convenient time. Often, he filled out two contracts at the same time, had them both signed, gave the original to the tenant, and kept the copy for himself, marking it as such. He paid little attention to dating these documents in the belief that exact dating was not important since the verbal agreement had preceded the written one. During the 1903 trial, he had dug out the white paper contract and, seeing that it was not marked as a copy, erroneously concluded that it had to be the original. This is why he introduced it as such in court. But that was inconsequential; the white and blue forms were identical except for the signatures.

Murray then contradicted earlier testimony heard at the trial. The printer had provided him with several lots of white forms before he sold him the February 1900 batch he had mentioned in his testimony. He had asked the Chatmans for five acres of their land to accommodate the Northwestern Railroad and to form the town site of Borden, but the land continued to belong to the Chatmans, and he compensated them fairly for its use. He owned about eight thousand acres in all, and he had made approximately one hundred sales contracts like the one he had made with the Chatmans, and there had never been a problem before. He had treated the Chatmans fairly; when they had remained in default, however, he had had no choice but to evict them.

Murray's wife, Ella, followed him to the stand. She was shown another white paper contract, dated January 1900, two months before the printer had allegedly printed any of that kind. She identified her signature as witness to the contract. Under prosecution pressure, ironically in the person of Harmon D. Moise, a relative of Murray's attorney and the surveyor of large sections of Murray's land,[5] she could not swear that the date on the contract was accurate. Several Sumter whites then testified to Murray's honesty and reliability, and the defense rested.

In its summation, the prosecution emphasized the existence of the two contracts: the blue one containing Scipio Chatman's signature, which was the true document, and the white one containing James Chatman's signature, which Murray had produced during the earlier trial. According to the solicitor, John S. Wilson, this discrepancy indicated Murray's intent. Murray had forged the white contract with James's signature on it in order to regain possession of the land, made more valuable by the new railroad line. The contract's terms stipulated abandonment as one of the causes of default. James Chatman had abandoned the land, while Scipio Chatman had not. Murray's desire to cheat the Chatmans had prompted him to introduce the forged instrument in court.

The defense responded that the Chatmans had violated the contract's terms by defaulting on their payments; Murray did not have to allege abandonment to evict them. In fact, he had leniently waited several years before taking legal action. This forgery accusation, Murray's lawyer, Marion Moise, concluded, was "a conspiracy to damage Murray and put him in serious trouble in revenge for his lawful efforts to secure his rights."

The jury (which one newspaper characterized as "composed of the best men in the country," that is, whites) was supposedly more partial to Murray than to "the ignorant negroes who prosecuted him." Yet this allegedly sympathetic jury took only one hour to find Murray guilty, though recommending mercy. Moise immediately announced his intention to appeal.

The next day, Saturday noon, Judge R. O. Purdy heard what a local newspaper characterized as Moise's "most eloquent and pathetic speech," unfortunately nowhere preserved. Moise's written statement argued that there was insufficient evidence to prove Murray's guilt of uttering a fraudulent document. The original case had "not involve[d] the question as to the validity or invalidity of the paper alleged to have been fraudulently uttered." The terms of the blue and white contracts were the same. Murray gained nothing by introducing the one over the other. Murray "was not seeking to avoid the contract, but was acting under it throughout." His only purpose in introducing the white contract had been to document the terms of the agreement. The jury, in finding him guilty, had not taken into account that Murray had gained nothing by introducing an allegedly fraudulent document. They had also ignored his "good character," a factor with direct bearing on his "intent and motive." Finally, Moise concluded, the prosecution had not proven that Murray had introduced a document he had known was false.

The two prosecutors briefly responded that "no other decision could have been returned by an intelligent and honest jury." The judge agreed. He ruled that Murray's guilt had been proven "beyond a reasonable doubt" and that the evidence warranted that verdict. He fined Murray $250 and sentenced him to three years at hard labor on the county chain gang or in the state penitentiary. A black fifty-five-year-old former congressman could hardly survive the anti-black severity of either confinement. This was a harsh sentence typical of South Carolina justice toward black people during that period. Murray's lawyer immediately applied for bail and gave notice of an appeal to the South Carolina Supreme Court. Judge Purdy set bond at $2,000 and required that two to five persons serve as sureties. Several white businessmen met these conditions, and the sheriff released the convicted former congressman to await the results of the appeal.[6]

The two day trial had attracted a jammed courtroom of interested spectators and reporters.[7] The spectacle of a black former congressman and the county's largest landowner being accused of dishonesty by two of the poor blacks he said he was trying to help caused wide commentary. The South Carolina press saw Murray's guilt as another proof of black venality. The black press, in contrast, split over the issue, being influenced as much by internal conflicts in the black community as by the merits of the case.

The Charleston *News and Courier*, the state's leading white newspaper, feigned sorrow over this alleged reflection on the whole black race, "the elevation and instruction of which the white people of South Carolina have contributed hundreds of thousands of dollars since Reconstruction days." This case and others like it only proved again the ridiculousness of the federal government's long insistence on special rights for blacks "without regard to the rights and interests or welfare of the general community." Even a Northern liberal newspaper agreed. The New York *Evening Post*, whose publisher, Oswald Garrison Villard, would later be a founder of the NAACP, published a stinging attack on Murray. The article said Murray's case proved again that "the inferior races thrown among Caucasians suffer more damage proportionately from men of their own blood than from the Caucasians." "All kindhearted Southerners will agree," said the *Post*, "that the brunt of their trouble in trying to protect the ignorant and helpless negro is caused by the colored brother who is 'smarter.'" Several other northern papers agreed, and the South Carolina press expressed pleasure at such surprising northern insight.[8]

Initially, black newspapers hoped that the reports of the guilty verdict against Murray were incorrect. When it became obvious that the accounts were accurate, most papers questioned the decision. A black Charleston newspaper recalled the earlier lynching scare and pointed to the "jealousy and prejudice" against the ex-congressman because of his ownership of "something like fifty or sixty thousand acres of land." The Cleveland *Gazette*, which had criticized Murray for accepting office from Koester, now attacked other newspapers for devoting excessive space to his legal problems. So much of what was being printed, said the *Gazette*, was "but a rehash from southern Negro-hating daily papers, that are constantly trying to lower our people in the estimation of the people of the world." Most black newspapers saw the trial and decision as a "political scheme" against Murray, "by a jury of 'crackers.'"⁹

Murray did not respond until late June, and then he lashed out, not against white justice, but against T. Thomas Fortune of the New York *Age*. Fortune's discussion of the trial included an alleged conversation he said he had once had with Murray. The ex-congressman had told him, Fortune reported, that even before the passage of Jim Crow legislation he had ridden outside of railroad coaches "to keep from giving offense to white passengers." For the same reason, Murray had confided, he never wore "fine clothes or jewelry." Murray angrily denied these allegations. He wondered why Fortune, "whom I have always admired and honored, should take this mean little slanderous way of striking me below the belt." Fortune's motive was never disclosed, but perhaps it was a delayed repercussion from the Koester controversy. Or, perhaps, this was just another example of the outrageous prose Fortune was famous for. The words attributed to Murray are out of character. Whatever the motive, Fortune's attack showed that Murray did not have unanimous black support in his battle with Palmetto State justice.¹⁰

While he waited for his state supreme court appeal, Murray continued his land dealings. Sumter County records are full of post-trial property transactions between Murray and small tenants like the Chatmans. He also expanded other business operations. In November 1904, he and two other blacks incorporated the Sumter Commercial and Real Estate Company with a capital stock of $10,000. A black reporter, attending a 1905 convention in Sumter, wrote of this "well organized and splendidly managed Investment Company" "doing good business," which had recently built a two-story cement-block building and had established a "Colored Dry Goods Company." Other 1905 reports told of Murray making a $15,000 commercial transaction and completing a land deal worth more than $60,000. According to yet another black reporter, Murray was "safely ahead in the 'get the quality'" race. In Sumter he was considered "more sinned against than sinful."¹¹

Murray's conviction clearly created no significant problems for him. In October 1904, a newspaper mistakenly even announced his appointment to a fourth-class postmastership. In March 1905, he traveled to Washington to support his former business partner, J. Milton Turner, in his candidacy for the position of recorder of deeds. He even visited the White House, though he did not see the president. Murray's conviction did not prevent him from dealing with the highest echelons of government, and the people of Sumter noticed.[12]

There is no indication, however, that he took any part in South Carolina Republican politics during this period.[13] The national convention that June had rejected Lily Whites throughout the South, and the South Carolina Regulars had benefited, although remaining a shell. The Regular Republican Executive Committee announced in September that there would be no state convention or state ticket; Republican electors pledged to Roosevelt were chosen without recourse to the depleted rank and file.[14]

No Republican had even the slightest hope of winning any election. In Murray's old congressional district, the first, the Republican campaign was particularly distressing. Claiming that he already had the nomination, A. P. Prioleau, a perennial candidate under indictment for mail theft, did not even appear at the district convention. A white man, John A. Noland, won the nomination, and the already impotent party split again in a key district. Then there was the white Republican Col. T. Barker Jones. During the convention, he placed himself in nomination by crying: "Ecce Homo—behold the man! I claim to be a Christian statesman and I believe I can reach the hearts of the people all over the district. I am the logical candidate!" He did not receive one convention vote, but he campaigned anyway, repeating his "Ecce Homo" speech and referring to himself as the savior of the Republican Party. In the middle of the campaign, he suddenly decided to campaign for U.S. marshall, though he did not indicate how this action fit into his plan of Republican redemption. Prioleau campaigned by appearing at Noland rallies and winning over the assembled crowds. Noland did not know what to do, and, in the middle of October, he suffered the additional indignity of losing his job at a Charleston retail dry goods store because of his Republican activities. All this would be humorous were it not so tragic. The South Carolina Republican Party was suffering a public collapse from the intense pressure and prejudice it had experienced since the passage of the 1895 constitution. In this campaign Republicans not only projected their frustration on to each other, but their reaction displayed an irrationality, a neuroticism not evident before.[15]

Murray had no time to dwell on the depressing plight of his party, which his own condition continued to mirror. On June 17, 1905, while he awaited the outcome of his appeal, his legal burden increased. Someone named J. Mood Brown swore out a warrant for his arrest, claiming that by introducing the allegedly fraudulent document in the 1903 Chatman eviction case Murray had committed perjury. Murray was arrested, but he was immediately released on bond for later trial. Whatever the unknown accuser's motivation, and it was never made public, even if the state supreme court reversed his forgery conviction, Murray would be right back in court on the perjury charge. On way or another, he seemed destined for prison.[16]

In August of that same year, there was further evidence of a determination to prejudice Murray's case and undermine his reputation. A Sumter newspaper reporter interviewed an Orangeburg black man named Hilliard Bostick, a person the reporter described as "a manly man with limited education, but well informed, with a great big head packed full of good, hard common sense" and "a safe leader of his people." Bostick had known Murray since the ex-congressman's first entry into politics, he said, and Murray had even conducted a political campaign out of his house. He said that Murray's "inordinate love of money" had led to his conviction. Murray had used the funds raised for the 1895 registration court cases to buy land. He was also a shabby dresser. Thomas Miller, said Bostick, now there was a man who never forgot those who had helped him. Old Republican political feuds died hard in the repressive South Carolina climate.[17]

In early September, the harassment crested. While Murray was away on vacation, a fire of unknown origin ravaged his house. A black newspaper blamed the fire on "the rebels of South Carolina," but a local newspaper intimated that Murray was responsible himself because, after all, he had a fire insurance policy on the property. Within the space of eighteen months, then, Murray was convicted of a felony, charged with perjury, accused of assorted wrongs, and suffered the destruction of his house. Even a successful appeal of his conviction would not restore matters to their pretrial status. Like so many other successful blacks, Murray paid the price for his impudence toward white supremacy.[18]

In early October 1905, Murray's appeal failed. The South Carolina Supreme Court reaffirmed the lower court's decision; Murray was guilty as convicted, and he had to serve his sentence. The decision refuted his contentions point by point. Murray's lawyer had argued that the judge had allowed the prosecution more than the legal two peremptory challenges. The supreme court ruled that five such challenges were permissible. The attorney, Moise, had also argued that the decision was unconstitutional. The high court disagreed. Finally, Moise said the judge had erred in not directing a verdict of not guilty because of insufficient evidence. The court responded in detail. The decision said that "in order to constitute forgery by uttering or publishing a forged instrument of writing," these conditions had to be met: "1. It must be uttered or published as true and genuine. 2. It must be known by the party uttering or publishing it as false, forged or counterfeited. 3. It must be uttered or published with intent to prejudice, damage or defraud another person." The court unconvincingly ruled that there was "abundance of testimony to the effect that said writing was forged." "No other than a fraudulent intent can be inferred, when a man makes or passes a false deed, as and for a true one." Finally, testimony showed clearly that Murray was trying to cheat Scipio Chatman out of his land. "The question whether there was a fraudulent intent depended upon all facts and circumstances of the case, and we are unable to say that the verdict is without any testimony to support it." "It is the judgement of this Court, that the judgement of the Circuit Court be affirmed."[19]

Murray had been confident his appeal would be successful, so "he showed much feeling" when he learned of the court's decision from a Columbia *State* reporter on Sumter's main street. He regained his composure quickly, however, and expressed confidence that the court would allow him a rehearing. If it did not, he believed the governor would grant him a pardon at the request of leading Sumter citizens. Few if any people believed him "morally guilty," he said; he had been convicted "on a technical rule of law" and was a "victim of circumstances over which he had no control."[20]

This account of the meeting between Murray and the reporter was fair to the ex-congressman. The editorial in the same newspaper was not, however; it accused him of immorally victimizing "a poor ignorant man of his own race." Murray's attorney found the editorial so offensive that he wrote a long letter in response, arguing that his client was guilty of nothing but "a technical rule of law." He followed this letter with an appeal for a stay of remittitur (a delay on the order sending Murray to jail). He also circulated a petition among Sumter attorneys asking the state supreme court to rehear the case and, if that failed, asking the governor to pardon his convicted client. A rumor circulated that Murray had left the state, but he was actually attending to his usual business in Sumter.[21]

On October 18, Moise made his formal appeal for a stay of remittitur before the author of the previous supreme court opinion, Judge Eugene B. Gary. Moise's argument emphasized the lack of proof that Murray had tried to gain or indeed had gained anything by introducing a forged document in the original 1903 court action. He had only introduced the document to clarify his point, Moise contended: "he was standing upon the contract as set up by the plaintiffs and not against it." His legal problem with the Chatmans in the 1903 case involved interpretation of the contract, not its existence. The court took Moise's appeal under consideration and granted a temporary stay.[22]

While the court deliberated, the press pondered. A Sumter newspaper, which had previously been silent, opposed the talk of a gubernatorial pardon. "To pardon Murray," it said, "would be a miscarriage of justice and a slap in the face of the courts." Murray's successful business life did not earn him any special favors. The Charleston *News and Courier* said Murray's case showed that the claim of discrimination against blacks in southern courts was false. Murray's ability to stay out of prison showed clearly "that if a person has money, race has nothing to do with it." The black Washington *Bee* disagreed. Murray's case was no example of equal justice; it was another indication "of the nefarious acts of Southern demagoguery."[23]

On October 30, 1905, Murray ran out of chances. The South Carolina Supreme Court ruled that "no material question of law has been either overlooked or disregarded" and ordered the enforcement of the lower court sentence. Murray now had only three possibilities, a newspaper taunted: he could "petition for a pardon, run away, or serve his sentence." When Governor Duncan C. Heyward said he had received no petition for a pardon, this option seemed closed. Murray either had to run away or go to prison. Despite the earlier rumor of his departure, the public was sure he would soon be incarcerated. In the penitentiary, one newspaper predicted, Murray would provide the state "a good deal better service than he has ever done before."[24]

The clerk of the Sumter County Court of General Sessions received the remittitur, but then he could not find the ex-congressman. Murray had disappeared. Unbeknownst to the public, he had put all of his holdings into a trust a few days previously and had given Marion Moise, his lawyer, power of attorney. On October 17, less than a week after the original state supreme court decision, he had also turned over eight hundred acres of land plus personal property to Moise because of "personal misfortune" "so that his business affairs may receive prompt and regular attention, and may be wound up in an orderly and proper manner." He directed that his debt be paid in the following manner: the mortgage he had with Moise, taxes, a mortgage with Harby and Company, "other indebtedness," and his wife's living expenses. Murray had probably run away soon after making these arrangements and before Moise had made the appeal for a rehearing. He escaped successfully, and Moise was never accused of any complicity.[25]

No one seemed to know where Murray had gone. Someone guessed Canada, and someone else told the county sheriff that the former congressman had gone to Washington. The Charleston *News and Courier* did not know where he was but called his escape further proof of black-white legal equality; the black man was equal to the white man in his right to run away. Interest in Murray's whereabouts subsided quickly. The last newspaper reference to him on November 4 was a reader's protest of the paper's use of the term "Mr." in a story about the fugitive. "If Murray is worthy of that recognition so is any and every other colored man. Yours for Constancy." The newspaper replied that the reader missed a more significant point; the paper had also referred to Murray as "Honorable," and, considering the contents of the story, "the use of this word was more remarkable." Murray departed South Carolina with a minimum of bother because white society was content to see him go. Like jail, departure separated him from the community, and whites seemed content as long as he was gone.[26]

Murray's case both exemplified and contradicted southern justice for black people. On the one hand, in many southern communities, blacks did not even have the chance to defend themselves in court; they were summarily lynched or thrown on the chain gang without benefit of counsel. On the other hand, the purpose of the justice system was to keep blacks suppressed. In Murray's case, he had benefit of good counsel, yet a white judge and jury found him guilty on specious grounds. The result was the same, no matter how done. A black man, even a well-known successful black man, had no hope in the judicial system.[27]

Several contemporary events help put Murray's case into particular perspective. At that time, he was not the only black public figure facing trial in South Carolina. In 1902, a U.S. District Court grand jury indicted A. P. Prioleau, another former First District Republican congressional candidate, for allegedly stealing while on duty as a mail clerk. Later he was also put on trial for forgery. In June 1903, while waiting for his trial to begin, he demanded protection from the governor against mobs who had earlier murdered his brother and were then threatening his life and property. His trials and appeals dragged on into 1907. In September 1904, a black preacher in Lancaster, South Carolina was accused of changing a $3 check to make it read three hundred dollars. When arrested, he was found to be carrying a concealed weapon, and this crime was added on to the original charge. He was sentenced to a $1 fine and three years on the chain gang or in the state penitentiary.[28]

Prosecution of prominent South Carolina blacks was not, therefore, unusual. As a successful black man apparently growing wealthier each year, Murray was living refutation of the stereotype that all blacks were incompetent.

Any wealthy black man was a threat to a white supremacist society; one like Murray who was simultaneously increasing the number of other successful blacks was an even graver threat. Throughout the South during the 1890s and early 1900s, whitecapping often eliminated successful blacks. Whites drove blacks off the land or from successful businesses. Sumter County, like other communities, had such activities; in 1897 the local newspaper even entitled an article "White Caps in Sumpter."[29] It was not clear until later, but Murray's trial was an example of legal whitecapping, a way to rid the community of a troublesome black. Courts of law, which in 1895 had helped disfranchise Murray out of office, had now driven him out of the state. Like the Republican Party he had been so much a part of, Murray could no longer exist in the Palmetto State.

Tragically, it could have been worse. Murray might have faced the horror that numerous blacks in South Carolina and throughout the South experienced in these years. To cite but one of many examples, Anthony Crawford, the wealthiest black property owner in Abbeville, South Carolina, was summarily stoned, stabbed, dragged through the streets, hanged, and repeatedly shot because he dared argue with a white merchant over the fair price for the black man's cotton seed. A newspaper man justified it all in this way: whites could not tolerate having "a 'nigger' forge ahead of them, and they lay for a chance to jump him."[30]

# In Chicago and on Tour

Though no one seemed to know where George Washington Murray had run to escape South Carolina justice, he had actually traveled to Chicago. Murray's reasons for going there are not clear. In the future, the Illinois city would become a major northern magnet for southern black migration, but as early as 1905 it already had a substantial black population on its South Side. His son always maintained that his father moved to Chicago because he knew numerous black businessmen there and because the former Mississippi congressman John R. Lynch was a resident of the city. In family memories, too, Murray made his escape not from justice but from violence. He was afraid, his family remembered, that he would be killed or he would kill someone defending himself and his property. He left so quickly that he had to sell his land at a loss, they maintained, but he arrived in Chicago with a substantial sum of money anyway.[1]

Murray entered Chicago in 1905 as he had left South Carolina—unnoticed. It was not until June 1906 that a small announcement about him appeared in a black Chicago newspaper. The brief note announced that the ex-congressman George W. Murray would be making a speech before the St. Mark's Church Literary Society, 47th and State Streets, on the "Opportunities of the Literary Societies for Race Development." The stark news release did not indicate how long Murray had been in town or what he was doing. The city directory listed his address as a boarding house at 2840 South State Street, but no other information on him appeared anywhere else.[2]

In 1907, Murray became involved in a substantial black financial venture: he became treasurer of the recently founded Sandy W. Trice and Company department store. The store had a complete line of goods at its 2818 South State Street location, and it enticed customers with Fish Trading Stamps. Sandy W. Trice, the president, had migrated from Tennessee in 1880 and had previously owned a men's clothing store. He was later to become president of the Chicago Colored Men's Business League, the local branch of Booker T. Washington's organization. He was also briefly president of a black newspaper, the Chicago *Conservator*, and, during the 1920s, he was an Illinois Central Railroad red cap and president of the Red Cap Club. The store's secretary was a black lawyer named Walter Farmer, and he may well have been Murray's conduit into the company. Before coming to Chicago, Farmer had practiced law in St. Louis for sixteen years. Perhaps he met Murray or knew of him through Murray's earlier manufacturing arrangement with J. Milton Turner.[3]

The amount of Murray's financial investment in this business and the extent of his duties are unknown. It may be revealing that he patented a hoisting mechanism during these years. Perhaps Murray did more than tally debits and credits; perhaps he was also involved in the physical side of the business. Whatever the case, the store lasted only about three years. In 1910, because of what Trice later called the "dissatisfaction of the stockholders," the business was dissolved.[4]

Murray's personal life during these early Chicago years is similarly unrecorded. He made several housing moves, and on November 25, 1908, he was remarried at St. Mark's Methodist Episcopal Church, the site of his first Chicago speech. His wife Ella had refused to accompany him to Chicago, and, since South Carolina law did not recognize divorce, the two had decided on a permanent separation. The state did not keep marriage license records until well into the twentieth century, so this fact made a mutual dissolution possible. Ella, like George Murray, later remarried without incident.[5]

Murray's new wife was a recent widow who ran "a fashionable boarding and rooming house" at 3254 Wabash. She was a black woman of some wealth named Cornelia Martin. Her husband, a white man, had been killed in a job-related accident at a freight yard, and she had only recently received a settlement of several thousand dollars. According to her family's recollections, she was financially secure and hoped that Murray's position as a former black congressman would gain her entry into black Chicago society. Murray, the remembrance continues, married her for her money.[6]

The available information indicates that by the time of this second marriage, Murray had lost much of the money he had brought from South Carolina. He may well have suffered financially in the department store, and perhaps his investment in the Black Diamond Development Company, a Chicago black business sinking gas wells in Kansas, proved unprofitable. The company had some early successes, but it folded sometime after 1910. When the department store closed, Murray became secretary of Crump's Sanitary Street Sweeping Company at 3704 South State Street; he either still had money to invest, or he had to take a job to make a living.[7]

Cornelia Martin Murray's alleged status seeking is equally hard to document. Whether or not she desired social status, she never gained it. She and her husband were never mentioned in contemporary newspaper accounts of the major social events of Chicago's black community. Ex-congressman though he was, Murray took no part in the social or political life of black Chicago. His job with the street sweeping company also bothered his wife. In later years, long after Murray had died, his son and family were visiting her. Edward Murray spied a sweeper cleaning a nearby street and told his daughter that her grandfather had once worked for such a company. Cornelia angrily retorted that George Washington Murray had been a congressman, not a street sweeper.[8]

In 1909, Murray's former position as congressman was prominently advertised, and it undoubtedly was the reason for his invitation to be "orator of the day" at the August 2 Emancipation Day celebration sponsored by the Colored Men's Industrial League of Milwaukee, Wisconsin. He and his wife traveled to Chicago's neighboring city, where they stayed with a prominent black family and where Murray addressed two thousand people at the celebration. Sharing the podium with Milwaukee's mayor and the city's only black lawyer, Murray told his audience what had been a familiar theme in his speeches: whites and blacks had to recognize that men should be judged on ability not color. Blacks had to rid themselves of inborn color inferiority if they were to become an integral part of American society.[9]

After his speech Murray granted an interview to a local reporter. He was asked to comment on a recent incident involving the assault on a black dining-car waiter by Senator William J. Stone of Missouri. Murray replied that Stone's actions were not indicative of "the best element of statesmen in the South." Sounding like a southern apologist, he praised southern attitudes on race while condemning northern ones. He admitted the prejudice of southern whites but insisted that they were not as obsessed with race as northerners were. In fact, southern segregation helped the black man by forcing him "to deal largely with the members of his own race." A black Chicago newspaper reprinted this interview and excoriated Murray for his comments. Where was all the southern love for the black man, the editor asked, when Murray was forced to escape from South Carolina at night after supposedly selling two hundred thousand dollars worth of property for forty thousand? Murray, the editorial continued, was an example of the "would-be" black leader who loved to defend lynching southerners and to criticize northerners "because they do not lynch a 'Nigger' every morning in the year before breakfast." Blacks would never amount to anything until they produced "some new manly leaders." Black leaders had to "learn to respect themselves before they . . . [could]

command the respect of the people." This sharp attack stung Murray, and he answered in the time-honored way: he accused the Milwaukee reporter of misquoting him. The Chicago *Broad Ax* accepted his denial and counseled him to ask the editor of the Milwaukee paper for a correction, which he apparently never did.[10]

Murray's willingness to appear in public indicates that he had no fear of South Carolina justice. He was a fugitive and susceptible to arrest, but Sumter seemed more interested in obtaining his bail money than in apprehending him. In the Sumter court's April 1906 term, the presiding judge had ruled that Murray's bond was forfeited because of his escape. In March 1907, the county's Board of Supervisors voted to accept a $2,500 settlement on the $2,600 forfeited bonds. After the forfeiture, the seemingly complete trial records in Sumter County indicate no official attempt to locate Murray.[11]

In September 1909, however, South Carolina newspapers suddenly announced that Palmetto State authorities had obtained Murray's arrest in Chicago. The ex-congressman refused to waive extradition, the paper reported, but the governor of South Carolina, Martin F. Ansel, was preparing the proper papers to obtain such a waiver. An unnamed Palmetto State Democratic politician also reported a bribe request for amnesty in return for Murray making a pro-Democratic tour of the West. This proposition, the Democrat indignantly sniffed, had been rejected. Murray had to go to jail.[12]

The extradition attempt bogged down into local and interstate jurisdictional conflicts. Disagreements among newspaper accounts only added to the confusion. Of all the papers discussing the case, the lowly Sumter *Watchman and Southron* provided the most accurate reports. As a hometown biweekly, it not only had the advantage of viewing events first hand, but it was also able to digest the reports of the daily press before printing its own account.

According to press accounts,[13] the sheriff of Sumter County apparently received a telegram from Chicago on Monday, September 21, 1909, indicating that Murray was in custody. (Who instigated the arrest or why it occurred at that time was never reported.) The sheriff's department immediately obtained the necessary court orders to begin extradition proceedings. On Thursday, a deputy sheriff went to Columbia to obtain Governor Ansel's requisition (formal demand) upon the governor of Illinois. Ansel then agreed to furnish the requisition, but he refused to pay for transporting Murray back to South Carolina. He said that Sumter County should use the forfeited bond to cover the expense. During a Saturday morning meeting, the county attorney told the Sumter County Board of Commissioners that the county did not have the authority to pay extradition expenses. The board agreed. The sheriff immediately sent the governor a telegraphic warning that, unless the state paid the expenses, Murray would "be set at liberty." Ansel then agreed to supply the necessary funds. On Sunday, the deputy sheriff and J. H. Grady, the person retained to go to Chicago, went to the state capital, where they obtained two requisitions: one on the forgery conviction and a second on the never-tried perjury charge. Grady then left for Chicago. Murray seemed close to a rendezvous with the chain gang.

That same Sunday, some Sumter citizens began to have second thoughts about Murray's return. They circulated an anti-extradition petition, arguing that the county would be better off with Murray a free man in Chicago than with him a convict or ex-convict in Sumter. His return might make him a hero to the black population. Besides, Murray had paid for his crime by forfeiting his bond and selling his property at a loss. Sumter residents saw no reason to bring him back.

The Sumter County Board of Supervisors received an out-of-state petition from the former Illinois senator William E. Mason, Murray's lawyer, arguing against his client's extradition. He enclosed affidavits contesting the testimony of James and Scipio Chatman, Murray's two black accusers in the original trial. The affidavits, one by James Chatman and the other by a Hampton Peters, swore that unnamed persons had paid the Chatmans $105 to take legal action against Murray. (Peter's affidavit alleged that the Chatmans had earlier told him of this scheme.) Mason also argued that Murray believed the $3,000 bail was a fine and that its payment guaranteed his freedom as long as he stayed out of South Carolina. Finally, Mason said, a group of Chicago blacks had defrauded Murray out of the little money he had been able to take with him from South Carolina, and they now wanted to escape payment by having him placed in jail.[14]

Before Sumter authorities could act on these petitions, J. H. Grady returned empty-handed from Chicago. Senator Mason had convinced the Illinois governor to delay extradition for thirty days so Sumter residents could present their pardon petition to the South Carolina governor. Grady also reported strong pro-Murray feeling in the Chicago area. Blacks there were talking of mobilizing ministers to raise $100,000 on his behalf. They considered him a victim of racial and political persecution. Murray was free on his own recognizance pending the thirty-day delay.

The black and white Chicago press remained silent on the matter. South Carolina papers synopsized the case and supported the petition of Sumter

County residents for gubernatorial clemency. Those who thought Murray was innocent and those who thought he had already paid enough for his crime and did not want him back in the state under any conditions had the right idea, they believed. "Ethically it may not be the best solution to the matter," a Sumter paper concluded, "but practically it is the most desirable."[15]

On October 23, 1909, *The Freeman* of Indianapolis announced that Murray had been "vindicated." "The governor of South Carolina refused to allow Cook County, Illinois any money to prosecute Mr. Murray confessing that there was no case against him in the courts of that state." This announcement, though incorrect, indicated the conclusion of extradition attempts. Precisely what happened is cloudy because neither the South Carolina governor nor his Illinois counterpart left any official documents about the case. The matter was probably handled informally. The two governors accompanied President William Howard Taft on a Mississippi River boat ride in late October and probably discussed the problem face to face. C. S. Deneen, the governor of Illinois, autographed Governor Ansel's October 25 cruise dinner program, proof the men were together. It seems logical to assume, therefore, that they resolved the Murray imbroglio then. As Ansel told a reporter on his return, "It was not altogether a pleasure trip, for the Governors held daily conferences and discussed questions that proved to mutual benefit." Solving the Murray problem was certainly such a matter.[16]

Upon returning from the cruise, Ansel was presented with the now well-known Sumter citizens' petition. The signees included the foreman of the jury that had convicted Murray, a supervisor of the county at the time of the trial, and one of those who posted Murray's bond and received a large chunk of his land in return. The petitioners urged the governor to pardon Murray, clearly indicating the reasons why: "Without comment upon the question as to his conviction, the fairness of the charges or anything of that sort, it appears to us that it would be for the great disadvantage of the white people of Sumter County to bring Murray back and have him undergo his term of imprisonment. If this is done, Murray will be looked upon in the light of a martyr by the negro population and will tend to keep race feelings stirred up." In short, Sumter whites did not want Murray to go to jail because imprisonment would strengthen his role in the Sumter black community. Thereafter the matter simply faded away. The governor did not mention Murray's case in his 1909 report on the year's pardons and commutations, but, at a governor's conference in early 1910, he made a speech on the legal aspects of extradition. No doubt the Murray case had provided him with the necessary expertise.[17]

In Sumter there occurred a shocking finality to the long-fought legal battle. Three months after the controversy had subsided for good, Marion Moise, Murray's lawyer, unaccountably committed suicide. He had recently been upset over a house fire and the accidental shooting of his nephew, but he had given no indication of considering self-destruction. There is no evidence of any connection between this death and the Murray controversy, but it was a symbolic indication that Murray's separation from Palmetto State law was permanent.[18]

Where Murray was jailed during this extradition controversy, how he felt about it, who he blamed for instigating it, what he did to try to maintain his freedom, whether the former senator William Mason was simply his lawyer or whether there was a closer tie, what role if any he played in the Sumter petition, and whether there were any conditions to his freedom are all a mystery. Murray left Chicago after his freedom was insured, and he did not return permanently for ten years. He spent most of his time traveling the country and perhaps visiting Europe. By 1917 he had visited thirty states. One might surmise that he was running from the law, but he kept himself much too visible to be a fugitive from justice. He was a professional lecturer, and his travels were far ranging. He visited Port Arthur, Texas in 1912; Indianapolis in 1915; Richmond in 1917; and Washington, New York, and New Jersey in 1917 and 1919.

When he arrived at a locality, he spent several months there, moving from town to town in the immediate area. During one week in Washington, D.C., for example, he spoke in Culpepper, Virginia on Monday and Wednesday evening, and went to Warrenton on Friday, Saturday, and Sunday. He returned to Washington on Monday. The nearest black newspaper usually carried information on his schedule. Notice of his appearance would normally be placed in the religion section of the paper because he usually spoke at black churches. The brief statement would cite him by name and indicate that he was an ex-congressman (this fact was always mentioned), give the title of his speech, and indicate the time and place of its presentation. The area's white press would normally ignore him as they ignored most other black activities. His departure would receive less notice than his appearance; even the black press rarely mentioned it. Local politicians of both races ignored him, and his speeches provoked no response from any source but the black press.[19]

Murray's 1914 visit to Indianapolis received the widest newspaper coverage of any of his tour stops. *The Freeman* extensively wrote about him, and the city's white paper announced his presence in the column it reserved for black news. These articles give a clue as to Murray's activities during a visit to a specific city. In Indianapolis, he spoke at the black YMCA on two separate evenings under the sponsorship of the Good Citizens League, and he also appeared at Jones Tabernacle, Allen Chapel, and the Second Baptist Church. He and his wife lived with a local black resident during their two-month stay, and Madame C. J. Walker, the black cosmetic millionaire, honored Mrs. Murray with a reception. There may have been other social festivities, but Murray seemed to spend most of his time on the platform. He made an impressive sight—"black but comely," as *The Freeman* described him, about six feet tall, "straight as an Indian," "of good speech, emphatic and enthused with his subject," "a blend of the older Negro and the new." His hair had turned white from age, but he had not lost the striking appearance of his congressional days.[20]

The titles of his speeches varied: "Race Ideals," "The Spiritual Man," "The Second Emancipation," "The Second or Spiritual Emancipation," "Why the Afro-American Is Producing an Undesirable Man in His Native Environment," "Spiritual or Psychological Man," and "The Relation of Philosophy and Psychology to the Solution of the Negro Problem." Newspaper accounts of several of these speeches indicate that although they had different titles they were all basically the same.[21]

The speeches had the same thesis as his pamphlet/book, *Race Ideals: Effects, Causes, and Remedy for the Afro-American Race Troubles*, apparently first published in 1910 and revised at least four more times by 1914. The first version contained thirty-six pages, and the final surviving edition consists of one hundred pages, including twenty-one pages of self-study questions.[22] The book's main aim, like that of Murray's speeches, was to analyze the lowly black role in American society. Unlike Booker T. Washington, who talked of industrial education, W. E. B. DuBois, who emphasized a highly educated "Talented Tenth," Marcus Garvey, who tied black pride to Africa, and William Monroe Trotter, who castigated whites, Murray advocated, as a solution to black subordination, the importance of the spiritual ideals of the black man. If blacks had proper "race ideals," he argued, they would become important members of American society.

In his 1890 Charleston speech, Murray had emphasized economics, but here he said that black feelings of inferiority were the root cause of the inferior status of blacks in American society. He sounded like a black accommodationist, but he emphasized black pride in the psychological terms of his age and did not even infer a continued black subordination. His solution was modern yet old. He sounded like a "black is beautiful" advocate of the 1960s, but he also reflected contemporary black thinkers such as W. E. B. DuBois, Henry M. Turner, and Marcus Garvey, and he applied to blacks Harriet Beecher Stowe's admonition to whites in *Uncle Tom's Cabin*, that is, end slavery by thinking good thoughts. Murray argued that black subordination would end if blacks had good thoughts about themselves. He reflected the predominant ideas of group solidarity, self help, and racial pride prevalent in black thought since Reconstruction, but he gave these ideas a novel modern-sounding twist.[23]

Murray blamed black people's condition in early twentieth-century America on their lack of pride in their blackness. Their "race ideals" were white. Blacks saw whiteness as the norm and their blackness as inferior. Their acceptance of the term "Negro" indicated this self-defeating attitude; a "Negro," Murray said, was neither white nor black, he was nothing—spiritually white and physically black. (To use a later term, Murray was saying a "Negro" was an "Oreo cookie.") The "Negro" was torn between his black outside, which he despised, and his white inside, which directed his being. The proper term was not "Negro." It was "black" or "Afro-American." The "Negro" did not realize this fact.[24]

In contrast to blacks who rejected their blackness and developed a racially "depreciated ego," whites reveled in their whiteness and developed "an extravagant ego or magnified spirit." This difference, Murray insisted, "constitutes the real difference between white men and colored men in this country." Whites and blacks both perpetuated the idea of white supremacy and black inferiority, the black man being "an unconscious propagandist of his own undesirable state." All his models were white, and, since he was black, he always fell short in his own mind. His belief in a white God caused him to wonder "how he will ever reach a heaven filled with white gods and angels." His white attitude made "the ideal woman white, but when he strives to reach the ideal, he is shot down like a mad dog and burned at the stake."

Murray said the black man should be pitied, not blamed, for this attitude. Centuries of slavery had "developed a white man's spirit in a black man's body." The former slaves had gained physical freedom on Emancipation Day, but they were still in spiritual slavery. Another emancipation was needed, a spiritual one. Until the day of spiritual emancipation, Murray insisted (in a gentle slap at Booker T. Washington's philosophy) all the industrial training in the world would not help. Putting a black man in a school that expressed white ideals only maintained his spiritual slavery.

The solution to the problem, Murray insisted, was scientific education. Each student had to be diagnosed in four areas: physical, mechanical, intellectual, and spiritual. Then, he had to be given remedial help where he needed it. In such diagnoses, Murray predicted, "it would be established that traditions and environments had given the southern white child a magnified ego, too much spirit, and the Afro-American child a dwarfed ego or too little spirit." "All educational plans" for the "development and spiritual freedom" of the black child had to be "laid with a view of restoring the spiritual being to a normal state."[25]

This spiritual revival could be accomplished in various ways, Murray advised. From birth, Afro-American children should have "race models" placed in their hands. They should play with black dolls, their rooms should be filled with pictures and paintings of black people,[26] and their books should include black heroes. The textbooks used in their schools should discuss history and literature, and black teachers should be present as role models. In short, Afro-Americans should be taught to think black. The black race "has all the elements of success except the proper pride in itself."

The second way to enhance the black role in society, Murray argued, was through economic training. In slavery, blacks had been kept economically ignorant, and, after emancipation, they had similarly been excluded "from all participation in the economic world above menials and scavengers." Consequently, they spent their money unwisely in white businesses. Like the Negro Business League, Murray argued that blacks needed to realize that money spent in black businesses aided the entire race. Blacks needed to be taught that it was "a great thing to save money, but a greater thing to use it wisely." The black man required this special economic education to "enable him either to break down the [segregation] barriers which prevent him from occupying his place in the general economic world . . . or to establish an independent economic system in which he and his progeny will have a chance to display their genius, prove their commercial equality, and enjoy the resultant fruits of their labor."

The expanded fourth edition of *Race Ideals* put even greater emphasis on proper race attitude as the way to eradicate black subordination. Attacking the pseudo-scientific racism of the early twentieth century, Murray denied that science had found "one atom of difference between the anatomical, physiological or psychological construction of white men and black men." No innate inferiority caused the black man's low societal status; his spiritual deficiency did. Blacks accepted white values and patronized white businesses instead of supporting black values and black businesses. Blacks even used "artificial methods" to try to look white.

Murray absolved whites from any wrongdoing against blacks except for slavery. Jim Crow segregation, for example, would be less oppressive if blacks established and supported their own "decent places of public accommodation and amusement." Whites excluded blacks because of the Afro-American's "objectionable spiritual characteristics," not because of color. Slavery had victimized blacks, but they had to forget that time, develop new race ideals, and improve themselves. They were no different than whites and were capable of self-improvement.

Modern sounding rhetoric aside, Murray was extolling self-help as the solution to black problems. Like Booker T. Washington, he believed that black improvement would result in societal acceptance. He did not consider white racism to be a major problem. He was clearly reacting to the anti-black prejudice he had experienced all his life by internalizing the basic arguments whites used to justify this subjugation in the first place.

This revised edition contains about twenty-five pages of questions, indicating that it was written as a study handbook. In the introduction, Murray urged the formation of reading clubs, asking organizers to write him at "Princeton University, Princeton, Indiana." He promised to register each club and forward new information as appropriate.

Murray's association with "Princeton University" was brief. In 1914, when he arrived in Indianapolis, he was called "dean of the Progressive Psychology Department of Princeton University at Terre Haute." The school was not in Terre Haute; it was located in the small northwest Indiana town of Princeton. It had been founded in 1907 as Princeton Normal College and Industrial University on the Tuskegee Institute model, apparently under the auspices of the local chapter of the Negro Business League. It leased the grounds and the one building of a former poor farm.[27]

Originally, the school was scheduled to begin classes on March 1, 1907, but construction problems delayed its opening until June. A correspondence course had begun on schedule, and a law school was also promised. The original faculty consisted of five instructors and the school president, a black educator from nearby Vincennes. The local press at first showed a great deal of interest in the institution, but newspapers soon ignored it. So too did the important black newspaper published in nearby Indianapolis. In 1911 *The Freeman* printed a long article on black life in Princeton, but it did not mention the school by name. It referred only to a "correspondence school, having many students."[28]

If the figures in the yearly reports of the U.S. Commissioner of Education are to be believed, the school's fortunes rose and fell dizzily. The 1911 report indicated the presence of sixteen teachers and an enrollment of about six hundred students, while the 1912 roll showed sixteen teachers and less than two hundred students. The 1916 report listed only five teachers and seventy-five students, but 1917 saw this increase to seven and two hundred respectively. After 1917, no individual statistics were published, and a search of the *Bureau of Education Biennial Survey* for 1916 to 1926 turned up no mention of the school. The institution apparently faded out of existence. It also disappeared from the community's memory. According to the Princeton town librarian during the 1970s, "No one knows of a Princeton University existing at any time." Like other unsuccessful black institutions, this school had little permanent impact.[29]

When Murray issued the fourth edition of his book sometime in 1914, he no longer listed the school address; now he instructed his readers to write to him in care of his step-son-in-law in Chicago. When he published another book in 1922, however, one of the founders of the school wrote the introduction. Because of Murray's important work, he said, "besides the title of Ph.D., Princeton University Extension school had coined and conferred on him also the title of Psy.D."[30]

Murray's precise relationship to Princeton University is unknown. Was he ever in residence as a faculty member as the 1914 newspaper account seemed to indicate or was his connection less formal? The school apparently at least used his book in some of its correspondence courses. The conferral of a Ph.D. and the invention of a new degree ("Psy.D.") indicates the low academic quality of the institution, and the fact that it was not even an object of curiosity or animosity in its community indicates its lack of importance.

Princeton University's lack of reputation despite Murray's association with it highlights an inescapable fact about him and his long tour of the United States. Like the school, he had little impact. People came to listen to him when he spoke before all black audiences in black churches, but once he departed (and he usually left without fanfare), he apparently left no mark. Contemporaries ignored him, and later historians have similarly not noted his strikingly modern-sounding philosophy. Even black newspaper editors, who commented freely on most matters affecting the black community, had little to say about Murray.

There are only scattered comments on his book and his speeches. *Southern Life Magazine* reviewed his book favorably, particularly approving his call for black teachers, but only one black newspaper mentioned this review or the book itself. During Murray's tour stop in the nation's capital, the editor of the Washington *Bee*, W. Calvin Chase, used Murray's ideas in a long editorial entitled "What Is a Negro?" In phrases taken from Murray's book and speeches, he protested the use of the word "Negro" and demanded the use of the term "Afro-American" instead. The *Bee* praised Murray's ideas grandiosely, but the only other black newspaper to comment on them, *The Freeman*, was less enthusiastic. This paper agreed with his call for black ideals but insisted it was possible only if blacks lived in "experimental communities" away from white ideals. Blacks lived in a multiracial society, *The Freeman* argued, and "after all, there has been efficacy in the white man's ideals." Murray "presents no new thing," *The Freeman* concluded, "nor anything not thought or said before. He simply arrayed his thoughts systematically...." "It would not do to take all on of what he suggests for that would arrest the progress of the race." Perhaps, said *The Freeman*, the Japanese model was a good one—the Japanese were adopting European ways, while simultaneously maintaining their identity. Murray's ideas might make sense in such a context.[31]

Despite such a limited response, Murray remained on tour from late 1909 to 1920. He also frequently returned to South Carolina during this eleven-year period; according to his descendants, he was "back and forth there all the time." He regularly visited his former wife in company with his new wife. In 1909, when his son bought some property and began his medical practice in Marion, South Carolina, Murray helped him with the details. A friend of his granddaughter vividly remembered the day in 1924 or 1925 when Murray appeared with the principal during an assembly at Sumter's Morris College. He embraced his granddaughter in front of the whole school and then gave a speech. In 1915 he even addressed a letter to the Washington *Bee* from Sumter. Murray obviously did not fear South Carolina law because of the forgery sentence, the perjury charge, the extradition fright, or any bigamy accusations. As long as he did not return to stay, he apparently was safe.[32]

In 1920, Murray decided it was time to settle down. By then he was sixty-seven years old, and the grind of almost constant travel was taking its toll. There is no way of knowing when he made Chicago his permanent home or under what monetary conditions he arrived. The first indication of his return was a small notice in a local black newspaper. At the last moment, he appeared as one of the two negative speakers at the Bethel Literary Society debate on U.S. entry into the League of Nations. The brief news account of the debate mentioned that he was an ex-congressman, but it said nothing about his present residence, his book, or his tour. He must have made a favorable impression on his audience because the society (whose president was Murray's former business associate Sandy W. Trice) invited him back to give a speech. This time another former black congressman, John R. Lynch, then a leading citizen of Chicago's black community, introduced him. He also spoke the following week at another black church, but then his activities in Chicago for the next five years were not publicized. He did, however, speak at least at Wendell Phillips High School and in the Hyde Park district of the city.[33]

Once more, Murray was no celebrity in Chicago's black community. His son, Dr. Edward Murray, who had moved to Illinois in 1921, received more public notice than he did. George Murray was mentioned as living in Chicago in a black newspaper article written by Dr. M. A. Majors, the author of the introduction to the 1910 edition of *Race Ideals*, but he was not mentioned in Major's later series of articles on leading blacks in the Windy City. In 1925, a black newspaper briefly summarized his South Carolina political life (the account obviously taken from the *Congressional Directory* of the 1890s), and his congressional speech supporting a federal election law was simultaneously reprinted. The article gave no indication that he lived in Chicago, and it mistakenly placed him in Congress during Reconstruction.[34]

During the 1920s Murray was quietly living in South Chicago at 4725 South Evans Avenue, a middle-class street near the black community's prestigious Grand Avenue (now Martin Luther King Drive). He and his wife purchased the home on October 23, 1920, and it remained in family hands until 1965. (In 1972, the city purchased it, and it was later demolished to allow the widening of a street.) The house was a Victorian-style, two-story, ten-room, gray frame house with a bay window, a tower, and a front stoop at the top of a front flight of stairs. Murray and his second wife, Cornelia, did not live there alone. Cornelia's daughter, Gaynell, and her husband, William J. Burks, an insurance salesman, resided with them. Sometime in the 1920s, Murray and his wife adopted a ten-year-old boy named Donald, who in later years moved to Los Angeles and lost contact with other members of the family. The Murrays were also foster parents for the county, so various children lived with them. (In 1944, years after Murray's death, Cornelia Murray still had two foster children under her care.)[35]

Murray's South Carolina family had gone in various directions. Nothing is known of his brother Prince, but his brother Frank remained a farmer in Sumter County. Murray's first wife, Ella, remarried and continued to live in South Carolina until her death in 1939. She remained in the same house she had earlier shared with Murray until a tornado destroyed the structure in the 1920s.

Murray's daughter, Pearl, married a Baptist minister, the Reverend Pharish Pinckney, and they spent much of their lives in Detroit tending to a church and raising a family of five children. Murray's son, Edward, was a graduate of Biddle College (now Johnson C. Smith University in Charlotte, North Carolina), and, in 1904, he received his M.D. from Meharry Medical College. He set up his first practice in Quitman, Georgia, but practiced medicine in Marion, South Carolina from 1906 to 1921. His first wife died in 1919, and he went to Chicago in 1921, where he met and married Thelma L. Stewart in 1926. In 1930, they moved to Norfolk, Virginia, where he remained a leading eye, ear, nose, and throat specialist until his death in 1956. Edward did a great deal of charity work in addition to carrying on a busy practice. He had one daughter, Louisa, by his first wife and two daughters and a son, June, Thelma, and Edward, by his second. William, a son Murray fathered out of wedlock during his political days in South Carolina in the 1890s, lived most of his life at sea and out of touch with the rest of the family. He suddenly reappeared one day and lived the remaining years of his life in Norfolk near his physician half-brother.

Murray did not stay close to his family nor did he have much of a social life in Chicago. His family remembers that his closest friend was another former Sumter County resident, Ransom W. Westberry, a preacher without a church. Edward lived with Murray when he first arrived in Chicago to practice medicine, but after he moved into his own home they did not see each other regularly. The two men were not close, the result of the long periods of separation when Edward was a young boy and Murray was a leading South Carolina politician. Edward was closer to his mother, often visiting her in South Carolina. Still, he admired his father and later often talked of him to his family. "My dad would buck a circle saw," he would frequently say with pride.

Murray apparently had no outside employment during the 1920s. The city directory for these years lists him as a writer, and apparently he spent most of his time working at this task. In 1922, he borrowed money from his son to print *Light in Dark Places*, volume 1 (listing himself under his home address as publisher). His daughter-in-law and granddaughter remember visiting Chicago in 1944 long after his death and seeing his old desk and two of his trunks in the attic of the Evans Street house. One trunk was filled with some of his old clothes, including a morning coat, and the other one contained books, papers, and at least three other manuscripts. His desk held photographs and more papers. Cornelia Murray would not part with any of this material despite

Edward's repeated requests, and it was apparently lost either when Cornelia died or the house was demolished.

The only available copy of *Light in Dark Places*, volume 1, is in family hands. The book repeats the arguments of *Race Ideals . . .* and the tour speeches, but it goes into much more detail. In 246 pages of text, Murray discussed what the book's subtitle suggests: that man is composed of "Environmental, Mental, Spiritual, Physical and Mechanical" sides, and that all of these elements combine to make him what he is, what he thinks, and how he acts. Man upon birth is a blank tablet and, as he develops these various facets, he also develops what he is and what he thinks. Murray's point is clear: American society is the result of the environmental impact of slavery on both whites and blacks, and consequently their attitudes toward themselves and toward each other are conditioned to admire whiteness and denigrate blackness. Over and over, he insisted, man is the result of environment, not inherited characteristics, but he can change himself by spiritual regeneration. *Light in Dark Places* was Murray's attempt to buttress his *Race Ideals . . .* argument with a more complete explanation of man's total being. The result, unfortunately, is a book whose attack on contemporary scientific racism is nearly lost in a maze of philosophical and pseudo-philosophical verbiage. This book had even less of an impact than his earlier one. It received no mention in the contemporary press, and today it appears in no bibliographies or libraries as the earlier one does. Murray had become so obscure that no one paid any attention to his book. Once the most famous black man in South Carolina and the highest-ranking black politician in the country, he had become an unknown.

In January 1926, he began to complain of excruciating pains in his lower abdomen. His son examined him and immediately took him to a specialist, who ordered him to Wilson Hospital, a small black medical institution in South Chicago. He underwent unsuccessful surgery on April 16, and he died on April 21. The cause of death was "carcinoma [cancer] of prostate and bladder" complicated by "Gen'l carcinomatosis."[36]

His death temporarily restored his fame: he received front-page coverage in the leading black newspaper in Chicago, the *Defender*. The white Chicago newspapers ignored him completely, as did the Chicago *Broad Ax*, the other black newspaper in town. His funeral was held at the large Pilgrim Baptist Church, even though he was a member of the Baptist Metropolitan Community Center. The church was packed. Pastors of various black churches in the area spoke, and the black dignitaries John R. Lynch, Ida B. Wells-Barnett, and

Judge William Hueston of Gary, Indiana were present. One of the honorary pallbearers was A. L. Williams, a leading black politician most famous for his work as an attorney following the 1919 Chicago race riot. The pallbearers were ordinary blacks, perhaps neighbors or friends.

The newspaper account discussed Murray's life, including his political career and his land sales plan in South Carolina. He had come to Chicago, the account read, because of "misunderstanding between him and his foes." Mistakenly too, the article said that several times he had been a delegate to national Republican conventions. He was, the newspaper charitably commented, "well known in political circles here and was on the verge of receiving an appointment from Senator Charles Deneen" (ironically the man who was the governor of Illinois during the extradition proceedings).[37]

Murray was buried in Lincoln Cemetery, the black burial grounds on the city's outskirts. He remained in the poorest part of the cemetery until 1940, when his body was moved into Lot 387 in the newly opened Oddfellows section. His grave is located at the foot of a large monument, but this huge tribute is not to him but to Col. John C. Buckner, a distinguished black military and political leader in Chicago. The Murray family later remembered Edward agreeing to the movement of Murray's body in 1940, and they believed he made a contribution for a suitable monument. They also remembered that he did not attend the accompanying ceremony. There is granite on Murray's grave site, but it is only a cemetery row marker that accidentally happens to be located there. The man who for years was a leading black politician and the owner of vast acreage of land today lies unremembered in an unmarked plot in a black Chicago cemetery. He left no will, and, from all appearances, he died virtually penniless.[38]

# Conclusion

George W. Murray and the South Carolina Republican Party fought long and hard, yet they failed completely. Murray died a penniless man and was buried in an unmarked grave far from the scenes of his political triumphs and defeats. The South Carolina Republican Party ceased being an effective political force until its resurrection as a white conservative entity in the 1960s. The Palmetto State was not alone in seeing its black politicians defeated and its Republican Party destroyed because disfranchisement movements existed in every southern state in the late nineteenth century and the early twentieth. Every Republican Party in the South was marginalized during these years. The Republican demise throughout the South does not explain the failure of Murray and his South Carolina Republican colleagues, but it does place that failure into context. Republican failure in South Carolina was neither unique nor does it reveal a peculiarly glaring incompetence.

Still, the belief remains that in South Carolina, Republican corruption, incompetence, and venal lust for office were singularly responsible for the party's demise. This is simply not accurate. The private lives of the Republican leaders clearly suggest that political greed was not at the heart of their politics. Many were financially secure from nonpolitical sources, so, as a group, they were not in politics to gain financial success through patronage jobs. Some no doubt benefited financially from their political participation, but most would have done better out of politics or as Democrats. Wallace, Melton, or Capers would have been honored members of their communities had they not been Republicans, but instead they suffered ostracism and other indignities, and such treatment was personally and financially draining. Black Republican leaders, who were already ostracized because of their race, were further stigmatized because of their Republican activities. Republican leaders were no paragons of virtue, but to equate their concern for black political participation only with selfish motives is to ignore the facts and accept white supremacy ideology.

The systematic disfranchisement of most black voters in the late nineteenth century and the early twentieth meant that federal patronage and participation in national nominating conventions was the only available political opportunity for South Carolina Republicans. It is only reasonable, therefore, that they should try to stay in existence by utilizing these political options, the only ones open to them. They reached out for anything that might save them, and, in the process, like other doomed people, they fought among themselves. Fighting over a life raft does not cause a ship to sink; the intra-party battles and the striving for patronage did not sink the Republican Party. Had Republicans never disagreed on anything, white hostility would still have destroyed their party. In their frustration over their hopeless predicament, Republicans exhibited a wide range of unflattering human reactions, but these reactions did not cause their destruction. These reactions exemplified their humanity rather than proved abnormal incompetence and mediocrity.

As this book has argued, Republican factionalism was not the result of color, economic, geographic, philosophical, or patronage differences. South Carolina Republicans angrily battled at their conventions, factionalized, and disputed with one another over patronage, and in doing so they were displacing their frustration-spawned aggression. Hounded out of the political process by white society's legislative and constitutional assaults, constantly threatened with physical, economic, and social harm, South Carolina Republicans had few available channels open to them to vent their frustration. Consequently, they displaced the aggression they felt toward white South Carolina society to one another. Divisions occurred and factional opponents were fought sometimes because of valid disagreements but more often because of bottled-up anger over white society's intense and continuous discrimination. Republicans fought other Republicans because they were unable to battle their true opponents.

South Carolina Republicans did not respond to their problems alone. During the 1880s, a group of New England reformers advised Benjamin Harrison to intervene in South Carolina, but, like them, he could do little to improve the position of Republicanism in the Palmetto State. Later, William McKinley, Theodore Roosevelt, and Mark Hanna all personally attempted to strengthen the party in the state, but the only result was more frustration and more failure. If persons of superior political talents could not solve let alone even understand Palmetto State Republican problems, it is not surprising that the less accomplished men on the scene were equally frustrated.

The actions of the Republican hierarchy in Washington, in fact, added to the South Carolina Republican burden. National Republicans worried less about improving the lives of their Palmetto State supporters and more about strengthening the party there for national purposes. The national party needed South Carolina and other southern state parties only to gain nominating convention votes and to keep northern black voters in the fold. What happened to the rank and file was not important. Consequently, Palmetto State Republicans were not only frustrated by the racism of their enemies but also by the manipulation of their alleged friends. They displaced the resulting frustration to one another.

It might be argued, however, that if Republicans had only been wise enough to recognize the inevitability of black disfranchisement and determined enough to establish a white party in South Carolina, such a party would have survived, and the frustration-producing prejudice would have been eliminated. This was precisely the argument advocates of several Lily White Republican strategies used in the South. The problem with this scenario is that it presupposes black willingness to leave politics and white willingness to become Republican. An all-white South Carolina Republican Party would have required blacks to turn over their party to white men willingly, and whites to flock eagerly into the GOP fold. Neither was feasible. Blacks refused to step aside voluntarily, and whites did not step forward eagerly. When Palmetto State Democrats talked of politics for whites only, they meant white Democrats like themselves. The reaction to John McLaurin's and John Capers's Republican efforts show this attitude clearly. Republicans of any color or persuasion were not welcome in the state.

In short, there was nothing Palmetto State Republicans could do to insure their survival. They tried various means to become viable, some wise, some unwise, but they always failed. The race issue and the anti-Republican feelings were too strong to permit any success. Republican failure was the result of white racism, not GOP venality and incompetence.

George W. Murray's political career is understandable within this context, while also illuminating to it. As a black Republican, Murray carried a double burden; he was an unwelcome part of the state's political process both because he was black and because he was a Republican. Still, he resolutely strove to have a political career. In his successes and in his failures, he mirrored the fortunes of the entire state party. He was its most militant spokesman; he was its highest-ranking elected official; he served on its Executive Committee; he chaired its conventions; he was prominent in its splits; and he led its major battle against disfranchisement. When the party reached its nadir, he dejectedly withdrew, only to be called back as a compromise patronage candidate during a major controversy. He then withdrew again when he failed to serve his compromise function. In the end, he found himself on the outside looking in. He displaced his final frustration by supporting a dissident attempt to prevent the 1904 rapprochement between two Republican leaders, Edmund Deas and John Capers.

George W. Murray was a leader of the South Carolina Republican Party, and thus he shared major responsibility for that party's failure. His particular reaction to the discrimination against him reflected general Republican reaction to the prejudice they faced. Like other state GOP leaders, he was not an incompetent; in fact he displayed obvious political abilities. His experiences on his farm, in education, with the Colored Alliance, in county politics, and with patronage provided him with a solid background when he entered congressional politics. He had learned on the stump how to speak his mind forcefully and fearlessly, and he recognized the necessity for political compromise and change. He was an advocate of black pride, yet he was willing to work with several so-called Lily White factions when he saw them as the best hope for the state GOP. He recognized the dominance of the Tillman forces and cleverly tried to cultivate their favor. When he believed a free silver stand would enhance his political position, he bucked national Republican policy and backed silver. Later he needed national Republican support, so he had no trouble extolling gold. His congressional district was gerrymandered, so he quickly organized his candidacy in the new district. He was not even above using dirty tricks in the form of oral and written propaganda. He recognized early the danger to his constituents and his race from the South Carolina constitution and militantly organized the opposition effort. He tirelessly fought a legal battle all the way to the U.S. Supreme Court. Failing there, he even threatened to stop the electoral count of his party's own president. Despite the prejudice he faced, Murray exhibited many of those characteristics associated with a successful partisan politician. He was clever, pragmatic, hard working, untiring, dedicated, ambitious, and demagogic. Had he been a white Democrat, he would have been a success. But he had the wrong skin, and he belonged to the wrong political party to succeed in South Carolina.

Murray's nonpolitical life also indicated his wide-ranging abilities and his consuming drive to overcome prejudice and be a success in white society. He was an advocate of black pride and used these exhortations to encourage blacks to develop the inner strength he felt they needed to survive in white society. His invention patents, his railroad deals, and especially his land plan were all attempts to make himself wealthy and, at the same time, gain a measure of political and economic status for other blacks. Murray's prosecution on forgery charges and eventual acceptance of his removal rather than his incarceration indicate that his land plan was probably working. Successful outspoken blacks, who were continually attempting to overthrow the system, were dangerous and had to be removed.

Murray's post–South Carolina years saw him continue his efforts to survive as an oppressed black member of white society. He wrote books, and he gave speeches that, in strikingly modern prose, emphasized the basic worth of black people and their rightful place in the United States. In these years, he played no role in politics. Yet he still symbolized the plight of his former party. Like it, he had become inconsequential; he gave speeches and perhaps people listened, but they certainly did not hear or remember, nor were they impressed. Like the South Carolina Republican Party, Murray did not receive much attention after 1905; he was an echo from the past with little to say to a present that had effectively eliminated blacks and southern Republicans. Even in death he was unheralded. By 1926 there had been no black congressman for twenty-five years, and the South Carolina Republican Party had long since ceased to play even a token role in the state's politics.

Both George W. Murray and the South Carolina Republican Party ultimately failed. Yet in their failure they tell us much about the society in which they lived and the people, white and black, who inhabited it. In a wider perspective, they tell us that, despite overwhelming odds and dangers, human beings do continue to battle—though not always in the most efficient way. That Murray and the South Carolina GOP failed was not a mark of their deficiency as much as it was the result of the unbending racism they faced. Disfranchisement and failure in South Carolina came not because of acquiescence, incompetence, or venality, but because of the brute power of uncompromising racism.

# Appendix: Late-Nineteenth-Century South Carolina Republican Leaders

| Name | Birth Date | Birth Place | Residence | Education | Occupation | Political Position |
| --- | --- | --- | --- | --- | --- | --- |
| *Regular Republicans* | | | | | | |
| Adams, J. D. | 1860 | Laurens County | ? | ? | Merchandise clerk; Traveling salesman | Dep. U.S. marshall for S.C. 1902; Dep. coll. of Internal Revenue, S.C. 1902–3; U.S. marshall for S.C. 1905 |
| Crum, William D. | 1859 | Charleston County | Charleston County | Avery Norman Inst. 1875; Howard Univ. Medical School 1881 | Physician; Various business enterprises | Charleston customs coll. 1903–9; Minister to Liberia 1910–12; State Republican official 1880s to 1900s |
| Cunningham, G. I. | 1834 | E. Tenn. | Charleston County | ? | Cattle driver; Grocery owner; President of Charleston Water Works; Bd. of Dir. of Charleston Savings Institution; Real estate | Charleston alderman 1868; Charleston mayor 1873 (2 terms); Charleston Bd. of Commissioners; Chairman (3 terms); U.S. marshall for S.C. 1889–93, 1902; Charleston postmaster 1898–1902 |

| Name | Birth year | Birthplace | County | Education | Occupation | Career |
|---|---|---|---|---|---|---|
| Deas, E. A. | 1855 | Georgetown County | Darlington County | ? | Politician | Dep. coll. of Internal Revenue, S.C. 1884–1901; State Republican Party chairman, official, candidate, 1870s to 1900s |
| Ensor, J. P. | 1834 | Butler, Maryland | Richland County | ? | Physician | Freedmens Bureau physician 1868–; Supt. of state hospital 1870–78; Columbia postmaster 1897–1907 |
| Johnston, T. B. | 1838 | Ireland | Sumter County | ? | Brevet Major 6 Mass. Regt.; Extensive property holdings | Sumter provost marshall (appointed by Grant); S.C. legislator; Sumter postmaster (appointed by Grant); Charleston customs coll. 1881–85, 1889–93 |
| Lathrop, Abial | 1845 | Western New York | Orangeburg County | ? | Lawyer (in N.Y, Ill., S.C.); Bank director; Director of Electric Light Company; Director of a wood and material company | U.S. Circuit Court commissioner 1878–89; U.S. attorney for S.C. 1889–93; 1897–1901; Orangeburg City Council; Orangeburg mayor 1893–99 |
| Miller, Thomas C. | 1849 | Beaufort County | Beaufort County | Lincoln Univ. (Penn.) | Lawyer; College president | Beaufort school commissioner 1872; S.C. legislator 1874–86, 1886, 1888, 1894; U.S. congressman 1890–91; S.C. constitutional conv. 1895; State Republican Party official, candidate, 1870s to 1890s; College president 1896–1911 |

*continued*

| Birth Name | Birth Date | Place | Residence | Education | Occupation | Political Position |
|---|---|---|---|---|---|---|
| Smalls, Robert | 1839 | Beaufort County | Beaufort County | no college | Sailmaker; Ship pilot; Landowner | S.C. constitutional conv. 1868; S.C. legislator 1868–75; U.S. congressman 1875–79, 1882–83, 1884–87; Beaufort customs coll. 1889–93; 1898–1913 |
| Tolbert, John R. and R. R. | ? | S.C. | Abbeville County | ? | Slave holders; In Confederate Army; Owners of several thousand acres of land | County commissioner of education during Reconstruction (John R.); Charleston customs coll. 1898–1900 (John R.); State Republican Party chairman 1898–1900 (R. R.); State Republican Party officials and candidates 1870s to 1890s |
| Wallace, R. M. | 1837 | York County | Sumter County | Erskine College | Lawyer; Confederate Army P.O.W.; President of Nat. Bank of Sumter; Official of Sumter Cotton Mills, Sumter Telephone Co., Sumter Electric Light Co., ice plant | Coll. of Internal Revenue S.C. 1868 (succeeded his father); U.S. marshall for S.C. 1872–76 (?); Charleston customs coll. 1900–1902 |

| Name | Birth year | Birthplace | County | Education | Occupation | Political career |
| --- | --- | --- | --- | --- | --- | --- |
| Webster, E. A. | 1849 | Montpelier, Vermont | Orangeburg County | Wesleyan Univ. 1872; Wesleyan Univ. Masters degree 1875 | Teacher in S.C. 1866–68; Claflin College Faculty 1875–77; Founded and ran newspaper 1875–77; Lawyer; Active in ME Church | Orangeburg Co. trial justice 1876; Orangeburg Co. treasurer 1876; Coll. of Internal Revenue S.C. 1889–93, 1897–1901; State Republican Party chairman, official, 1870s to 1900s |
| *Reform Republicans* | | | | | | |
| Blaylock, L. W. C. | ? | S.C. | Newberry County | ? | Secretary and treasurer of a cotton mill | Mayor of Newberry |
| Brayton, Ellery M. | 1843 | Augusta, Ga. | Richland County | Brown Univ.; Harvard Law School | Lawyer | Coll. of Internal Revenue, S.C. 1880–85; State Republican Party chairman, official, and candidate, 1880s to 1900s |
| Capers, John G. | 1866 | Anderson County | Pickens County | Various prep schools and The Citadel | Lawyer; Columbia *Journal* editor 1893 | Greenville supt. of education 1887–89; State Militia captain; Ass't U.S. attorney at Washington, D.C. 1894–1901; U.S. attorney for S.C. 1901–5; U.S. commissioner of Internal Revenue 1907 |

*continued*

| Birth Name | Birth Date | Place | Residence | Education | Occupation | Political Position |
| --- | --- | --- | --- | --- | --- | --- |
| Koester, George R. | 1870 | Philadelphia Penn. (moved to Charleston at 3 mos. of age) | Richland County | Charleston public schools; Furman Univ. | School teacher 1887; Reporter 1888–; Founded Columbia *Record* 1897 | Coll. of Internal Revenue, S.C. 1901–2 |
| McLane, J. Hendrix | 1848 | Jackson County, Ga. | Fairfield County | Tufts Univ. | Farmer; Agrarian protester; Agrarian newsman; Ministerial student | Dem. and Greenback politician; Independent candidate for governor 1882; Independent candidate for Congress 1884; Independent movement organizer |
| Melton, Lawson D. | ? | S.C. | Richland County | ? | Lawyer | State Republican Party chairman and official 1890s |
| Murray, G. W. | 1853 | Sumter County | Sumter County | Univ. of S.C. | Farmer; Teacher; Landowner; Inventor | U.S. congressman 1893–97; Dep. coll. of Internal Revenue, S.C. 1901–2; State Republican Party official, candidate, 1880s to 1900s |

# Notes

## Preface

1. Samuel Denny Smith, *The Negro in Congress, 1870–1901* (Chapel Hill, 1940), 143–44.

2. James Welch Patton, "The Republican Party in South Carolina, 1876–1895," in *Essays in Southern History*, ed. Fletcher M. Green (Chapel Hill, 1949), 93, 95, 96, 99.

3. Harris M. Bailey, Jr., "The Only Game in Town: The South Carolina Republican Party in the Post-Reconstruction Era," *Proceedings of the South Carolina Historical Association* (1992): 86.

## Chapter 1. From Slavery to Public Life

1. Anne King Gregorie, *History of Sumter County* (Sumter, S.C., 1954), 132–35.

2. Ibid., 136–37, 139–40.

3. Ibid., 143–44, 244.

4. John F. Marszalek, "Resistance, Slave," in *Dictionary of Afro-American Slavery*, ed. Randall M. Miller and Josh David Smith (New York, 1988), 635–41.

5. Gregorie, 249–50.

6. Ibid., 259–71.

7. The sketch of Murray's early life found in this chapter, unless otherwise noted, is based on material available in the following sources: U.S. Congress, *Congressional Directory*, 53rd Cong. 1st, 2nd, 3rd sess., 54th Cong., 2nd sess.; Interview with Thelma L. Murray and June M. Davis, George Washington Murray's (GWM's) daughter-in-law and granddaughter, Norfolk, Va., November 30, 1973; *The Freeman*, March 25, 1893; Washington *Star*, October 28, 1893; Gregorie, 396; D. W. Culp, ed., *Twentieth Century Negro Literature* (New York, 1969), 230–31.

8. A Rafting Creek farmer named L. B. Murray was related to G. W. Murray, but the degree of relationship is unknown. *Johnston v. Stokes* (Washington, 1896), 288; see also U.S. Congress, House, HR 1229, 54th Cong., 1st sess. (1896).

9. This overview of black life in post–Civil War South Carolina is based on the following: Joel Williamson, *After Slavery: The Negro in South Carolina During Reconstruction, 1861–1877* (Chapel Hill, 1965); George B. Tindall, *South Carolina Negroes 1877–1900* (Baton Rouge, 1966); I. A. Newby, *Black Carolinians: A History of Blacks in South Carolina from 1895 to 1968* (Columbia, 1973).

10. Thomas Holt, *Black over White: Negro Political Leadership in South Carolina during Reconstruction* (Urbana, Illinois, 1977).

11. Map of Sumter County, South Carolina (1878) preserved in South Caroliniana Library, University of South Carolina (SCL, USC).

12. *Tindall*, 216–17. For other accounts of the problems of South Carolina education during this period, see Edgar W. Knight, "Reconstruction and Education in South Carolina," *South Atlantic Quarterly* 28 (October 1919), 350–64 and 19 (January 1920): 55–56; and Henry A. Bullock, *A History of Negro Education in the South From 1610 to the Present* (New York, 1967).

13. See Daniel W. Hollis, *University of South Carolina* (Columbia, 1956), vol. 2; Williamson, 232–33, 236. For a thoroughly hostile account of the 1870s university see Edwin L. Green, *A History of the University of South Carolina* (Columbia, 1916), 410–15. For a more sympathetic view, see the essays in James Lewell Underwood and W. Lewis Burke, Jr., eds., *At Freedom's Door: African American Founding Fathers and Lawyers in Reconstruction South Carolina* (Columbia, S.C., 2000).

14. Faculty Minutes Book, October 5, 1874, SCL, USC. Under white control in 1893–94, the university's enrollment was only sixty-eight students. Diane Neal, "Benjamin Ryan Tillman: The South Carolina Years, 1847–1874," (Ph.D. diss., Kent State University, 1976), 239–41.

15. Faculty Minutes Book and assorted documents, Folios 51 and 86 and Boxes 17 and 18, SCL, USC.

16. Ibid., Box 17, GWM to Faculty, January 4, 1876; GWM to Professor Brewer, chairman of faculty, March 7, 1877 in ibid., Box 18,; petition is preserved in Box 18.

17. Faculty Minutes Book, ibid. In the *Congressional Directory* biographical sketch mentioned in note 1 and in *The Freeman*, March 25, 1893 account, GWM listed himself as a junior. The records do not indicate that he reached that level. This mistake is repeated by A. A. Taylor, "Negro Congressman a Generation After," *Journal of Negro History* 7 (April 1922): 133.

18. Gregorie, 339–40.

19. Eric Foner, *Reconstruction, America's Unfinished Revolution 1863–1877* (New York, 1988), 570–75; Gregorie, 349; Walter Edgar, *South Carolina, A History* (Columbia, S.C., 1998), 407–14. For Benjamin R. Tillman's role in the Hamburg Massacre, see Stephen Kantrowitz, *Ben Tillman and the Reconstruction of White Supremacy* (Chapel Hill, 2002), 64–71.

20. Murray-Davis interview.

21. U.S. Census, *Agriculture, Industry, Social Statistics and Mortality Schedules for South Carolina, Pickens-Sumter Counties*, Tenth Census, 1880, deposited in South Carolina Department of Archives and History (SCDAH); Murray's holdings and production indicate he did as well as or better than the average farmer in Sumter County. He owned sixty-four acres whereas 70 percent of all farms in the county were forty-nine acres or less (48 percent of the farms cultivated by owners were one hundred acres or more; 20 percent were fifty to ninety-nine acres). The value of Murray's farmland and buildings amounted to $23.43 per acre compared to the county average of $5.35 per acre. His yearly farm production was $10.15 per acre compared to the county average of $4.02 per acre. His cotton, corn, and wood production was slightly better than the county average, and his egg and butter production was slightly less. In short, when compared to all black and white farmers, he was probably a better than average farmer

for his time and his county. Considering that these county figures included various types of farms and considering that the validity of the farm-holding figures of the 1880 census has been disputed (see, e.g., Fred Shannon, *The Farmers' Last Frontier: Agriculture, 1860–1897* [New York, 1945], 81) these statistics must be treated cautiously. For an in-depth analysis of black southern farming during these years, see Roger L. Ransom and Richard Sutch, *One Kind of Freedom . . .* (Cambridge, 1977). See also Orville Vernon Burton, "African American Status and Identity in a Postbellum Community: An Analysis of the Manuscript Census Returns," *Agricultural History* 72 (spring 1998): 213–40.

22. U.S. Census, Tenth Census, 1880, Sumter County, Microcopy T-9, Roll 1241, p. 213. See note 20 for agricultural schedule reference. Unfortunately this author was unable to discover, in the SCL, USC, or the National Archives and Records Administration (NARA), any records pertaining to Murray's Census Bureau service. For discussion of the South Carolina Republican Party in the post–Civil War period, see Thomas Holt, *Black over White: Negro Political Leadership in South Carolina During Reconstruction* (Urbana, 1977); Tindall, 41–54; William J. Cooper, Jr., *The Conservative Regime, South Carolina 1877–1890* (Baltimore, 1968); James W. Patton, "The Republican Party in South Carolina 1876–1895," in *Essays in Southern History,* ed. Fletcher M. Green (Chapel Hill, 1949); and Harris M. Bailey, Jr., "The Only Game in Town: The South Carolina Republican Party in the Post-Reconstruction Era," *Proceedings of the South Carolina Historical Association* (1992): 76–86.

23. See John F. Marszalek, *Court-Martial: A Black Man in America* (New York, 1971), paperback edition is *Assault at West Point* (New York, 1994). See also Marszalek, "A Black Cadet at West Point," *American Heritage* 22 (August 1971), 30–37, 104–6.

24. Charleston *News and Courier*, April 28, 29, 30, 1880.

25. Ibid., March 3, 8, 10, 1882; Edgar, 414.

26. The Seventh Congressional District (the "Black District") consisted of Orangeburg, Beaufort, Georgetown, Sumter, Colleton, and parts of Berkeley, Williamsburg, Richland, and Charleston Counties.

27. Charleston *News and Courier*, September 22–28, 1882; Columbia *Register*, September 27, 28, 1882.

28. Charleston *News and Courier*, September 20, October 14, 1882; circular in Republican Party Papers, SCL, USC; Charleston *News and Courier*, November 10, 1882; Gregorie, 358.

29. George B. Tindall, "The Campaign for the Disfranchisement of Negroes in South Carolina," *Journal of Southern History* 15 (May 1949), 216; Sumter *Watchman and Southron*, February 26, March 4, 1884.

30. Charleston *News and Courier*, March 11, April 16, 1884.

31. Ibid., September 17, 25, 1884; Sumter *Watchman and Southron*, September 7, December 2, 1884; Columbia *Register*, November 27, 1884; *The Freeman*, March 25, 1893.

32. Sumter *Watchman and Southron*, February 3, 1885, February 2, 9, 1886, February 3, 1887, February 7, 1888, February 6, 1889, May 21, 1890, May 30, June 6, 1882, May 8,

1883, June 17, 1884; *The Freeman*, March 25, 1893; Charleston *News and Courier*, September 10, 1883.

33. Charleston *News and Courier*, April 7, 23, May 2, 1888; Columbia *Register*, April 22, 1888.

34. Charleston *News and Courier*, August 21, 1888.

35. S.C. *Reports and Resolutions* 1888, 1: 556–64; Charleston *News and Courier*, October 1, 1888.

36. GWM to Benjamin Harrison, November 26, 1888, microfilm reel 59, Benjamin Harrison Papers, Library of Congress (LC).

37. Ellery M. Brayton, *An Address Upon the Election Law of South Carolina and the Methods Employed to Suppress the Republican Vote* (Columbia, 1889).

38. This overview of Republican policy toward the South is based on Vincent P. DeSantis, *Republicans Face the Southern Question 1877–1897* (Baltimore, 1959), and Stanley Hirshon, *Farewell to the Bloody Shirt . . .* (Bloomington, 1962).

39. See unpublished pamphlet written by McLane's son-in-law: Herbert J. Seligmann, "A South Carolina Independent of the 1880's J. Hendrix McLane," J. Hendrix McLane Papers, Yale University Library. SCL, USC also has a copy of this pamphlet.

40. See, for example, Edmund H. Deas to Harrison, January 8, 1889, Ellery M. Brayton to Harrison, January 10, 19, 1889, GWM to Harrison, January 8, 1889, microfilm reels 15 and 16, Harrison Papers, LC.

41. Charleston *News and Courier*, October 20, June 26, August 6, 10, 1889; Washington *Bee*, June 15, 1889; McLane Diary, June 22, July 26, 1889, McLane Papers, Yale University Library; see both DeSantis and Hirshon for fuller discussions of these Republican national plans.

42. *The Freeman*, March 25, 1893.

43. For accounts of blacks in the farmer movements, see Jack Abramowitz, "The Negro in the Agrarian Revolt," *Agricultural History* 24 (April 1950): 89–95; Herbert Shapiro, "The Populists and the Negro, a Reconsideration," in *The Making of Black America*, 2 vols., ed. August Meier and Elliott Rudwick (New York, 1969), 2: 27–36; Floyd J. Miller, "Black Protest and White Leadership: A Note on the Colored Farmers' Alliance," *Phylon* 33 (summer 1972): 169–74; William F. Holmes, "The Demise of the Colored Farmers Alliance," *Journal of Southern History* 41 (May 1975): 187–200; Robert C. McMath, *Populist Vanguard: A History of Southern Farmer's Alliance* (Chapel Hill, 1975); Joseph Church, "The Farmers' Alliance and the Populist Movement in South Carolina, 1887–1896" (master's thesis, University of South Carolina, 1953). South Carolina does not have a listing in Henry C. Dethloff, ed., *A List of References for the History of the Farmers' Alliance and the Populist Party* (Davis, 1973); Francis Butler Simkins, *Pitchfork Ben Tillman, South Carolinian* (Baton Rouge, 1944), 147–48, 204; Neal, "Tillman," chapter 7; Tindall, *South Carolina Negroes*. 117–19.

44. Simkins, 204; Neal, 140–44; Tindall, *South Carolina Negroes*, 117–19; Charleston *News and Courier*, May 10, 1888, April 25, June 20, 21, 1889; Cleveland *Gazette*, July 13, 1889 cites the forty thousand figure.

45. Sumter *Watchman and Southron*, September 18, 1889; Charleston *News and Courier*, September 11, 1889.

46. Charleston *News and Courier*, November 9, 10, 1889, February 28, August 29, 1890, January 12, September 10, 1891; Sumter *Watchman and Southron*, November 13, 1889; Cleveland *Gazette*, May 3, 1890, July 18, 1891; Columbia *State*, August 14, 1891; Holmes, 196–99; Neal, 148.

47. Charleston *News and Courier*, June 27, July 17, 1890.

48. Ibid., December 8, 1890, May 22, 1891; New York *Age*, July 12, August 2, 1891.

## Chapter 2. The 1890 Election: Success and Failure

1. In his speech at the inaugural meeting of the Farmers Association, Pitchfork Ben Tillman had similarly referred to the farmers' problem of mental and physical slavery. Francis Butler Simkins, *Pitchfork Ben Tillman, South Carolinian* (Baton Rouge, 1944), 102.

2. For examples of South Carolina's black leaders making similar pro-business exhortations in 1883 and 1898, cf. George B. Tindall, *South Carolina Negroes, 1877–1900* (Baton Rouge, 1966), 140.

3. GWM, *An Oration Delivered in the City of Charleston on the Twenty-Seventh Anniversary of the Emancipation Proclamation* (Charleston, 1890).

4. See Louis R. Harlan, *Booker T. Washington: The Making of a Black Leader, 1856–1901* (New York, 1972), 225, 269; see also ibid., 266–67 for a discussion of W. E. B. DuBois' similar words in 1899.

5. See chapter 11 for a discussion of GWM's 1910 to 1922 speeches and writings on the same topic; Columbia *Register*, January 2, 1890; GWM to T. B. Johnston, January 2, 1890, U.S. Customs Records, R.G. 56, NARA.

6. Charleston *News and Courier*, January 3, 1890; Columbia *Register*, January 3, 1890.

7. Simkins, *Tillman*, 138–51; Diane Neal, "Benjamin Ryan Tillman: The South Carolina Years, 1847–1894" (Ph.D. diss., Kent State University, 1976), 152–66. Stephen Kantrowitz, *Ben Tillman and the Reconstruction of White Supremacy* (Chapel Hill, 2000) discusses Tillman's attack on both black and white opponents and agrees with the premise of this book that whites in South Carolina agreed on the suppression of blacks and differed not in that goal but in the way to achieve it.

8. The following discussion of Democratic factionalism is based on Simkins, 93–309, and William J. Cooper, Jr., *The Conservative Regime 1877–1900* (Baltimore, 1969).

9. Simkins, vii.

10. Walter Edgar, *South Carolina, A History* (Columbia, 1998), 436, 439.

11. Ellery M. Brayton to Benjamin Harrison, February 27, 1890, microfilm reel 25, Benjamin Harrison Papers, LC; Charleston *News and Courier*, February 27, March 19, 20, 1890.

12. Charleston *News and Courier*, April 1, March 24, 1890; E. A. Webster to Thomas E. Miller, March 21, 1890, enclosed in Miller to Harrison, April 17, 1890, microfilm reel 26, Harrison Papers, LC.

13. Charleston *News and Courier*, April 8, 1890.

14. Ibid., April 11, 30, June 15, July 8, 11, 1890.

15. Ibid., April 11, June 15, July 13, 1890.

16. T. B. Johnston to William Windom, February 5, 12, 1890, G. S. Botcheller, acting secretary of the Treasury, to Johnston, February 15, 1890, Charleston Customs Collector's Letter Book, 413, 432, 96, National Archives and Records Administration's South East Region (Atlanta, Ga.) (NARA's-SE); Charleston *News and Courier*, March 1, 1890; *Charleston City Directory, 1891–1892* (courtesy of Virginia Rugheimer, Charleston Library Society, to author, May 7, 1975). There is no indication that Murray's family lived with him in Charleston. Interview with Thelma L. Murray and June M. Davis, Norfolk, Va., November 30, 1973; G. W. Botcheller to collector of customs, Charleston, June 8, 1890, Charleston Customs Records, NARA's-SE.

17. Charleston *News and Courier*, July 17, 30, 1890; Washington *Bee*, September 27, 1890; Cleveland *Gazette*, September 27, 1890; New York *Times*, July 31, 1890 in Charleston *News and Courier*, August 2, 1890.

18. Charleston *News and Courier*, July 4, 6, 14, 29, 1890.

19. Ibid., August 2, 6, 11, 1890; Sumter *Watchman and Southron*, August 13, 1890.

20. Charleston *News and Courier*, August 13, 15, 18, 25, 1890; Thomas Holt, *Black Over White: Negro Political Leadership in South Carolina during Reconstruction* (Urbana, 1977).

21. Charleston *News and Courier*, August 17, 1890.

22. Ibid., September 15, 1890.

23. Ibid., September 17, 1890.

24. Ibid., September 17, 18, 19, 1890; Columbia *Register*, September 17, 18, 19, 1890; Sumter *Watchman and Southron*, September 24, 1890.

25. Simkins, 164–65; Neal, 190–97.

26. Charleston *News and Courier*, October 16, 1890; Columbia *Register*, October 16, 1890; Sumter *Watchman and Southron*, October 22, 1890; Tindall, *South Carolina Negroes*, 52 cites the *Register* account to indicate that there were sixty-five persons at the convention. I have accepted the *News and Courier* estimate of eighty because I found the *News and Courier* account of the convention to be generally complete and thorough.

27. Charleston *News and Courier*, October 25, 1890.

28. Ibid., October 14, 16, 23, 28, 30, 31, 1890; Simkins, 167.

29. Charleston *News and Courier*, November 9, 1890; Cleveland *Gazette*, November 15, 1890; Robert M. Burts, *Richard Irving Manning and the Progressive Movement in South Carolina* (Columbia, 1974), 15. Miller was later seated by the House of Representatives. George B. Tindall, "The Campaign for the Disfranchisement of Negroes in South Carolina," *Journal of Southern History* 15 (May 1949): 216.

## Chapter 3. White Republicans but One Black Victory

1. See the appendix for a chart containing the data on which the following analysis is based.

2. McLane Diary, March 13, 1891, J. Hendrix McLane Papers, Yale University Library.

3. Columbia *State*, January 8, 1892; Charleston *News and Courier*, January 9, 1892; Francis Butler Simkins, *Pitchfork Ben Tillman, South Carolinian* (Baton Rouge, 1944), 198–99; Diane Neal, "Benjamin Ryan Tillman: The South Carolina Years, 1847–1894" (Ph.D. diss., Kent State University, 1976), 272–75.

4. Tindall does not mention McLane's major role. He cites Memminger as the major leader. George B. Tindall, *South Carolina Negroes 1877–1900* (Baton Rouge, 1966), 49–50.

5. McLane Diary, March 29, 31, 1892, McLane Papers, Yale University Library; Columbia *State*, April 14, 1892; Charleston *News and Courier*, April 14, 1892.

6. Columbia *State*, April 20, 21, 1892; Charleston *News and Courier*, April 21, 22, 1892.

7. Columbia *State*, April 22, 1892; Ellery M. Brayton to Benjamin Harrison, April 25, 1892, microfilm reel 81, Benjamin Harrison Papers, LC.

8. Charleston *News and Courier*, May 11, 1892; Columbia *State*, May 11, June 1, 1892.

9. Charleston *News and Courier*, June 7, 1892; Columbia *State*, June 9, 11, 1892; *Proceedings of the Tenth Republican National Convention . . .* (1892), microfilm, 45, 92, 116. White Republicans from other states were also denied seats. Stanley Hirshon, *Farewell to the Bloody Shirt* (Bloomington, 1962), 239; Vincent P. DeSantis, *Republicans Face the Southern Question* (Baltimore, 1959), 228–29.

10. Simkins, 195, 215. A Columbia newspaper warned that the "uneducated classes of Democrats" did not know the Democratic presidential electors by name and might vote for Weaver electors by mistake. Columbia *State*, October 29, 1892.

11. Columbia *State*, July 31, September 1, 3, 29, 30, October 20, 1892; DeSantis, 227–62; Columbia *Register*, September 2, 1892; Charleston *News and Courier*, October 1, 1892.

12. Columbia *State*, February 15, 17, July 31, September 2, 3, 1891; Sumter *Watchman and Southron*, August 31, 1892. GWM to T. B. Johnston, September 8, 1892, U. S. Customs Records, R.G. 56, NARA; Johnston to GWM, September 9, 1892, Charleston Custom Collector's Letter Book, 170, NARA's SE; Beckett got the job. Secretary, Department of Appointments, Treasury Department to Collector of Customs, Charleston, September 15, 1892, No. 20, NARA's SE.

13. Barnett A. Elzas, *The Jews of South Carolina . . .* (Philadelphia, 1905), 248–51; Harry Simonoff, *Saga of American Jewry . . .* (New York, 1959), 80–83; J. C. Garlington, *Men of the Time . . .* (Spartanburg, 1902), 313; Sumter *Watchman and Southron*, July 6, 1892; Columbia *Register*, October 1, 1892; Columbia *State*, September 12, 1892.

14. Sumter *Watchman and Southron*, October 5, 1892; Charleston *News and Courier*, September 29, October 1, 22, 27, November 4, 5, 9, 1892.

15. Charleston *News and Courier*, October 31, 1892.

16. Ibid., October 27, 1892.

17. Ibid., November 6, 8, 1892; Sumter *Watchman and Southron*, November 9, 23, 1892.

18. Sumter *Watchman and Southron*, November 2, 1892; Charleston *News and Courier*, November 3, 5, 6, 1892; Columbia *State*, November 6, 8, 1892.

19. Charleston *News and Courier*, November 11, 12, 1892.

20. Tindall, *South Carolina Negroes*, 44 cites the Charleston *News and Courier*, October 1, 1892, to state that the Republicans ran a state ticket headed by Webster. What the newspaper actually reported was that the Republican state convention passed the time, while waiting for the Elector Committee to make its report, by jokingly naming a state ticket. But, the *News and Courier* reporter wrote: "No one seriously thought of making nominations . . ."; DeSantis, 243 says that Republicans supported Tillman in this election. Some surely did, but the party as a whole did not. Charleston *News and Courier*, November 11, 18, 21, 22, 1892.

21. Charleston *News and Courier,* November 17, 1892; Columbia *State*, November 21, 1892.

22. Minutes of the State Board of Canvassers, vol. 1, 1867–97, 393–409, Records of the State Election Commission, SCDAH. Published accounts appeared in Charleston *News and Courier*, November 26, 1892, and Columbia *State*, November 26, 28, 1891; Neal, 306 mistakenly says the Tillman board seated Murray over William Elliott in 1894.

23. Columbia *State*, November 27, 28, 1892; Charleston *News and Courier*, November 28, 1892; Sumter *Watchman and Southron*, November 30, 1892.

24. Washington *Post*, in Columbia *Register*, December 2, 1892; Pittsburgh *Gazette*, in Charleston *News and Courier*, December 6, 1892; Huntsville *Gazette*, December 3, 1892; Washington *Bee*, December 3, 1892.

25. Sumter *Watchman and Southron*, December 7, 1892 published clippings from newspapers all over the state. Columbia *State*, November 28, 1892; Charleston *News and Courier*, November 28, 29, 1892; Sumter *Watchman and Southron*, December 7, 1892.

26. Columbia *Register*, November 27, 29, 30, 1891. As early as November 20 and 22, 1892, the *Register* had called on Democrats to stand for "justice with an evenly-balanced hand" arguing for the "right" and "privilege" of blacks to elect one of their own if they could. See Sumter *Watchman and Southron*, December 7, 1892, for the few papers that agreed with the *Register*.

27. Columbia *State*, November 28, 1892; Charleston *News and Courier*, December 6, 1892.

28. Sumter *Watchman and Southron*, November 30, December 14, 1892; Columbia *State*, December 2, 14, 1892; Columbia *Register*, December 13, 1892.

29. David D. Wallace, *The History of South Carolina*, (New York, 1934), 3: 442, 443, 443n; Columbia *State*, August 3, 1930, in Samuel D. Smith, *The Negro in Congress* (Chapel Hill, 1940), 107n. In 1897 John McLaurin's office issued a denial that he had voted for Murray and appended documents from the Board of Canvassers to prove it.

Sumter *Herald*, August 27, 1897; Sumter *Watchman and Southron*, September 1, 1897; Tindall, *South Carolina Negroes,* 57–58.

30. Tompkins to GWM, July 31, 1893, Governor Benjamin R. Tillman Letterbooks, SCDAH cited in Stephen Kantrowitz, *Ben Tillman and the Reconstruction of White Supremacy* (Chapel Hill, 2000), 351n.

31. Columbia *Register*, November 29, 1892, December 3, 1892; Charleston *News and Courier*, December 25, 1892.

## Chapter 4. Congressman

1. Columbia *State*, March 23, 1893; Huntsville *Gazette*, April 8, 1893. The *State* said that Murray should have called for the appointment of Tillmanites not blacks since the former not the latter had made him congressman.

2. *Colored American*, in Huntsville *Gazette*, March 17, 1893.

3. Francis Butler Simkins, *Pitchfork Ben Tillman, South Carolinian* (Baton Rouge, 1944), 173–74, 224–25; Diane Neal, "Benjamin Ryan Tillman: The South Carolina Years, 1847–1894" (Ph.D. diss., Kent State University, 1976), 211, 220, 258–59, 280–81, 307–16.

4. Savannah *Tribune*, May 6, 1893; Columbia *State*, May 19, 1893; Cleveland *Gazette*, May 27, 1893; Columbia *Register*, May 19, 1893.

5. Columbia *Journal*, June 28, 1893.

6. *Congressional Directory*, 53rd Cong., 1st sess., 2nd ed., 329; Joseph W. Moore, *The American Congress . . . 1774–1895* (New York, 1895), 511; for a discussion of Washington during this period, see Constance M. Green, *The Secret City, a History of Race Relations in the Nation's Capital* (Princeton, 1967) and *Washington,* vol. 2, *Capital City 1879–1950* (Princeton, 1963).

7. Biographical information on the South Carolina delegation was gleaned from the *Biographical Directory of the American Congress 1774–1949 . . .* (Washington, 1950) and *Congressional Directory*, 53rd Cong., 1st sess.

8. When Brawley resigned, he was succeeded on April 12, 1894 by James F. Izlar, a Conservative Democrat who did not run for reelection.

9. Roger E. Stroup, "The Congressional Career of John L. McLaurin, Independent Tillmanite" (master's thesis, University of South Carolina, 1972), 13.

10. Latimer, Strait, McLaurin, and Shell all wrote to Grover Cleveland protesting their Democratic allegiance and denying membership in any third party alliance. Latimer, Strait, McLaurin to Cleveland, March 28, 1893, Shell to Cleveland, April 27, 1893, microfilm reels 74, 84, Grover Cleveland Papers, LC.

11. Champ Clark, *My Quarter Century in American Politics*, 2 vols. (New York, 1920), 1: 270.

12. *CR*, 53rd Cong., 1st sess. (August 7, 1893), 204; Huntsville *Gazette*, August 8, 1893; *CR*, 53rd Cong., 2nd sess., 1st ed., 190–91; Columbia *State*, August 8, 1893; Charleston *News and Courier*, August 8, 1893.

13. *CR* (August 21, 1893), 554–55. Other South Carolina congressmen did equally poorly. All received what a Charleston newspaper called "rather obscure committees."

Only Shell was awarded a chairmanship and that was of the Committee on Ventilation and Acoustics. Charleston *News and Courier*, August 22, 1894. The slim records of the Education Committee are preserved in Records of the House of Representatives, R.G. 233, NARA. During Murray's second abbreviated term, the committee never met. For a discussion of the retraction, see Minutes of the House Committee on Education, March 7, 1894, in R.G. 233, NARA; see also *CR* (March 13, 1894), 2902–10.

14. Unnamed tally sheet dated "[August 1893?]" microfilm reel 79, Cleveland Papers, LC.

15. Columbia *State*, August 10, 1893.

16. Ibid. The Conservative Democrat Charleston *News and Courier*, August 2, 1893, called free silver a worst danger to the South than federal interference in elections.

17. *CR* (August 21, 1893), 546; Charleston *News and Courier*, August 25, 1893.

18. New York *Times*, August 25, 1893; Columbia *Register*, August 25, 1893.

19. *CR* (August 24, 1893), 858–62; see also New York *Times*, August 25, 1893, and Sumter *Watchman and Southron*, August 30, 1893.

20. Sumter *Watchman and Southron*, August 30, 1893; Charleston *News and Courier*, August 26, 1893; Columbia *Register*, August 30, 1893; Sumter *Watchman and Southron*, September 1, 6, 1893; Charleston *News and Courier*, September 2, 1893; Sumter *Watchman and Southron*, September 20, 1893.

21. Charleston *News and Courier*, September 10, 1893; Columbia *Register*, September 10, 1893; *CR* (September 11, 1893), 1392–93; Columbia *State*, September 12, 1893; Savannah *Tribune*, September 16, 1893.

22. Simkins, 218; Neal, 316–18.

23. *CR* (September 26, 1893), 1823, (September 29, 1893), 1939. A useful account of the passage of the federal election law is Xi Wang, *The Trial of Democracy, Black Suffrage, and Northern Republicans, 1860–1910* (Athens, 1997), 254–59.

24. *CR* (October 2, 1893), 2048–49.

25. Isaiah Montgomery was the founder of the all-black town of Mound Bayou, Mississippi and a delegate to the 1890 Mississippi Constitutional Convention. His support for the disfranchising constitution has never been adequately explained.

26. *CR* (October 3, 1893), 2092.

27. Tindall is not aware of this speech, citing Murray's silver speech as "his only major effort on the floor during the one full term he served." George B. Tindall, *South Carolina Negroes, 1877–1900* (Baton Rouge, 1940), 57.

28. *CR* (October 4, 5, 1893), 2146–50, 2158–63, (October 6, 1893), 2256.

29. New York *Tribune*, October 5, 1893; Washington *Star*, October 28, 1893.

30. Columbia *State*, September 23, October 7, 1893; Columbia *Register*, October 6, 1893; Atlanta *Journal*, in Columbia *Register*, October 7, 1893.

31. *The Freeman*, October 14, 1893; New York *Age*, in Charleston *News and Courier*, October 28, 1893; Cleveland *Gazette*, October 21, 1893. A brief account of the speech without comment appeared in the Savannah *Tribune*, October 14, 1893. Two weeks after its original opinion, the Cleveland *Gazette* read a text of the speech in the New York *Age* and now considered it "a multiplication of almost meaningless and ridiculous

sentences." The *Gazette's* original statement must have been a reaction to the fact that Murray had given the speech; its second statement must have been an indication of the paper's disagreement with his silver ideas. Cleveland *Gazette*, November 4, 1893; *CR* (October 10, 1893), 2378.

32. Philadelphia *Record*, in Charleston *News and Courier*, August 17, 1893; New York *World*, in Huntsville *Gazette*, September 9, 1893; *Congressional Directory*, 53rd Cong., 1st sess., 2nd ed., 106; Indianapolis *Sentinel*, in Columbia *State*, August 28, 1893.

33. Philadelphia *Record*, in Charleston *News and Courier*, August 17, 1893; Washington *Post*, September 5, 1893, in Charleston *News and Courier*, September 15, 1893.

34. New York *Times*, in Sumter *Watchman and Southron*, March 11, 1903.

35. Charleston *News and Courier*, September 11, 1893; New York *Press*, in Charleston *News and Courier*, April 25, 1894; Columbia *State*, April 27, 1894; interview with Thelma L. Murray and June M. Davis, Norfolk, Va., November 30, 1973.

36. *CR* (October 6, 27, 1893) 2258, 2901; Columbia *State*, October 15, 28, 1893; *The Freeman*, November 15, 1893; Huntsville *Gazette*, November 18, 1893.

37. Murray-Davis interview.

38. Charleston *News and Courier*, August 28, 1893; the data for the voting analysis were supplied by the Interuniversity Consortium for Political and Social Research.

## Chapter 5. The Congressman Runs for Reelection

1. Francis Butler Simkins, *Pitchfork Ben Tillman, South Carolinian* (Baton Rouge, 1944), 223; Columbia *State*, December 9, 15, 16, 17, 20, 1893; Columbia *Register*, December 20, 1893.

2. *CR*, 53rd Cong., 2nd sess. (December 16, 1893), 307; Charleston *News and Courier*, January 1, 1894; Sumter *Watchman and Southron*, December 12, 1894.

3. Charleston *News and Courier*, January 5, 18, 1894; *CR* (February 6, 8, 1894), 1971, 2045.

4. *CR* (February 23, 1894), 2399, 2400; see Index under H.R. 7071 in ibid.; U.S. Congress, House, House Report 892, 53rd Cong., 2nd sess., 1894. Technically, the committee substituted H.R. 7071 for Murray's bill, but the substitute differed little from the original.

5. Washington *Bee*, March 10, 1884; see Simkins, 234–61, especially 251–59 for a discussion of the dispensary law controversy.

6. Columbia *State*, April 7, 1894.

7. Ibid., April 9, 1894.

8. *CR* (April 17, 1894), 3797; Murray to William McKinley (WMcK), April 25, 1894, Carter G. Woodson Papers, Library of Congress (CGW, LC); Charleston *News and Courier*, April 23, 1894. There is no mention of this campaign nor of Murray in Okon Edet Uya, *From Slavery to Public Service, Robert Smalls, 1830–1915* (New York, 1971).

9. Charleston *News and Courier*, April 23, 1894.

10. Columbia *Journal*, in Sumter *Watchman and Southron*, May 23, 1894; Columbia *Register*, May 16, 1894.

11. Columbia *State*, May 16, 19, 31, June 2, 5, 7, 1894; Columbia *Register*, June 5, 1894.

J. Morgan Kousser argues that southern state disfranchisement indeed affected lower-class whites as well as blacks. Kousser, *The Shaping of Southern Politics* . . . (New Haven, 1974).

12. Columbia *State*, June 12, 1894.

13. Ibid., June 8, 9, 12, 1894; Columbia *Register*, June 8, 9, 1894.

14. Columbia *State*, June 23, 1894.

15. *CR* (May 25, 1894), 5303; Louis R. Harlan, *Booker T. Washington: The Making of a Black Leader, 1856–1901* (New York, 1972), 192; Savannah *Tribune*, March 24, June 16, 1894; Booker T. Washington to GWM, May 11, 1894, Booker T. Washington Papers, LC (courtesy Louis R. Harlan to author, March 19, 1973); *Southern Workman* 23 (August 1894), 148.

16. *CR* (June 12, 1894), 6177–178, (July 12, 1894), 7356; see the few records of the Committee on Education, 53rd Cong., 2nd sess., Records of the House of Representatives, R.G. 233, NARA.

17. GWM to Washington, July 7, 1894, in *The Booker T. Washington Papers,* ed. Louis R. Harlan et al. (Urbana, 1974), 3: 451–52; Louis R. Harlan to author, March 19, 1973.

18. Columbia *State*, July 11, 13, 1894; *CR* (July 14, 1894), 7497; Columbia *Register*, July 11, 1894.

19. Sumter *Watchman and Southron*, July 18, 1894.

20. *Colored American*, in *The Freeman*, June 23, 1894; *The Freeman*, July 7, 1894; Washington *Post*, in Charleston *News and Courier*, July 31, 1894.

21. Columbia *State*, August 18, 1894; Harlan, *Booker T. Washington*, 205–7; *CR* (August 10, 1894), 8382–83. An excerpt of Murray's speech appears in William L. Katz, ed., *Eyewitness: The Negro in American History* (New York, 1967), 301–2 (he is erroneously listed as George H. Murray); Murray's inventions are discussed in detail in chapter 9 of this book.

22. Charleston *News and Courier*, August 24, 1894; Columbia *State*, September 28, 1894; see George B. Tindall, "The Campaign for the Disfranchisement of Negroes in South Carolina," *Journal of Southern History* 15 (May 1949), 212–34.

23. Columbia *State*, September 13, October 3, 1894; Columbia *Register*, October 3, 1894; Charleston *News and Courier*, October 3, 4, 1894; Columbia *State*, October 4, 20, 1894.

24. Columbia *State*, October 4, 11, 1894; Columbia *Register*, October 11, 1894.

25. GWM to WMcK, October 9, 1894, CGW, LC; Columbia *State*, October 10, 1894; Charleston *News and Courier*, October 11, 15, 1894.

26. Charleston *News and Courier*, September 25, 26, 28, 29, 1894; Sumter *Watchman and Southron*, October 3, 1894, said he came out "on top" in the feud.

27. Columbia *State*, September 15, 1894; Columbia *Register*, September 15, 1894; Tindall, "Disfranchisement," 222–23; Columbia *State*, October 23, 1894; Charleston *News and Courier*, November 3, 1894.

28. Charleston *News and Courier*, October 27, 30,1 1894; Columbia *State*, September 29, October 29, 30, November 1, 3, 1894.

29. Columbia *State*, November 3, 5, 1894; Murray made a speech in Port Royal near

the end of the campaign, but he did not discuss this issue. *Palmetto Post*, in Charleston *Post*, October 29, 1894.

30. Charleston *News and Courier*, October 19, 31, November 1, 1894.

31. Simkins, 281–82; Charleston *News and Courier*, November 7, 12, 1894; the certificates have been preserved in House Committee on Elections, Records of the House of Representatives, 54th Cong., 2nd sess., R.G. 233, NARA; election records that show that Murray voted in the first ward of Charleston are located in there as well.

32. Columbia *State*, November 14, 16, 1894. On October 9, 1894, GWM asked WMcK to "see Wheeler" for him and ask him "to reply to my favor of a recent date." CGW, LC; Minutes of the State Board of Canvassers, vol. 1, 1867–97, 489–91, Records of the State Election Commission, SCDAH.

33. GWM to WMcK, November [?] 1894, CGW, LC. The letter was written in Concord, North Carolina, but it is unknown what GWM was doing there.

34. Minutes of the State Board of Canvassers, vol. 1, 1867–97, 489–93, 498, Records of the State Election Commission, SCDAH; Columbia *State*, November 23, 1894; Columbia *Register*, November 23, 1894; Charleston *News and Courier*, November 23, 1894; Diane Neal erroneously indicates that the board chose Murray, and she then utilizes this error to argue that, on occasion, Tillman cooperated with blacks. Diane Neal, "Benjamin Ryan Tillman: The South Carolina Years, 1847–1894" (Ph.D. diss., Kent State University, 1976), 316.

35. Savannah *Tribune*, December 1, 1894; Sumter *Watchman and Southron*, December 12, 1894.

36. Tindall, "Disfranchisement," 231.

37. Charleston *News and Courier*, January 16, 1894.

38. *Journal of the [S.C.] House of Representatives* (December 11, 1894), 264; Sumter *Watchman and Southron*, December 12, 19, 1894; Columbia *State*, December 12, 1894; Simkins, 272n erroneously says that Butler and Crum received 21 votes to Tillman's 102. He does not mention GWM.

## Chapter 6. Fighting Constitutional Disfranchisement

1. *South Carolina Statutes at Large*, 17: 1110–15. A thorough discussion of Tillman and the constitutional convention is found in Stephen Kantrowitz, *Ben Tillman and the Reconstruction of White Supremacy* (Chapel Hill, 2000), 198–242.

2. Columbia *State*, January 5, 22, 1895; Columbia *Register*, January 5, 22, 1895; Charleston *News and Courier*, January 22, 1895. Webster's circular was dated January 12, 1895; the reason for the delay in publication is unclear. Tindall refers to Ellery Brayton as the state Republican chairman and does not seem to know about the split in the party and the resulting establishment of two separate factional organizations. George B. Tindall, *South Carolina Negroes 1877–1900* (Baton Rouge, 1966), 76.

3. Columbia *State*, January 20, 1895; Charleston *News and Courier*, January 21, 1895; Columbia *Register*, January 21, 1895.

4. Columbia *State*, February 1, 1895; Columbia *Register*, February 1, 1895.

5. In discussing this issue, one historian surmised that "The Negroes had little or no

leadership. . . ." Anne King Gregorie, *History of Sumter County* (Sumter, S.C., 1954), 385.

6. Columbia *State*, December 13, 1894, January 8, 1895; Charleston *News and Courier*, February 18, 1895.

7. Charleston *News and Courier*, January 2, 1895; Sumter *Watchman and Southron*, January 9, 1895.

8. Columbia *State*, February 7, 1895; Charleston *News and Courier*, February 7, 1895; Columbia *Register*, February 7, 1895; Sumter *Watchman and Southron*, February 13, 1895.

9. Columbia *Register*, February 15, 1895; Columbia *State*, February 20, 1895.

10. Francis Butler Simkins, *Pitchfork Ben Tillman, South Carolinian* (Baton Rouge, 1944), 287–89; Columbia *State*, February 7, 1895; Charleston *News and Courier*, February 7, 9, 1895; Charleston *Post*, February 16, 1895.

11. *CR*, 53rd Cong., 3rd sess. (February 1, 24, 1895), 1652, 2669; Cleveland *Gazette*, February 16, 1895; Charleston *News and Courier*, February 24, 25, March 5, 1895.

12. *Wiley v. Sinkler*, 179 U.S. 58 (1900); Charleston *News and Courier*, March 13, 1895; Columbia *State*, March 13, 1895.

13. *Butler v. Ellerbe*, 44 S.C. 256 (1894).

14. Charleston *News and Courier*, March 9, 15, 1895; Columbia *State*, March 9, 15, 1895; Columbia *Register*, March 14, 15, 1895; Columbia *State*, March 14, 1895; Charleston *News and Courier*, March 14, 1895; Columbia *Register*, March 14, 1895; Georgetown *Semi-Weekly Times*, March 16, 1895; Sumter *Watchman and Southron*, March 20, 1895.

15. Georgetown *Semi-Weekly Times*, March 16, 1895; GWM to WMcK, March 21, 1895, CGW, LC.

16. Columbia *State* , March 20, April 23, 1895; Charleston *News and Courier*, April 4, 17, 24, May 3, 1895; Sumter *Watchman and Southron*, April 3, 1895; GWM to WMcK, April 2, 1895, CGW, LC.

17. Columbia *State*, March 23, 1895, also in Sumter *Watchman and Southron*, March 27, April 3, 1895.

18. Thomas E. Miller to GWM, March 29, 1895, in Charleston *News and Courier*, March 30, 1895; Columbia *State*, April 12, 1895. General Sam Lee, the long-time black Republican leader and ranking black militia officer, died while this controversy was going on.

19. *Palmetto Post*, April 4, 1895; Charleston *News and Courier*, March 30, 1895.

20. *Mills v. Green*, 67 Fed. Rep. 818 (1895); Charleston *News and Courier*, April 10, 19, 20, 22, 1895.

21. Charleston *News and Courier*, April 23, 1895.

22. Ibid., May 3, 1895.

23. Columbia *State*, May 3, 1895; Charleston *News and Courier*, May 3, 4, 5, 1895; *Mills v. Green*, 67 Fed. Rep. 818 (1895). That same day Judge C. H. Simonton declared the controversial South Carolina dispensary law unconstitutional and void. Charleston *News and Courier*, May 9, 10, 1895.

24. Simkins, 291; Charleston *News and Courier*, May 9, 10, 15, 23, 26, 29, 1895; Columbia *State*, May 9, 11, 27, 1895; Columbia *Register*, May 9, 1895; Columbia *Post*, May 9, 1895.

25. Columbia *State*, May 10, 1895; Georgetown *Semi-Weekly Times*, May 22, 1895; Charleston *News and Courier*, June 12, 1895; Columbia *State*, May 18, 1895; Columbia *Register*, May 18, 1895; Georgetown *Semi-Weekly Times*, June 15, 1895; Charleston *News and Courier*, May 29, June 5, 15, 1895; Columbia *State*, May 27, 1895.

26. 69 *Fed. Rep.* 852 (1895); Charleston *News and Courier*, June 12, 1895; Columbia *State*, June 18, 1895; Sumter *Watchman and Southron*, June 19, 1895.

27. Charleston *News and Courier*, June 19, 20, 1895; *Palmetto Post*, June 20, 1895; Columbia *State*, June 21, 1895; *Butler v. Ellerbe*, 44 S.C. 256 (1894); Columbia *State*, July 7, 9, 1895; Charleston *News and Courier*, July 7, 1895; Columbia *Register*, July 7, 1895.

28. Columbia *Register*, June 22, 1895; Columbia *State*, July 1, 1895; Charleston *News and Courier*, July 1, 1895; Columbia *State*, July 4, 1895; Washington *Star*, in Charleston *News and Courier*, July 5, 1895. No other information on this organization was discovered.

29. Charleston *News and Courier*, July 11, 1895; Columbia *State*, July 11, 1895; Sumter *Watchman and Southron*, July 1895.

30. Columbia *State*, July 11, 12, 1895; Charleston *News and Courier*, July 12, 13, 19, 22, 1895; Columbia *Register*, July 11, 12, 1895.

31. Charleston *News and Courier*, July 11, 22, 25, 1895; Columbia *State*, July 14, 1895.

32. Charleston *News and Courier*, July 22, 1895; Savannah *Tribune*, July 27, 1895; *Gowdy v. Green*, 69 *Fed. Rep.* 865 (1895).

33. *Gowdy v. Green*, 69 *Fed. Rep.* 865 (1895); Charleston *News and Courier*, July 29, August 7, 1895; Columbia *State*, July 30, August 7, 1895; Columbia *Register*, August 7, 1895.

34. Obear and Douglass to GWM, n.d., in Columbia *State*, August 16, 1895. This letter also requested payment of the remainder of the legal fees, indicating that, despite Murray's touring, his campaign suffered from a scarcity of funds.

35. Columbia *State*, August 21, 1895; Charleston *News and Courier*, August 21, 1895. An editorial in the Columbia *Register*, August 21, 1895, reminded the lawyers that the state's newspapers had been very fair to them considering the issue in litigation.

36. Sumter *Watchman and Southron*, August 7, 26, 1895.

37. Columbia *State*, August 10, September 24, 1895; Georgetown *Semi-Weekly Times*, August 24, 1895. For discussions of the convention, see Simkins, 285–309; Tindall, *South Carolina Negroes*, 80–88; and Tindall, "The Question of Race in the South Carolina Constitutional Convention of 1895," *Journal of Negro History* 37 (July 1952): 277–303.

38. Tindall, "The Question of Race,"; Booker T. Washington delivered his "Atlanta Compromise" speech on September 18, 1895, soon after the South Carolina convention began. The Washington *Bee*, October 19, 26, 1895, wrote: "While Professor Washing-

ton was apologizing for the Southern white people, the South Carolina Constitutional Convention was disfranchising the Negro." Washington wrote a conciliatory letter to Ben Tillman hoping to prevent total disfranchisement, but it was to no avail. Louis R. Harlan, *Booker T. Washington: The Making of a Black Leader, 1856–1901* (New York, 1972), 290; Columbia *State*, October 12, 1895; Charleston *News and Courier*, October 14, 1895.

39. Charleston *News and Courier*, October 10, November 4, 1895; Columbia *State*, October 10, 28, 1895; Columbia *Register*, October 26, 1895.

40. Columbia *State*, November 27, December 8, 1895.

41. *Mills v. Green*, 159 Sup. Ct. 40 L. Ed. 293 (1895); the Charleston *News and Courier* never even reported this decision, and the Columbia *State*, November 26, 1895, mentioned it only briefly. The Columbia *Register*, November 26, 1895, editorially attacked Judge Goff for his original decision.

42. Charleston *News and Courier*, December 3, 1895; *Wiley vs. Sinkler*, 179 U.S. 58 (1900). There is no published record of the Circuit Court action (Iris C. Stevenson, librarian, U.S. Court of Appeals for the Fourth Circuit, to author, July 22, 1977); *Gowdy v. Green*, 363 Sup. Ct. 41, L. Ed. 1179 (1897).

43. Charleston *News and Courier*, December 3, 1895; Savannah *Tribune*, November 30, 1895.

## Chapter 7. Reaction to Disfranchisement

1. Columbia *State*, February 24, 1896, December 16, 18, 1895, January 3, 1896.

2. Charleston *News and Courier*, February 26, March 21, 1896; Columbia *State*, March 29, 1896. On New Year's Day, Murray attended a Washington dinner given by Recorder of Deeds C. H. J. Taylor in honor of North Carolina banker Isaac H. Smith. *The Freeman*, January 18, 1896.

3. U.S. Congress, House, *George W. Murray vs. William Elliott*, H.R. 1567, 54th Cong., 1st sess., 1896; Chester H. Rowell, . . . *Digest of All the Contested Elections in the House . . . 1789–1901*, House Document no. 510, 56th Cong., 2nd sess., 543–46; Charleston *News and Courier*, January 8, April 4, 9, 1896; Columbia *State*, April 5, 1896; *CR* (December 17, 1895), 222.

4. U.S. Congress, House, *George W. Murray vs. William Elliott*, H.R. 1567, Pt. 2, 54th Cong., 1st sess., 1896.

5. Charleston *News and Courier*, April 16, 1896; *Palmetto Post*, May 7, 1896. In 1899 when Reed resigned in protest against the nation's expansionist policy, he told a friend he believed that "we had niggers enough in this country without buying any more of 'em." George H. Mayer, *The Republican Party, 1854–1964* (New York, 1964), 268.

6. Sumter *Watchman and Southron*, April 15, 1896; Richmond *Planet*, April 18, 1896; Savannah *Tribune*, April 11, 1896; *The Freeman*, April 18, 1896; Washington *Bee*, May 2, 1896.

7. Charleston *News and Courier*, April 15, 1896; Columbia *State*, April 15, 1896; Columbia *Register*, April 15, 1896.

8. GWM announced his intention to make another congressional election run, is-

suing a statement telling blacks to try to register, new constitution or not. Charleston *News and Courier*, April 16, 23, 1896.

9. *CR*, 54th Cong., 1st sess. (May 1, 1896) (June 3, 4, 1896), 4673, 6072–78, 6110–11, Appendix 445–52; Columbia *State*, May 2, June 5, 1896; *Palmetto Post*, May 21, June 11, 1896; Charleston *News and Courier*, June 4, 5, 10, 15, 1896; Sumter *Watchman and Southron*, June 10, 1896; Columbia *Register*, June 15, 1896; Charleston *Post*, June 5, 1896.

10. *CR* (June 4, 5, 1896), 6111, 6174; Charleston *News and Courier*, June 5, 1896. On June 9 Murray was appointed to the Education Committee and the Expenditures in the Treasury Department Committee. *CR* (June 9, 1896), 6364; *Review of Reviews* 14 (July, 1896): 12–13.

11. Charleston *News and Courier*, July 29, 1897. *Official Proceedings of the Eleventh Republican National Convention* . . . (1896), microfilm, 123.

12. Charleston *News and Courier*, June 21, 1896.

13. Columbia *Register*, June 20, 1896, in Sumter *Herald*, June 26, 1896; Charleston *News and Courier*, June 14, 16, July 14, 31, August 21, 1896; *Palmetto Post*, June 18, 1896; Columbia *State*, June 28, 1896.

14. Washington *Bee*, August 8, 1896; Columbia *State*, August 21, 23, 1896; Charleston *News and Courier*, August 23, 1896; Columbia *Register*, August 23, 1896; Charleston *News and Courier*, September 12, 16, 17, 1896; Columbia *State*, September 16, 1896; Columbia *Register*, September 17, 1896.

15. The account of the two meetings is based on the following newspaper stories: Charleston *News and Courier*, September 18, 1896; Columbia *State*, September 18, 1896; Columbia *Register*, September 18, 1896.

16. *U.S. Statutes at Large* 15, ch. 70, 73 (1867).

17. Columbia *State*, September 19, October 4, 5, 1896; Sumter *Watchman and Southron*, September 23, 1896; Charleston *News and Courier*, October 3, 5, 1896; Sumter *Herald*, October 16, 1896; Columbia *Register*, October 13, 1896. There is no record of this case (*Williams vs. McCoy, Bridges, and Green*) ever reaching the South Carolina Supreme Court (Elizabeth A. Sprott, librarian, the Supreme Court of South Carolina, to author, May 22, 1978). Other Supreme Court cases that allowed black disfranchisement to stand included *Giles v. Harris* (1903) and *Giles v. Teasley* (1904).

18. Charleston *News and Courier*, October 4, 1896; GWM to WMcK, September 26, 1896, CGW, LC.

19. Columbia *Register*, October 2, 1896; Columbia *State*, October 3, 5, 7, 1896.

20. Charleston *News and Courier*, October 14, 15, 19, 21, 30, 31, 1896; Columbia *State*, October 12, 24, 1896; Columbia *Register*, October 13, 16, 1896.

21. Cleveland *Gazette*, October 10, 1896; Charleston *News and Courier*, October 8, 11, 1896; Columbia *Register*, October 7, 1896; Charleston *Post*, October 10, 1896; Cleveland *Gazette*, October 10, 1896; Charleston *News and Courier*, October 11, 1896; Columbia *State*, October 11, 1896.

22. Charleston *News and Courier*, October 16, 20, 1896.

23. Charleston *News and Courier*, October 27, 28, 29, 30, November 1, 1896; Colum-

bia *Register*, October 27, 1896; Charleston *News and Courier*, October 21, November 4, 1896.

24. Columbia *State*, November 21, 22, 1896; Charleston *News and Courier*, November 21, 24, 1896; SC, *Reports and Resolutions*, 1897, 4–12.

25. GWM to WMcK, November 6, 1896, CGW, LC.

26. Minutes of the State Board of Canvassers, vol. 1, 1867–97, 545–73, Records of the State Election Commission, SCDAH; Charleston *News and Courier*, November 24, 1896; Columbia *Register*, November 24, 1896.

27. Charleston *News and Courier*, December 15, 1896; Sumter *Watchman and Southron*, December 16, 1896; *CR* (December 19,1896), 320.

28. Charleston *News and Courier*, February 6, 7, 10, 1897; Columbia *Register*, February 7, 1897.

29. The Columbia *Register*, February 26, 1897, particularly attacked the petition signed by white businessmen of Charleston. The paper saw this memorial as an affront to Democratic unity and as proof that the Haskellite Conservatives were still fighting the Tillmanites. "It is an ill bird which fouls its own nest," the *Register* warned the Conservatives. *CR* (February 8, 9, 11, 12, 1897), 1167, 1689, 1757, 1787; the original petitions are preserved in Committee on the Election of President, Vice President, and Representatives in Congress, Records of the House of Representatives, 54th Cong., 2nd sess., R.G. 233, NARA; Charleston *Post*, February 8, 1897; Charleston *News and Courier*, February 7, 9, 1897; *The American Citizen*, February 12, 1897.

30. Savannah *Tribune*, February 13, 1897; Columbia *Register*, February 11, 1897; *CR* (February 15, 1897), 1868; Tindall, 90–91 argues that GWM withdrew his threat because he was "still hopeful for the new Republican movement to attract white voters into the party and conscious of the futility of any effort to overthrow the new constitution by action of Congress." Considering the beating the Republicans had taken in the recent 1896 elections, the first part of this interpretation is not plausible. It was national Republican pressure and the promise to consider the matter in the House that convinced Murray to drop his plan.

31. "No minutes of the committee for the 54th Congress have been located, nor is there any information as to the disposition of them available." George P. Perros, NARA, to author, April 5, 1977.

32. Charleston *News and Courier*, February 19, 26, 1897; Columbia *Register*, February 20, 26, 1897.

33. Charleston *News and Courier*, February 26, 27, March 3, 1897; U.S. Congress, House, H.R. 3065, 54th Cong., 2nd sess.; Committee on the Election of President, Vice President, and Representatives in Congress, Records of the House of Representatives, 54th Cong., 2nd sess., R.G. 233, NARA.

34. Savannah *Tribune*, February 20, 1897; *The Freeman*, February 13, 1897; Columbia *State*, in *Palmetto Post*, February 18, 1897.

35. Charleston *News and Courier*, February 16, 1897; *Palmetto Post*, February 25, 1897.

36. Cleveland *Gazette*, February 23, 1897; *CR* (March 1, 1897), 2591.

## Chapter 8. Political Nadir

1. H. Wayne Morgan, *William McKinley and His America* (Syracuse, 1963), 287–88.

2. Charleston *News and Courier*, July 25, 1897, November 10, 1897, March 11, 19, June 7, 12, 1898.

3. Ibid., September 14, 16, October 7, 9, 19, 1897, February 18, 28, March 2, 1898; *Palmetto Post*, October 14, 1898; Charleston *News and Courier*, October 16, 1897; Sumter *Herald*, July 2, 1898; Charleston *Post*, June 7, 1898.

4. Charleston *News and Courier*, February 23, 1898; Columbia *Register*, February 23, 1898 reported that the baby was in its mother's arms, and Baker fell dead upon the child.

5. Charleston *News and Courier*, March 2, 4, 1898; Columbia *Register*, March 4, 1898; Cleveland *Gazette*, April 15, May 20, December 9, 1899; *Colored American*, May 20, September 30, October 14, December 2, 1899; Charleston *News and Courier*, August 9, 1899, March 2, 3, 1900. In late April 1900, McKinley reopened the post office under the management of a white woman. *Colored American*, May 5, 1900; Cleveland *Gazette*, April 13, 1901; Washington *Bee*, October 11, 1898.

6. Charleston *News and Courier*, November 8–16, 28, 1898, March 14, 1899; Columbia *Register*, November 8–16, 1898; Savannah *Tribune*, August 19, 26, 1899; George B. Tindall, *South Carolina Negroes 1877–1900* (Baton Rouge, 1966), 256–58; Tom H. Wells, "The Phoenix Election Riot," *Phylon* 31, no. 1 1970): 58–69. The noted black educator Benjamin E. Mays was five years old and living in the area when these events took place; his father's mistreatment by armed whites on horseback was his first childhood memory. Benjamin E. Mays, *Born to Rebel: An Autobiography of Benjamin E. Mays* (New York, 1971), 1.

7. For a discussion of Murray's land business, see chapter 9.

8. Charleston *News and Courier*, May 17, 1897; GWM was in Washington during late June, early July, but his activity is unknown. See Joseph O. Thompson to Booker T. Washington, July 2, 1897, Louis R. Harlan, et al., eds., *The Booker T. Washington Papers* (Urbana, 1975), 4: 307; *Colored American*, May 14, 1898; Washington *Bee*, May 20, 1899.

9. Washington *Bee*, December 31, 1898; *Colored American*, May 14, 21, 1898; New York *Times*, December 21, 1898.

10. Emma Lou Thornbrough, "The National Afro-American League, 1887–1908," *Journal of Southern History* 27 (November 1961): 494–512; Louis R. Harlan, *Booker T. Washington: The Making of a Black Leader, 1856–1901* (New York, 1972), 263–68, 270; Emma Lou Thornbrough, *T. Thomas Fortune, Militant Journalist* (Chicago, 1972), 178–89.

11. GWM was one of those who responded to Bishop Alexander Walters's call for the meeting, but he was not identified with the Protective League. Alexander Walters, *My Life and Work* (New York, 1917), 100, 102.

12. Cleveland *Gazette*, January 7, 1899; *The Freeman*, January 14, 1899; *The Appeal*, January 21, 1899. Bishop Walters devotes a chapter in his book to the Washington meet-

ing, but most of the account is a verbatim reprint of his speech and the meeting's later address to the nation. The meeting's agenda and other speakers are not mentioned. Walters, *Life and Work*, 94–140; August Meier, *Negro Thought in America, 1880–1915* (Ann Arbor, 1963), 172–73.

13. Charleston *News and Courier*, December 31, 1898, January 1, 1899; Sumter *Watchman and Southron*, January 4, 1899; *The Freeman*, January 14, 1899, February 23, 1901.

14. Sumter *Herald*, January 7, 1898; Charleston *News and Courier*, August 12, 1898. It is uncertain whether he attended the organizational meeting of the "state Colored Farmers' Congress" called by Thomas E. Miller's state black college. Charleston *News and Courier*, April 30, 1898.

15. *Palmetto Post*, March 4, 1897; Charleston *News and Courier*, December 4, 1897, January 11, 1898; *The Freeman*, December 11, 1897; *Colored American*, June 4, 1898; Washington *Bee*, May 21, 1898; Chester H. Rowell, . . . *Digest of All the Contested Elections in the House . . . 1789–1901*, House Document No. 510, 56th Cong., 2nd sess., 13–14, 20–21.

16. Charleston *News and Courier*, August 29, 30, 31, September 18, 28, 29, October 1, 4, 1898. Obviously Jones had not noted Murray's 1896 shift from free silver to gold.

17. GWM to WMcK, October 12, 1898, CGW, LC; Charleston *News and Courier*, November 5, 7, 1898; *Palmetto Post*, October 4, 1989.

18. Charleston *News and Courier*, November 30, 1898; SC, *Reports and Resolutions*, 1899, vol. 1, 252–56.

19. GWM to WMcK, November 4, 1898, CGW, LC; Minutes of the State Board of Canvassers, vol. 2, 3–13, Records of the State Election Commission, SCDAH; Charleston *News and Courier*, December 3, 1989.

20. Columbia *State*, February 8, 9, March 21, 1900; Charleston *Post*, March 21, 1900; Charleston *News and Courier*, March 22, 26, 28, 1900.

21. Charleston *Post*, October 4, 1900; New York *Times*, October 4, 1900 reported that this was the first time there had been all black leadership in the state. Columbia *State*, October 4, 1900; Charleston *News and Courier*, October 4, 1900; Sumter *Herald*, October 5, 1900; Thomas Cripps, "Lily White Republicans: The Negro, the Party, and the South in the Progressive Era" (Ph.D. diss., University of Maryland, 1967), 76–77.

22. Charleston *News and Courier*, October 4, 1900; Columbia *State*, October 4, 1900.

23. Charleston *News and Courier*, November 7, 19, 1900; S. C. *Reports and Resolutions*, 1901, vol. 2, pt. 1, 796–801.

24. Sumter *Watchman and Southron*, November 21, 1900; *Colored American*, December 1, 1900; Charleston *News and Courier*, November 12, 1900, January 2, 4, 1901. In 1902 in answer to the question "What should be the Negro's attitude in politics?" GWM repeated a number of these ideas, once more emphasizing the need for black economic power in order to gain true political power. As for the disfranchisement movement, Murray could only counsel prayer, hard work, and hope in God's help. D. W. Culp, ed., *Twentieth Century Negro Literature* (New York, 1969), 231–35.

## Chapter 9. Economic Success and Political Failure

1. Information on Murray's land dealings is derived from property records located in the Clerk's Office, Sumter County, South Carolina. The dates indicate when each transaction was recorded; there was often a considerable time lapse from the date of the transaction to its recording. See, for example, Sumter *Herald*, December 8, 1899, which mentions Murray's purchase of fifty acres of land. This purchase was not recorded until February 1900. Such lapses were normal during that period.

2. *Colored American*, November 30, 1901; Cleveland *Gazette*, December 14, 1901; *The Freeman*, September 27, 1902; D. W. Culp, ed., *Twentieth-Century Negro Literature* (New York, 1969), biographical sketch located between 230 and 231.

3. For a discussion of blacks in South Carolina agriculture at the turn of the century, see I. A. Newby, *Black Carolinians: A History of Blacks in South Carolina from 1895–1968* (Columbia, 1973), 124–33. Newby does not mention anything like Murray's plan, nor does the most important book on poor blacks in post–Civil War Southern agriculture, Roger L. Ransom and Richard Sutch, *One Kind of Freedom . . .* (Cambridge, 1977).

4. GWM to WMcK, May 12, 1899, January 9, September 4, 6, 1901, CGW, LC.

5. 1900 census, Sumter County, South Carolina, T-1070, microfilm reel 80, NARA; Title Records, Clerk's Office, Sumter County, South Carolina. There is no mention of Murray in Loren Schweninger, *Black Property Owners in the South, 1790–1915* (Urbana and Chicago, 1990).

6. *Annual Report of the Commissioner of Patents for the Year 1894* (Washington, 1895); *Official Gazette of the United States Patent Office* 67 (April 10, June 5, 1894), 185–86, 1242–44; Records of the United States Patent Office, R.G. 241, NARA. Actually Murray also patented a hoisting mechanism, but this patent is never credited to him whenever his inventions are discussed. This invention is discussed in chapter 11. See *Colored American*, November 14, 1903; H. E. Baker, "The Negro Inventor," in Culp, *Negro Literature*, 403, 409–10; H. E. Baker, *The Colored Inventor: A Record of Fifty Years* (New York, 1913), 9; Frederic H. Robb, ed., *1927 Intercollegian Wonder Book, or, The Negro in Chicago 1779–1927* (Chicago, 1927), 98; St. Louis *Post-Dispatch*, March 6, 1898.

7. St. Louis *Post-Dispatch*, March 6, 1898; *The Freeman*, January 15, 1898. For accounts of Turner's life, see Lawrence O. Christensen, "J. Milton Turner: An Appraisal," *Missouri Historical Review* 70 (October 1975), 1–19; and Gary R. Kremer, *James Milton Turner and the Promise of America . . .* (Columbia, Mo., 1991).

8. GWM to WMcK, March 25, April 3, 13, 24, May 12, 1899, January 22, 1900, W. S. Duvall to WMcK, undated, CGW, LC.

9. Records of the United States Patent Office, R.G. 241, NARA; *Scientific American*, April 21, 1894, 253; Bishopville *Eagle*, in Sumter *Watchman and Southron*, January 29, 1890.

10. See, for example, Herbert Aptheker, "The Negro Scientist and Inventor," *Masses and Mainstreams* 4 (February 1957), 80–89. The historian of Sumter County mentions several white inventors, including some who were denied patents, but she does

not mention GWM. Anne King Gregorie, *History of Sumter County* (Sumter, 1954), 471–75; John Schlebecker, Smithsonian Institution, to author, November 4, 1976.

11. Thomas R. Cripps, "Lily White Republicans: The Negro, the Party, and the South in the Progressive Era" (Ph.D. diss., University of Maryland, 1967), 92.

12. Charleston *News and Courier*, September 18, 1901. The best account of the controversial dinner is Willard B. Gatewood, Jr., "Square Deal for Dr. Crum," in *Theodore Roosevelt and the Art of Controversy* (Baton Rouge, 1970), 90–133. John L. McLaurin to Theodore Roosevelt (TR), October 21, 1901, microfilm reel 21, TR Papers, LC; New York *Times*, October 22, 1901; Charleston *News and Courier*, October 22, 1901.

13. Charleston *News and Courier*, September 24, 1901, in Sumter *Watchman and Southron*, October 30, 1901; TR to Booker T. Washington, November 2, 1901, TR to George R. Koester, October 31, 1901; Koester to TR, November 3, 1901; George B. Cortelyou to Koester, November 7, 1901, TR to Koester, November 8, 1901, Koester to TR, November 4, 1901, microfilm reels 21, 327, 415, TR Papers, LC.

14. Columbia *State*, November 4, 1901; Charleston *News and Courier*, November 8, 1901. The only public reference to GWM immediately prior to his appointment was the report of his participation in a Sumter church debate and a Washington newspaper comment that he resembled a District of Columbia resident. Columbia *State*, October 27, 1901 and *Colored American*, March 23, 1901. Charleston *News and Courier*, November 10, 1901; Columbia *State*, November 13, 1901.

15. Columbia *State*, November 11, 1901; Charlotte *Observer*, in Columbia State, November 5, 1901; Anderson *Mail*, in Columbia *State*, November 16, 1901; Rock Hill *Messenger*, in Columbia *State*, November 22, 1901; Cleveland *Gazette*, November 16, 1901; New York *Times*, December 8, 1901; Charleston *News and Courier*, December 8, 12, 1901; Columbia *State*, February 21, April 9, 10, May 26, 1902; Washington *Bee*, February 22, April 5, 1902; *Colored American*, June 7, 1902; Savannah *Tribune*, June 21, 1902.

16. GWM to WMcK, December 13, 1901, May 13, 1902, June 20, 1902, CGW, LC; *Colored American*, February 1, 1902. Despite this call for moderation, GWM was reported to have given an "incendiary" speech to a black audience in Goodwill, South Carolina. Columbia *State*, April 1, 1902.

17. TR to Booker T. Washington, December 12, 1901, microfilm reel 327, TR Papers, LC; Charleston *News and Courier*, April 8, 9, 10, 1902; TR to Micah Jenkins, March 3, 1902, in TR, *The Letters of TR*, ed. Elting E. Morison (Cambridge, 1951), 3: 237–38; Charleston *News and Courier*, April 15, 1902; John G. Capers to Mark Hanna, April 12, 1902, Hanna to TR, April 23, 1902, TR to Hanna, April 24, 1902, microfilm reels 26, 328, TR Papers, LC; Columbia *State*, May 5, 1902; Charleston *News and Courier*, May 5, 1902; TR to Koester, June 18, 1902, microfilm reel 329, TR Papers, LC; Charleston *News and Courier*, June 29, 1902; Columbia *State*, July 4, 6, 1902.

18. Cleveland *Gazette*, July 5, August 2, 1902; Cleveland *Plain Dealer*, in Washington *Bee*, July 19, 1902; GWM to WMcK, July 25, 1902, CGW, LC; GWM to Editor, *Colored American*, September 20, 1902.

19. *Southern Christian Advocate*, in Washington *Bee*, August 9, 1902.

20. This feeder line was completed in October 1900. Charleston *News and Courier,* October 18, 1900. The train that ran on this line was, according to one account, operated like "The Cannon Ball" on *Petticoat Junction,* a 1960s television comedy. It was a mixed freight and passenger service and one of its engineers, "Cap'n Bowen," accommodated tardy passengers by delaying departure from a station for as long as one hour. Cassie Nicholes, *Historical Sketches of Sumter County . . .* (Sumter, 1975), 116.

21. 64 S.C. 520 (1902); Columbia *State,* October 21, 1902; Sumter *Watchman and Southron,* October 22, 1902.

22. Sumter *Watchman and Southron,* October 15, 1902; Columbia *State,* October 15, 1902; Charleston *News and Courier,* October 16, 1902; Sumter *Herald,* October 17, 1902; interview with Thelma L. Murray and June M. Davis, Norfolk, Va., November 30, 1973; *Colored American,* January 1, 1903.

23. George B. Tindall, *South Carolina Negroes, 1877–1900* (Baton Rouge, 1966), 233–59; I. A. Newby, *Black Carolinians, a History of Blacks in South Carolina from 1895 to 1968* (Columbia, 1973), 61–62; Columbia *State,* August 26, 1904.

24. GWM to Northwestern Railroad Company, May 8, 1903, Title Book TTT 47, Clerk's Office, Sumter County, South Carolina; interview with Borden residents Mark Myers and Louise Myers, May 12, 1977, and letter from Borden resident H. H. Sanders to author, May 28, 1977.

25. Columbia *State,* July 3, August 22, 24, 26, 27, 1903; Charleston *Post,* August 26, 1903; Charleston *News and Courier,* August 26, 27, 1903.

26. Columbia *State,* January 19, 1901; New York *Age,* in Sumter *Watchman and Southron,* February 24, 1904; Charleston *News and Courier,* February 16, 1904; *Colored American,* February 4, 1904, quoted in Gatewood, *Theodore Roosevelt,* 124.

27. *The Southern Reporter,* in Charleston *News and Courier,* February 16, 1904; Sumter *Watchman and Southron,* February 24, 1904; Columbia *State,* February 18, 1904; *Southern Reporter,* in Columbia *State,* February 21, 1904 and Charleston *News and Courier,* February 22, 1904.

28. Charleston *News and Courier,* February 25, 1904; Columbia *State,* February 25, 1904; Charleston *Post,* February 25, 1904; Sumter *Watchman and Southron,* March 2, 1904; printed excerpts of Capers platform presentation speech have been preserved in Box 1, Booker T. Washington Papers, LC.

29. Leon Litwack, *Trouble in Mind: Black Southerners in the Age of Jim Crow* (New York, 1998), 366.

30. Edward L. Ayers, *The Promise of the New South: Life after Reconstruction* (New York, 1992), 88.

## Chapter 10. On Trial

1. Sumter *Defender,* in *Colored American,* April 23, 30, 1904; GWM to WMcK, May 5, 1904, CGW, LC.

2. GWM to WMcK, May 5, 1904, CGW, LC. The two Supreme Court cases were *Carter v. Texas,* 177 U.S. 442 (1900) and *Rogers v. Alabama,* 192 U.S. 226 (1904). They were largely ignored; juries remained all-white through out the South.

3. Information on the trial is taken from Court of General Sessions, Sumter County, May 1904 Term, Roll 1835, Courthouse, Sumter County, South Carolina. These records do not include a trial transcript. The fullest account of the trial is found in the Sumter *Daily Item*, May 20, 1904, reprinted in Sumter *Watchman and Southron*, May 25, 1904. The historian of Sumter County utilized the *Daily Item* to provide an account of the trial, but she made several errors. For example, she mistakenly said that the litigation took place in 1905. Ann King Gregorie, *History of Sumter County* (Sumter, 1954), 398–400. Ms. Gregorie's notes are deposited in the South Carolina Historical Society, Charleston, South Carolina. See also Columbia *State*, May 20, 1904, Charleston *News and Courier*, May 21, 1904, and Marion Moise to Editors, October 13, 1903, in Columbia *State*, October 15, 1905.

4. John S. Hoar, "George Washington Murray," a paper, March 1980, in James Mitchell Reames Papers, South Caroliniana Library.

5. Ibid.

6. Court of General Sessions, Sumter County, May 1904 Term, Roll 1835, Courthouse, Sumter County, South Carolina; Sumter *Daily Item*, May 21, 1904, in Sumter *Watchman and Southron*, May 25, 1904; Columbia *State*, May 22, 1904. For a discussion of the South Carolina penal system and blacks, see George B. Tindall, *South Carolina Negroes, 1877–1900* (Baton Rouge, 1966), 265–76.

7. Columbia *State*, May 21, 1904; Sumter *Herald*, May 27, 1904.

8. Charleston *News and Courier*, May 23, 1904; New York *Post*, in Charleston *News and Courier*, May 29, 1904; Sumter *Watchman and Southron*, June 1, 1904; Sumter *Herald*, June 3, 1904.

9. Washington *Bee*, May 28, 1904; Charleston *Messenger*, in Washington *Bee*, June 4, 1904; Cleveland *Gazette*, June 18, 1904; Washington *Bee*, June 18, 1904; *Colored American*, July 23, 1904.

10. GWM to Editor, June 30, 1904, in Cleveland *Gazette*, July 23, 1904, and *Colored American*, July 23, 1904.

11. Sumter *Watchman and Southron*, November 16, 1904; Sumter *Herald*, November 18, 1904; Charleston *News and Courier*, July 28, 1905; Columbia *State*, October 12, 1905; *The Freeman*, January 14, 1905.

12. Charleston *News and Courier*, October 7, 1904; Sumter *Herald*, March 31, 1905; Turner did not get the post. *The Freeman*, February 24, 1906.

13. On April 25, 1905, GWM wrote WMcK explaining his role at the 1904 state Republican convention in assuring the delegate post for Crum. He also castigated Capers, Deas, and Crum, the latter for not paying Murray's convention expenses as he had promised. GWM to WMcK, April 25, 1905, CGW, LC.

14. Charleston *News and Courier*, June 20, 1905; Columbia *State*, June 29, September 15, 1904.

15. Sumter *Daily Item*, September 28, 1904, in Sumter *Watchman and Southron*, October 5, 1904; Charleston *News and Courier*, September 22, 28, October 7, 17, 26, 27, 29, November 1, 2, 3, 1904; Columbia *State*, October 20, 1904.

16. Court of General Sessions, Sumter County, May 1904 Term, Roll 1835, Court-

house, Sumter County, South Carolina. Brown is listed in the document as J. Mood Brown, but he signed his name "R. M. Brown." Sumter *Watchman and Southron*, June 28, 1905.

17. Sumter *Watchman and Southron*, August 2, 1905.

18. Sumter *Watchman and Southron,* September 6, 1905; Washington *Bee*, September 16, 1905. The historian Valerie Grim has concluded in her study of black property holders that white society used every imaginable method to squash black independence "so that blacks would be dependent on whites for survival." Valerie Grim, "African American Landlords in the Rural South, 1870–1950, A Profile," *Agricultural History* 72 (spring 1998): 406.

19. 72 S.C. 508 (1905); see also 52 *Southeastern Reporter* 189 (1906); Charleston *News and Courier*, October 2, 1905; Columbia *State*, October 12, 1905.

20. Columbia *State*, October 12, 1905.

21. Ibid., Marion Moise to Editor, October 13, 1905, in Columbia *State*, October 15, 1905; Charleston *News and Courier*, October 13, 1905; Sumter *Watchman and Southron*, October 18, 1905; Charleston *Post*, October 18, 1905.

22. Columbia *State*, October 19, 1905; Charleston *News and Courier*, October 19, 1905.

23. Sumter *Daily Item*, in Columbia *State*, October 20, 1905; Charleston *News and Courier*, October 20, 1905; Washington *Bee*, October 28, 1905.

24. 72 S.C. 516 (1905); Columbia *State*, October 31, 1905; Charleston *News and Courier*, October 31, 1905; Charleston *Post*, October 31, 1905.

25. Charleston *News and Courier*, November 1, 1905; Title books V.V. 650, V.V. 674, Clerk's Office, Sumter County, South Carolina.

26. Columbia *State*, November 2, 1905; Charleston *News and Courier*, November 2, 4, 1905.

27. Leon Litwack, *Trouble in Mind: Black Southerners in the Age of Jim Crow* (New York, 1998), 246–70.

28. Charleston *News and Courier*, December 4, 1902, May 11, December 14, 20, 21, 1904, January 4, 10, 1905; Columbia *State*, June 23, 27, 1903; Washington *Bee*, August 11, 1906; New York *Age*, June 6, 1907. The Charleston *Post*, May 20, 1904, in comparing the Prioleau and Murray cases, wrote: "We suppose those coincidences must be expected in Republican circles." Charleston *News and Courier*, September 27, October 21, 1904. In the early 1890s a black Sumter postmaster was also arrested on a forgery charge. Charleston *News and Courier*, February 12, 1891.

29. Sumter *Herald*, July 16, 1897; Tindall, 58, discusses whitecapping in Greenwood a year after the 1898 Phoenix riots, pointing out that the white cappers said they wanted to make blacks migrate in order to get their land at a low cost. See also William F. Holmes, "Whitecapping: Agrarian Violence in Mississippi, 1902–1906," *Journal of Southern History* 35 (May 1969): 165–85.

30. Loren Schweninger, *Black Property Owners in the South 1790–1915* (Urbana and Chicago,1990), 233–35.

## Chapter 11. In Chicago and on Tour

1. The best account of blacks in Chicago during this period is Allan H. Spear, *Black Chicago: The Making of a Negro Ghetto, 1880–1920* (Chicago, 1967); Professor Spear "did not run across any information on Murray" while researching this book. Allan H. Spear to author, April 29, 1973. Alfreda M. Duster, the daughter of nineteenth-century black leader Ida Wells Barnett and the editor of *Crusade for Justice: The Autobiography of Ida B. Wells* (Chicago, 1970), indicated she was "at a loss to know" why she had no information on GWM since her parents, she believed, must have known him. Duster to author, September 1, 1973. A letter requesting information on GWM from the author to the Editor, Chicago *Defender* was published on September 4, 1973, but it produced no data on Murray's life in Chicago; interview with Thelma M. Murray and June Davis, November 30, 1973, Norfolk, Va.

2. Chicago *Broad Ax*, June 23, 1906. The site of Murray's first Chicago residence later became a high-rise housing development near the Illinois Institute of Technology.

3. Chicago *Broad Ax*, March 2, 1907, September 12, 1905, December 28, 1907, August 24, 1907, July 13, 1907, February 3, 1923, May 11, 1907.

4. *Report of the Commissioner of Patents . . . 1910* (Washington, 1911); *Official Gazette of the United States Patent Office* 155 (June 18, 1910), 937–38. Records of the United States Patent Office, R.G. 241, NARA; Chicago *Broad Ax*, September 12, 1925.

5. *Chicago City Directories, 1908, 1909*, Chicago Historical Society; Bureau of Vital Statistics, Chicago, Illinois.

6. Chicago *Broad Ax*, January 2, 1909. On September 4 and 11, 1909, this same newspaper described the area as becoming a center for the "Sporting Element." After their marriage the Murrays moved to 3665 Wabash, *Chicago City Directories, 1910, 1911*, Chicago Historical Society. Dorothy Westbrooks to author, September 11, 1973. Ms. Westbrooks was a friend of Cornelia Murray's family.

7. Murray-Davis interview; Chicago *Broad Ax*, August 21, 1909; New York *Age*, February 7, 1907, October 29, 1908; Chicago *Broad Ax*, December 18, 1909, March 12, 26, 1910. During the late 1890s early 1900s, there was a white-owned Black Diamond Railroad Company planning a route from Toledo, Ohio, via Cincinnati and Columbia, South Carolina to Port Royal, South Carolina. The similarity in names is intriguing, but any connection is unknown. *Palmetto Post*, September 21, 1909; Charleston *News and Courier*, October 7, 1898, September 21, 1900; Columbia *State*, September 25, 1901; *Chicago City Directories, 1910, 1911*, Chicago Historical Society.

8. Murray-Davis interview.

9. Chicago *Broad-Ax*, August 14, 1909; Milwaukee *Sentinel*, July 20, August 1, 2, 3, 1909.

10. Milwaukee *Sentinel*, August 8, 1909, in Chicago *Broad Ax*, August 14, 1909. GWM's interview was not discovered in any issue of the Milwaukee paper for this period. Chicago *Broad Ax*, August 21, 1909.

11. Court of General Sessions, Sumter County, May 1904 Term, Roll 1835, Courthouse, Sumter County, South Carolina.

12. *The Southern Sun* reported GWM was in Africa. Columbia *State*, October 2, 1906, reprinted this article. Charleston *News and Courier*, October 11, 1909; Sumter *Watchman and Southron*, October 13, 1909; Columbia *State*, September 23, 1909.

13. The account below, unless otherwise indicated, is based on Sumter *Watchman and Southron*, October 2, 4, 13, 1909; Columbia *State*, September 24, 28, October 2, 9, 1909; Sumter *Herald*, October 15, 1909; and Charleston *News and Courier*, October 11, 1909.

14. Columbia *State*, October 2, 1909; Sumter *Watchman and Southron*, October 6, 1909.

15. Charleston *News and Courier*, October 11, 12, 1909; Sumter *Watchman and Southron*, October 13, 1909.

16. *The Freeman*, October 23, 1909; Martin F. Ansel, Governors' Papers, SCDAH; Wayne C. Temple, Archives Division State of Illinois, to author, January 16, 1974; "Program of Dinner on Mississippi River . . . October 25, 1909," Martin F. Ansel Papers, SCL, USC; Charleston *News and Courier*, November 2, 1909.

17. Charleston *News and Courier*, November 4, 1909; Columbia *State*, November 9, 1909; Sumter *Watchman and Southron*, November 13, 1909. In a 1911 article discussing the blacks who attended the University of South Carolina during the 1870s, the statement was made that efforts to extradite Murray "were successfully resisted, mainly by white citizens of South Carolina." Columbia *State*, May 8, 1911; *Statement of Pardons and Commutations Granted by Martin F. Ansel Governor of South Carolina* (Columbia, 1909); Martin F. Ansel, *A Brief Review of the Law of Extradition . . . Conference of Governors, Washington, D.C., January 18–20, 1909* (Columbia, 1918).

18. Sumter *Watchman and Southron*, February 2, 1910.

19. *The Freeman*, March 30, 1912; "Admission Souvenir" in possession of author, received from Dorothy Westbrooks, August 25, 1974; Washington *Bee*, December 11, 1915; Richmond *Planet*, May 20, July 8, 15, 22, 1916; Washington *Bee*, February 24, March 3, 17, 24, 31, April 21, 1917; New York *Age*, June 14, 1917; Baltimore *Afro-American*, June 16, 30, 1917; Philadelphia *Tribune*, September 27, November 3, 17, 1917; *The Appeal*, October 3, 1917; New York *Age*, August 3, 1918, March 8, 1919; Chicago *Broad Ax*, February 28, March 6, 20, 1920; Chicago *Defender*, March 13, 20, 1920; Philadelphia *Tribune*, November 3, 1917; Washington *Bee*, June 13, 1914.

20. *The Freeman*, May 23, June 5, 13, 1914; Indianapolis *News*, June 6, 1914; Indianapolis *Star*, June 7, 14, 21, 28, 1914.

21. *The Freeman*, March 30, 1912; "Admission Souvenir" in possession of author; Indianapolis *Star*, June 7, 1914; Richmond *Planet*, May 20, 1916; Washington *Bee*, February 24, March 17, 24, 1917; Chicago *Broad Ax*, March 6, 1920.

22. George W. Murray, *Race Ideals: Effects, Causes, and Remedy for Afro-American Race Troubles* (n.p., 1910; Newark, two different publishers, 1914; Princeton, Indiana, 1914).

23. See August Meier, *Negro Thought in America 1880–1915: Racial Ideologies in the Age of Booker T. Washington* (Ann Arbor, 1963). There is no indication in Murray's writings that he was responding to the "racist arguments and insulting language" of the

"embittered 'black' Negrophobe" William Hannibal Thomas, who in 1901 published *The American Negro*, a scathing defamation of black people as racial inferiors of the worst order. John David Smith's perceptive analysis of Thomas is found in *Black Judas: William Hannibal Thomas and the American Negro* (Athens, Ga., 2000). Quotes in the previous sentence are found on p. xxiii.

24. New York *Tribune*, June 10, 1906, published a poll of leading blacks and found that most preferred "Negro" to "Afro-American." For a discussion of the term "Afro-American" and the efforts of the newspaper editor T. Thomas Fortune to widen its use, see Emma Lou Thornbrough, *T. Thomas Fortune, Militant Journalist* (Chicago, 1972), 132–34, 134n.

25. In a public letter, GWM ridiculed the contemporary argument that blacks and whites were created differently and that each had different innate characteristics. He argued that "the fundamental and self-evident truths" were that every human being had within him the same capacity. Differences in human beings were the result "of the different thought which . . . [each] has cultivated." GWM to Editor, December 6, 1915, in Washington *Bee*, December 11, 1915.

26. There was an interest in black dolls and calendars in black America during these years, reflecting the growth of group consciousness. Meier, 270. In 1908, the National Baptist Convention, meeting in Lexington, Kentucky, called for black dolls for black babies. Surprisingly, a South Carolina newspaper agreed. Columbia *State*, October 4, 1908. The Reverend R. H. Boyd, who along with Nashville's National Baptist Publication Board, operated the National Negro Doll Company, orchestrated this resolution both to foster black pride and to sell dolls. Bobby L. Lovett to University Press of Florida, May 9, 2005.

27. *The Freeman*, June 5, 1914; Princeton *Clarion-News*, October 16, 26, December 8, 21, 1906.

28. Princeton *Clarion-News*, March 1, April 13, June 1, 27, 29, September 21, 1907; Indianapolis *News*, June 1, 1907; *The Freeman*, June 22, 1907, December 23, 1911.

29. *Reports of the Commissioner of Education . . . 1911, 1912, 1913, 1914, 1916, 1917*; Department of the Interior, Bureau of Education, *Biennial Survey 1916–1926*; Louise R. Falls, Princeton Public Library, to author, August 4, 1973; Tom Rumer, Indiana Historical Society Library, to author, January 14, 1974, June 10, 1975. The historian of black Indiana does not mention this institution. Emma Lou Thornbrough, *The Negro in Indiana: A Study of a Minority* (Indianapolis, 1957).

30. GWM, *Race Ideals . . .* , preface; GWM, *Light in Dark Places* (Chicago, 1922), 6.

31. *Southern Life Magazine*, in Pittsburgh *Courier*, April 27, 1912; Washington *Bee*, March 24, May 17, 1917; *The Freeman*, June 13, 1914.

32. Murray-Davis interview; Washington *Bee*, December 11, 1915; Dr. Murray's 1909–1921 property transactions are recorded in the Clerk's Office, Marion County, South Carolina; interview with Evelyn R. Cuthbert, Sumter, South Carolina, December 12, 1973.

33. Chicago *Broad Ax*, February 20, 28, March 6, 20, 1920; Chicago *Defender*, March 13, 20, 1920; Murray-Davis interview.

34. Chicago *Whip*, October 29, 1921, February 18, 25, 1922; Chicago *Broad Ax*, September 27, October 25, 1924, January 3, March 28, April 25, 1925, January 9, February 27, 1926 April 22, 1922, September 20, 1920 through 1921; Chicago *Defender*, December 19, 1925.

35. Doc. 6996895, 16333/363 Chicago Property Records Office; Murray-Davis interview. Unless otherwise indicated, information on Murray's life in Chicago is based on the Murray-Davis interview.

36. Death Certificate, Division of Vital Statistics, Chicago, Illinois.

37. Chicago *Defender*, May 1, 1926.

38. Grave records, Lincoln Cemetery, Chicago, Illinois; Murray-Davis interview; George B. Tindall, 285 points out that by 1890 the Oddfellows claimed sixty-seven lodges in South Carolina. Consequently, Murray probably belonged to the order even before he moved to Chicago. In 1992, a newspaper reporter writing a story on Murray in light of a new South Carolina black congressional district was erroneously told that Murray was buried in Sumter. Steve Piacente, "State's Last Congressman a Man with No Monument," *Charleston Post and Courier*, June 21, 1992, 15A.

# Bibliographical Essay

The research leading to this account of George W. Murray and the South Carolina Republican Party encountered many of the difficulties familiar to historians of most areas of black history. Neither Murray nor the other leading South Carolina Republicans left collections of personal papers. Consequently, Murray's story and that of his party had to be recreated, small piece by small piece, from public sources.

A few Murray letters have been preserved. Twenty-seven of his letters are located in the Carter G. Woodson Papers, Library of Congress, and there letters written by several other South Carolina Republicans are also found. There are also two Murray letters in the Benjamin Harrison Papers, Library of Congress. Murray's family, in the persons of his daughter-in-law, Mrs. Thelma L. Murray. and his granddaughter, Mrs. June Davis, both of Norfolk, Virginia, welcomed this author into their homes and provided information on Murray's personal life and permitted the use of a copy of one of his books and his photograph. Two friends of the family, Ms. Evelyn Cuthbert of Sumter, South Carolina, and Ms. Dorothy Westbrooks of Chicago, provided supplementary information.

A number of Murray's written works are also available. There are several editions of his *Race Ideals: Cause and Effect of and Remedy for the Afro-American Race Troubles*. The first edition was apparently printed around 1910, but it lists no publisher. In 1914, three separate publishers/printers issued new enlarged editions of this same book: Roosevelt Printing and Publishing Company of Newark, New Jersey, Smith and Sons Publishing Company of Princeton, Indiana, and New Jersey Rilograph Press and Investment Company of Newark, New Jersey. In 1922, Murray published *Light in Dark Places*, volume 1, under his own name; apparently the only copy of this book is in family hands. Murray's 1890 Charleston speech was similarly printed privately and a copy has been preserved in the South Caroliniana Library, University of South Carolina. Accounts of numerous other speeches were found in contemporary newspapers, but this 1890 speech is the only one preserved verbatim.

Several libraries proved indispensable in this research. The South Caroliniana Library, University of South Carolina, houses the best manuscript and secondary collection on Palmetto State history. The South Carolina Department of Archives and History in Columbia is the rich repository for the state's official documents. The Schomburg Center for Research in Black Culture, New York, contains a major collection of black history material. The Library of Congress has manuscript collections that were essential. The collections of the Chicago Historical Society provided information on Murray's later life, while the National Archives and Records Administration both in Washington and at the East Point, Georgia, branch contain official documents that touched on several governmental aspects of Murray's life.

The manuscript collections that proved to be the most helpful were those of the following individuals: James S. Clarkson, Grover Cleveland, Hanna McCormick Family, Benjamin Harrison, William McKinley, Theodore Roosevelt, Booker T. Washington, and Carter G. Woodson, all in the Library of Congress; J. Hendrix McLane Papers, Yale University Library; and the slim Governor Martin Ansel papers, South Caroliniana Library, University of South Carolina. A host of other collections were consulted, for example, the Benjamin Ryan Tillman Papers at the Clemson University Library, the South Caroliniana Library, and the South Carolina Department of Archives and History, but they contained little information pertinent to this study.

Public documents that were the most helpful included the records of the South Carolina Board of Canvassers and the 1880 Census and Agricultural Schedule both at the South Carolina Department of Archives and History; the records of the University of South Carolina at the South Caroliniana Library; the 1900 census, and records of the Internal Revenue Service, U.S. Customs Service, U.S. Patent Office, the U.S. House of Representatives, and the U.S. Census Bureau, at the National Archives, Washington; Port of Charleston Customs records and Internal Revenue Service records for South Carolina at the East Point, Georgia, branch of the National Archives and Record Administration; *Chicago City Directories* for Murray's years in Chicago (1905-26); telephone directories and miscellaneous other public biographical material at the Chicago Historical Society; property and court records, Sumter County Courthouse; Property Records Office and Vital Statistics Office, Chicago and Cook County, Illinois; records, Lincoln Cemetery, Chicago.

Printed public documents particularly useful in this study included *Congressional Record, Congressional Directory, House Reports*, 53rd and 54th Congresses; Roll Call Data, 53rd and 54th Congresses, Interuniversity Consortium for Political and Social Research; *Biographical Directory of the American Congress*; *Reports of the Commissioner of Education . . . 1911, 1912, 1913, 1914, 1916, 1917*; Bureau of Education, *Biennial Survey 1916-1926*; *Proceedings of the 10th and 11th Republican National Conventions*; *Charleston City Directory 1892-1899* (located at Charleston Library Society); *Journal of the [S.C.] House of Representatives* (1894); *South Carolina Statutes at Large*; *U.S. Supreme Court Reports*; *Federal Reporter*; *South Carolina Reports*; *United States Reports*; *United States Statutes at Large*; *Annual Report of the Commissioner of Patents for 1894, 1910*; *Official Gazette of the United States Patent Office* (1894, 1910).

The most useful of all the public documents were contemporary black and white newspapers, most of which are on microfilm. White South Carolina newspapers of this period were virulently anti-black and anti-Republican, but they still provided factual information not available anywhere else. Black newspapers all over the country were 4-8-page weeklies, often one man operations, and thus not very thorough. Still they provided data and a viewpoint not available elsewhere. The white newspapers most valuable for this book proved to be the Charleston *News and Courier*, 1880-1905, 1909; Columbia *State*, 1891-1905, 1909; and Sumter *Watchman and Southron*, 1881-1906, 1909-10 (manuscript in South Caroliniana Library). The most valuable black newspapers proved to be Chicago *Broad Ax*, 1899-1926; Chicago *Defender*, 1905-26;

and *The Freeman* (Indianapolis), 1888–1916. Other black and white newspapers utilized in this study in alphabetical order and with dates listed according to years available or consulted are *The American Citizen* (Kansas City), 1889–1907; *The Appeal* (St. Paul), 1897–1923; Baltimore *Afro-American Ledger*, 1892–97, 1905–6, 1917; Beaufort *Gazette*, 1903–5, 1909; Boston *Guardian*, 1902–4; Charleston *Post*, 1894–1905, 1909; Chicago *Record-Herald* Index, 1910–12; Chicago *Tribune*, 1926; Chicago *Whip*, 1919–22; Cleveland *Gazette*, 1892–1917; *Colored American* (Washington, D.C.), 1898–1904; Columbia *Journal*, September 1894 scattered; Columbia *News*, 1895; Columbia *Register*, 1880–98; Georgetown *Semi-Weekly Times*, 1895, 1896; Huntsville (Alabama) *Gazette*, 1892–94; Milwaukee *Sentinel*, 1909; New York *Age*, 1888–1900, 1905–26; New York *Times* Index 1880–1926; New York *Tribune*, 1893; Palmetto *Post* (Port Royal, S.C.), 1895–98; Philadelphia *Tribune*, 1912–21, 1923–26; Pittsburgh *Courier*, 1911–12, 1923–26; Princeton (Indiana) *Clarion-News*, 1907–8, 1918; Richmond *Planet*, 1895–1900, 1915–18, 1925–26; St. Louis *Post-Dispatch*, March 6, 1898, July 9, 1911; Savannah *Tribune*, 1897–1920; Sumter *Herald*, 1896–1906, 1909; Washington *Bee*, 1882–1922; Washington *Star*, October 28, 1893; Washington *Times*, 1894.

There are no monographs on George W. Murray, but there is one article: William J. Gaboury, "George Washington Murray and the Fight for Political Democracy in South Carolina," *Journal of Negro History*, 62 (July 1977), 258–69. Though this article presents a sketch of Murray's life, it concentrates on his 1895 battle against the proposed South Carolina constitution. Professor Gaboury was kind enough to provide me with a copy of his article before it was published. Sumter, South Carolina attorney John S. Hoar wrote a paper on Murray in the 1980s, a draft of which is present in the James Mitchell Reames Papers, South Caroliniana Library, University of South Carolina.

# Index

accommodationist attitude, 52–53, 96, 119

Afro-American Council, 115–16

Alabama, xiv, 17

Anderson, Robert B., 94

Andrews, W. T., 93

Ansel, Martin F., 147, 149

appeal of conviction, 139–40

Arkansas, xiv

arrest, warrant for, 138–39

Atwood, Harrison H., 109

Babcock, J. W., 105

Bailey, Harris M., Jr., xiii–xiv

bail money, forfeiture of, 147

Baily, Joseph, 65–66

Baker, Frazier B., 112–13

Baker, Henry M., 108–9

Bampfield, Samuel G., 112

barber shop, battle of, 77

Barnwell, lynchings at, 23

Barron, J. T., 46

Barton, Clara, 59, 71

Bates, W.T.C., 46, 47, 77

Beaufort County: constitutional convention and, 94; cyclone and, 59; dirty trick and, 117; fusion in, 78; Ministerial Union and, 91; Republican split in, 43–44; speech at, 69

Beckett, William W., 42–43, 119

Berkeley County, 78

"Black Bold Eagle" nickname, 14, 37

black church, 4

"Black Codes," 5

Black Diamond Development Company, 145

blacks: Conservative Democrats and, 84; education of, 4–5, 73–74; housing accommodations of, 4; meeting of, in South Carolina, 52–53; opposition of, to disfranchisement, 88–91; patronage jobs and, 112–13; population of, 83; skin color and, 6, 21–22, 37; southern justice for, 142–43; voting by, 113–14. *See also* disfranchisement; prejudice, anti-black; registration and voting law, anti-black; violence, anti-black

Blaine, James G., 39, 41

Blair Education Bill, 56

Blalock, Loomis L., 119

Bland, Richard "Silver Dick," 57, 65–66

Blaylock, L.W.C., 36, 130

Blease, Cole L., 46, 47, 80

Borden, 127, 129

Bostick, Hilliard, 139

Boutelle, Charles A., 60, 88

Boutwell, George S., 6

Brawley, William H., 54, 65

Brayton, Ellery M.: all-black conference and, 32; appearance before committee by, 109; as candidate, 43; Capers and, 130; chairmanship and, 28; Congressional campaign and, 27; as delegate, 40, 41; delegate election and, 91; GWM and, 71, 72; Harrison and, 14; McLane and, 17; Reformers and, 85–86, 98; registration efforts and, 25; Regulars and, 39; in Seventh District, 74, 79; state convention and, 83

Browne, R. C., 106

Bryan, William Jennings, 57, 65–66, 103, 119

Buckner, John C., 160

Bull Run, battle of, 2

Burks, William J. and Gaynell, 157

business, success at, 20–21, 121, 139, 142–43, 164

Butler, Matthew C., 8, 81, 87

*Butler v. Ellerbe*, 91

Cannon, "Uncle Joe," 60, 65–66

Capers, John G., 124–25, 127, 130, 161, 163

John F. Marszalek is Giles Distinguished Professor Emeritus of History, Mississippi State University. Among his publications are biographies of the Civil War generals William T. Sherman and Henry W. Halleck and the *Encyclopedia of African American Civil Rights: From Emancipation to the Twenty-First Century.*